HATING AMERICA

BARRY RUBIN | JUDITH COLP RUBIN

HATING A M E R I C A

A History

OXFORD
UNIVERSITY PRESS

2004

WINGATE UNIVERSITY LIBRARY

OXFORD

UNIVERSITY PRESS

Oxford   New York
Auckland   Bangkok   Buenos Aires   Cape Town   Chennai
Dar es Salaam   Delhi   Hong Kong   Istanbul   Karachi   Kolkata
Kuala Lumpur   Madrid   Melbourne   Mexico City   Mumbai   Nairobi
São Paulo   Shanghai   Taipei   Tokyo   Toronto

Copyright © 2004 by Oxford University Press, Inc.

Published by Oxford University Press, Inc.
198 Madison Avenue, New York, New York 10016

www.oup.com

Oxford is a registered trademark of Oxford University Press

All rights reserved. No part of this publication may be reproduced,
stored in a retrieval system, or transmitted, in any form or by any means,
electronic, mechanical, photocopying, recording, or otherwise,
without the prior permission of Oxford University Press.

Library of Congress Cataloging-in-Publication Data
Rubin, Barry M.
Hating America : a history / by Barry Rubin, Judith Colp Rubin.
p. cm.
ISBN-13 978 0-19-530649-1
ISBN-10 0-19-530649X
1. Anti-Americanism—History 2. United States—Foreign public opinion.
3. United States—Foreign relations.   4. United States—History.
5. National characteristics, American.   I. Rubin, Judith Colp.   II. Title.
E183.7.R89   2005
973—dc22   2004010808

9 8 7 6 5 4 3 2
Printed in the United States of America
on acid-free paper

As always to Gabriella and Daniel—our co-authored children

PREFACE

When writing a book, an author often has the sensation of being surrounded by that topic. In the case of anti-Americanism that experience was particularly strong. As the twenty-first century began it seemed as if the amount of criticism the United States was receiving around the world was matched only by the quantity of passionate debate about why this was happening. Almost every day brought more evidence that anti-Americanism was an omnipresent global phenomenon.

Yet as this project was being conceived the situation should have been the opposite. The United States had attained victory in the Cold War against communism, which had begun immediately after it had done the same thing in a war against fascism. Moreover, there had been the September 11, 2001, attack on America, the single most horrific terrorist attack in world history. Although the event itself showed the extent of anti-Americanism in the Middle East, the United States on September 12 should have been at the height of its global popularity, praised, appreciated, and sympathized with around the world, whatever undertone of reasonable criticism also existed.

Nevertheless, in the aftermath of September 11, although many in the world did sympathize with America, the response of others was that the United States somehow deserved it. That there could be such hatred after the death of so many of their fellow citizens was a shock to many Americans. The displays of hatred only increased as America sent troops to Afghanistan and then fought a war in Iraq.

Certainly, images of the American flag and effigies of the U.S. president being burned throughout the Middle East were disturbing, yet not new. But in Europe, which Americans considered their strategic ally and cultural partner, signs of this hatred were especially disturbing. The German chancellor used demagogic criticism of America to win an election, while one of his top aides likened the U.S. president to Hitler. In France, a book claiming that September 11 was a propaganda stunt by American intelligence agencies and the military-industrial complex to justify world conquest became a best seller. Even in Britain, America's closest friend, a former cabinet minister claimed the United States was planning to dominate space, cyberspace, and just about everything else.

Almost without exception, both the critics and those defending America viewed this outpouring of anti-Americanism as unprecedented, as the result of contemporary or at least recent events. But the tone of such rhetoric would not have been at all surprising for Americans living a century or two earlier. Only by understanding the historical development—and powerful continuity—of anti-Americanism can one comprehend it as a contemporary issue.

The American expatriate Henry James, who had little love for his native country, once mused, "It is, I think, an indisputable fact that Americans are, as Americans, the most self-conscious people in the world."

But given the historical evidence it was hard to see how Americans could feel otherwise. Indeed, even before it was a country, America was being harshly criticized. Thomas Jefferson and Benjamin Franklin spent much time and creative energy trying to prove to Europeans that their country was not inherently barbaric. There were always many intellectual figures in Europe who could not resist the facile put-down of America: "I am willing to love all mankind, except an American," said the British author Samuel Johnson in the eighteenth century. The respected British historian Thomas Carlyle in 1850 merely found Americans "the greatest bores ever seen in this world."

The French statesman Georges Clemenceau said that "America is the only nation in history which, miraculously, has gone directly from barbarism to degeneration without the usual interval of civilization," while Oscar Wilde, who would agree with Clemenceau on little else, declared, "America is the only country that went from barbarism to decadence without civilization in between." Decades later the British writer George Bernard Shaw jeered: "An asylum for the sane would be empty in America."[1]

This book in no way seeks to suggest that all criticism of America constitutes anti-Americanism or is invalid. One reason why it is important to examine the history of this debate is to see what can be learned about the real defects of the United States, as well as ways to communicate its virtues better. Similarly, those governments, classes, groups, ideologies, and individuals who have held anti-American views can be better understood by investigating the reasons for these attitudes.

In this book we have carefully defined anti-Americanism as being limited to having one or more of the following characteristics:

- An antagonism to the United States that is systemic, seeing it as completely and inevitably evil.
- A view that greatly exaggerates America's shortcomings.
- The deliberate misrepresentation of the nature or policies of the United States for political purposes.
- A misperception of American society, policies, or goals which falsely portrays them as ridiculous or malevolent.

We have also restricted our discussion to anti-American views held by non-Americans (or in a few cases to Americans who lived abroad for so long as to become virtually part of this category). Otherwise, the issues that must be dealt with more properly fall into the sphere of domestic political and partisan debate.

Of course, opposition to specific American actions or policies is easily understandable and may well be justifiable, but anti-Americanism as a whole is not. The reason for this conclusion is simply that the United States is not a terrible or evil society, whatever its shortcomings. It does not seek world domination and its citizens do not take pleasure in deliberately injuring others.

There are many occasions when decisions inevitably have drawbacks and bad effects. There are equally many times when mistakes are made.

But here is where the line can be drawn between legitimate criticism and anti-Americanism.

One of our most important conclusions is that there has been a historical continuity and evolution of anti-americanism, coinciding with the development of the United States, changes in other societies, and the world situation. We have detected five phases in this process:

The first phase (Chapter 1) began in the eighteenth century, when America was a little-understood place whose society was still under construction. At this time, criticism focused on the idea that it would be difficult or impossible to create any civilization there due to environmental conditions.

The second phase, from around 1800 to about 1880 (Chapter 2), was characterized by the idea that the United States was already demonstrably a failed society, ruined by democracy, equality, and other dangerous experiments. Its system was said to be so unworkable that no one elsewhere should view this new society as a model.

The third phase, from the 1880s to the 1930s (Chapter 3), took place when America's growing size, power, and economic might showed that it could no longer be described as a failure. Then, however, there was a growing fear abroad that the bad American model—populist democracy, mass culture, industrialization, and so on—might in the future take over the world and change the way of life of others in a dangerous and negative manner.

In this context, Chapter 4 discusses how the twentieth century's two main counter-ideologies—communism and fascism—dealt with the American challenge. Chapter 5 deals with the specific forms of anti-Americanism taking place in Latin America.

By the fourth phase, from the end of World War II in 1945 to the end of the Cold War by 1990 (Chapter 6), the fear of American domination was moved from the future to the present. The United States was supposedly in the process of taking over the world. During this phase, the Middle East (Chapter 7) became increasingly conscious of the United States and anti-Americanism became an important phenomenon there.

Finally, in the current phase (Chapter 8), those who hold anti-Americanism views see the U.S. domination, both as a great power and as a terrible model for civilization (as the centerpiece of globalization, modernization, and Westernization), to be an established fact. That is why it is the most angry and widespread exemplification of anti-Americanism ever seen. Moreover, hatred was intensified by a new doctrine that claimed that America's higher level of development was at everyone else's expense and, by the same token, the relative failure of others to duplicate this success was due to America's sins.

Chapter 9 analyzes anti-Americanism in the early twenty-first century, also summing up the book's main arguments and conclusions.

Finally, it is important to note the spirit in which this book is written. Our goal has been to produce a useful work of analysis and narration rather than one of preordained ideological content. Most of the conclusions were developed by the authors in the course of examining the evidence. There is nothing innately "liberal" or "conservative," left or right, about the line of reasoning used in this book. Rather than take sides in an ongoing partisan debate, the book tries to suggest the need for a totally new framework for understanding this vital issue.

ACKNOWLEDGMENTS

We want to thank our editor, Dedi Felman, who, as always, was a pleasure to work with. Thanks also to staff members at the Global Research in International Affairs (GLORIA) Center, especially Cameron Brown, Joy Pincus, and Ehud Waldoks. Many others have helped in various ways, and we wish to especially thank Mark Falcoff, Josh Pollack, Brian Loveman, Steve Grant, and Eleanor Howard.

CONTENTS

HATING AMERICA

A NATURALLY DEGENERATE LAND

America was a land before it was a society or country: a strange and mysterious place, virtually the first entirely new territory Europe discovered since starting its own modern civilization. The experience might have been the closest in history to finding another planet with alien life forms. Understanding what went on in this strange locale would always be difficult enough for Europeans despite the fact that their culture would be the biggest influence on it. Comprehension would be far more difficult for those from societies having even less in common with the United States.

Certainly, it seemed reasonable for people to expect that the climate, soil, and other physical features in such a thoroughly distinctive place would make for a very different type of human being and social order. The very fact that Europeans knew that the new world they found populated with Native Americans was technologically behind them, and the fact that they considered it to be spiritually inferior as well, made it easy for them to conclude that this relative backwardness had been inevitable. Obviously, too, the idea that America was inferior had a great appeal for

Europeans, since this validated the natural human propensity to believe in the superiority of themselves and their own way of life.

Perhaps, they thought, America was doomed and destined to be always inferior. If so, any effort to implant civilization there would fail or, even worse, produce a monstrous hybrid, a Frankenstein's monster that some day would menace its creators. Even those who accepted the basic principles on which the United States would be ostensibly based often strongly rejected the way they were implemented there.

Many themes of later anti-Americanism began to appear from this very start. A key, though often subtle, element would be the view of America as a separate civilization, at first by Europe and later by other parts of the world as well. Though descended from Europe, it was also different, an experiment with unique features. Long before America was a power on the world scene, it had power as an example, a role model to be exalted or despised.

Thus, while some Europeans as early as the eighteenth century would think that America offered the vision of a better future, others would consider it a horrifyingly distorted caricature of all that was good in their own society. The debate between these two standpoints, with many variations in each camp, would continue for centuries, shifting emphasis over time but maintaining the same basic themes down to the present. Such arguments, and the divisions between pro-American or anti-American sentiments, were always related to local political or philosophical conflicts as well.

This dispute's first round took place in the eighteenth century as part of a broader debate over the proper form of society. Was change a good thing or something better to avoid or limit? Would such new forces as a faster pace of life, lower class barriers, democracy, and a mass rather than elite culture advance or destroy civilized life? For better or worse, America was seen as a test case of these and other propositions.

Advocates of material progress, like the mercantilists, saw the development of America with its vast natural resources as a remarkable opportunity to enhance Europe's wealth. By providing raw materials and furnishing markets, colonies there would bring the mother country endless riches, though obviously only as long as they remained under European control. It was in this context that Anne-Robert-Jacques Turgot, an eighteenth-century French minister of finance and advocate of economic development, called America the "hope of the human race."[1]

But their rivals, the physiocrats, asked why Europeans should become involved in this far-off land instead of focusing on preserving their way of life at home, with an emphasis on agriculture rather than commerce or industry. They feared the coming of a new type of society whose shape had not yet even become clear. But they already felt that American products or ideas would undermine traditional life. It was a sentiment perhaps best put into words later by the romantic Italian poet Giacomo Leopardi, who warned in 1820 that America was a danger because it would destroy Europe's "supremely poetic" "other world" of "pleasant dreams" and "beautiful imaginings" with a soulless, low-quality, hard-edged society.[2]

America similarly became a test case in the debate over the nature of human beings themselves. Was America's newness a sign of unspoiled innocence or a rawness that would make it reject higher civilization? If everything good was already created by tradition, if European society was already at the peak of achievement, starting afresh was a dangerous and doomed enterprise. To the majority, the new land was simply backward, but a new wave of thinkers—whose agenda was also the renewal of Europe—argued that the very lack of deep-seated traditions and an established structure would let America create a successful society.

One of the American experiment's most passionate and articulate proponents was Michel Guillaume Jean de Crèvecoeur, a Frenchman who fought in his country's losing war against Britain and then became a farmer in upstate New York in 1765. When the United States gained independence two decades later, he wrote lyrically that America was "the most perfect society now existing in the world" because it was so fresh and flexible. It was welding together immigrants from all over Europe "into a new race of men, whose labors and posterity will one day cause great change in the world." In contrast to Europeans, Americans did not "toil, starve, and bleed" on behalf of princes but for their own benefit under leaders they freely chose. Europe would learn new ways of living and governance from this people's achievements.[3]

Crèvecoeur was in the minority. Most members of Europe's governing and intellectual elite believed that civilization was a delicate matter. They feared that any deviation from the existing order—a stable class system based on a monarch and an aristocracy setting standards—would be a catastrophic failure. From this perspective would arise the conservative version of anti-Americanism.

Not even all advocates of change in Europe liked the American experiment. Many of them had their own vision of society to propose that they considered better and more worthy of global imitation than what the United States offered. While conservatives disdained America's innovations as too extreme, adherents of the romantic cultural movement and radical political ideas, which spread at the eighteenth century's end, found them to be too limited.

Both schools would also have much in common, sometimes combining in strange and unexpected ways. When the United States was just a few years old, they were already agreeing to decry it as too materialistic and middle class. Its version of democracy was directionless, amplifying the worst impulses of the masses rather than the leadership of a cultured superior or intellectual elite. Radicals and conservatives certainly concurred that such a society would be a disaster if it was to be the model for their own countries or the world.

But the very first debate on America, in the eighteenth century and long before the United States even existed, was over whether civilization was possible there at all. The initial thought of eighteenth-century European science, then in its infancy and much taken by ideas of innate and permanent characteristics, was that something "degenerate" about North America's environment made it innately inferior. This degeneracy theory would be discredited and eventually forgotten, yet its basic concept continued to form the basis, a subbasement in effect, for the nagging proposition that the United States was certainly different and also somehow inevitably wrong, bad, or a lesser place altogether.

European civilization's striking discovery that it was more technologically advanced and the belief that it was more spiritually and culturally advanced than America's native inhabitants had to be explained. Why were the people of this little-known land relatively backward? Were they cursed by the lack of the proper religion, some racial handicap, or an environmental deficiency? Even if one recognized the advanced civilizations of the Aztecs and Incas in South America, why was there nothing remotely equal in the north?

The resulting theory would predict that the same plight of backwardness was a powerful natural force that could also strike white Europeans who tried to settle America. This was no abstract or marginal debate. It involved Europe's best minds, the leading naturalists, scientists, and philosophers of the day. Few of those who insisted that America was intrinsically inferior to Europe ever visited there. Like those of many later anti-Americans, their theories were based on ignorance and misinformation or a distortion of facts designed to prove some political standpoint, philosophical concept, or scientific theory.

These claims could also be based on some apparently self-evident observations. Why, European thinkers asked, was the American continent so sparsely populated? Didn't this imply that it lacked the essential requirements for human life? Even if America could eventually be civilized, this task just beginning would require, as it had in Europe, countless generations to achieve. Moreover, they added, in Europe nature was fairly benign and assisted humankind, while in America such features as hurricanes, floods, lightning storms, poisonous snakes, deadly insects, and epidemic diseases were a wild force that would have to be conquered with great difficulty.

The issue of climate obsessed the Europeans, especially since they heard most about the blizzards of frosty New England, or frigid French Canada, or the humid South. In the eighteenth and nineteenth centuries, with no air conditioning or effective central heating, people were the pawns of weather. The food one ate, health or infirmity, and wealth or poverty all depended on the climate. Extremes of hot or cold were said to create unstable people and conditions inimical to progress.

Equally, most Europeans considered the taming of nature to be the basis of civilization. The gardens of England and France were well-ordered affairs in which flowers, waterfalls, and trees were made to march in discipline. Wild nature meant wild men; a disorderly environment engendered a lawless and backward society. The French philosopher Jean-Jacques Rousseau might see Native Americans as exemplars of the "noble savage" who enjoyed freedom without the burdens of an oppressive social structure. But most of his contemporaries were convinced that they were only savages plain and simple.

And how could their environment permit anything else? For either it made civilization impossible or, at best, it might take many centuries to wrest a decent society from the hostile wilderness. European thinking leaned toward the view that success was impossible. In his noted 1748 work, *The Spirit of the Law*, the French philosopher Charles de Montesquieu said that the "temper of the mind" and "passions of the heart" are prisoners to climate. In cooler ones, such as in Northern Europe, people were more vigorous, possessing additional strength, courage, and frankness while being less prone to suspicion.⁴ But he also warned that a wilderness that had remained largely uninhabited must have a dangerous climate, perhaps fatal to any colonist who went there.⁵ Taming this hostile soil and climate would require a constant, probably losing battle.⁶

Most of the ammunition for the early anti-Americans came from another Frenchman, Georges-Louis Leclerc, Comte de Buffon. Although now largely forgotten, Buffon was considered to be the greatest biologist and naturalist of his time. His works were widely read and quoted. Born in 1707 into a family of minor officials in a provincial town, he was at first an indifferent student of law and later of mathematics at the University of Angers. Leaving school, he embarked on extensive travels throughout Europe.⁷

On returning to France in 1732, however, Buffon become both serious and ambitious. Ironically, as a social-climbing, innovative, aggressive self-promoter, Buffon seemed to embody the kind of figure who two centuries later would be the French intellectuals' negative stereotype of an American. Indeed, Buffon was such a good politician that he even survived the French Revolution with his head intact, no mean feat for a man who became a royal official and aristocrat.

Buffon's success began when he started translating into French works by the British scientist Isaac Newton and others. He networked with the aristocracy until his contacts brought him to the favorable attention of King Louis XV. As a result, in 1739, Buffon was elected to the prestigious Academy of Sciences and became director of the Royal Botanical Garden, making him officially the country's top expert on nature. He was a colorful figure known for fancy clothes (his lace cuffs were famous) and the pursuit of women, money, and power.

Despite cultivating a superb image, however, he was not a very good scientist. His theories and factual statements were often wrong, not surprising since he rarely did experiments. As an excuse, Buffon claimed that focusing too much on factual details would make it harder to understand the whole, an approach that would characterize the critique of America made by many future French intellectuals.

Buffon's main work was a multivolume natural history intended to summarize all human knowledge about geology, zoology, and botany. Each known animal, for example, was described in great detail. When the first three volumes were finally published in 1749, they were translated into most European languages. Buffon became an international celebrity. In honor of his accomplishments, the king made him a count in 1771.

Aside from classifying animals, vegetables, and minerals, Buffon also divided humanity into different subgroups along racial lines. All people, he believed, had originated in a single species but had been modified by the climate, diet, and physical conditions in which they lived. America's environment was so hostile that adaptation there was the opposite of growth: it was degeneration. America would remain backward because its environment was so hostile that it made civilization there virtually impossible.

Buffon, who never visited America, insisted that nature there was "much less varied and . . . strong" than in Europe.[8] Ignorant of such impressive American animals as the buffalo and grizzly bear, Buffon claimed that the biggest American animals were "four, six, eight, and ten times" smaller than those of Europe or Africa. There was nothing to compare to the hippopotamus, elephant, or giraffe.[9] Even if the same animal could be found in both the Old and New Worlds—like the wolf and elk—the former version was always better. For example, the American puma was "smaller, weaker, and more cowardly than the real lion."[10]

The most impressive proof of America's innate degeneracy, Buffon claimed, was that "all the animals which have been transported from Europe to America—like the horse, ass, sheep, goat, hog, etc.—have become smaller."[11] What went for animals also applied to people. The Native American "is feeble and small in his organs of generation; he has neither body hair nor beard nor ardor for his female; although swifter than the European because he is better accustomed to running, he is, on the other hand, less strong in body; he is also less sensitive, and yet more timid and more cowardly; he has no vivacity, no activity of mind." In sum, using phrases like those applied by anti-Americans two centuries later to the people of the United States, he concluded, "Their heart is frozen, their society cold, their empire cruel."[12]

What caused this degeneration? Buffon thought it was due to the New World being both too cold and too humid. Without ever inhaling a breath in America, he felt confident in concluding that its air and earth were permeated with "moist and poisonous vapors" unable to give proper nourishment except to snakes and insects.[13]

This pessimistic belief was widely accepted throughout Europe.

Among the many who echoed such views was the great French philosopher Voltaire, who said that the American climate and environment were so inimical to human life that it made no sense for France to fight to obtain "a few acres of snow" there.[14] Prospective immigrants, mostly from the poorer classes, either did not hear or ignored such claims and went to America anyway.

Adding grist to the argument, though, was the work done by Peter Kalm, a scientist sent by the Royal Swedish Academy on a three-year study tour of America in 1748. In contrast to Buffon, Kalm was a meticulous scientist who, for example, recorded daily temperature readings in Philadelphia over a four-month period in 1749. But his analysis was also colored by naïveté (he believed reports that rattlesnakes caught squirrels by hypnotizing them) and bias, especially against German immigrants he met there.[15]

Echoing Buffon in his book on America, Kalm claimed that cattle brought from England became smaller. Though he acknowledged that many of the settlers were robust, he also said that they had shorter life spans than Europeans, women ceased having children earlier, and everyone was weakened by the constantly changing weather. America's climate, Kalm concluded, inevitably made people there disease-ridden and beset by aggressive insects.[16] Reviews of Kalm's book in Europe highlighted, as happened with other anti-American works, his most negative remarks.[17]

But next to Buffon, the greatest eighteenth-century popularizer of anti-American thinking was Cornelius De Pauw. Born in Holland in 1739, he spent most of his life in Berlin, Germany at the court of the Prussian king. Somehow, De Pauw, who never visited America, became Europe's leading expert on that land following publication of his book, *Philosophical Research on the Americans*, in 1768. It was a big hit in both Germany and France.

Like many later anti-Americans, he had a hidden agenda. De Pauw worked for the Prussian ruler King Frederick II, who launched a systematic anti-American campaign. Thus, Prussia became the world's first state sponsor of anti-Americanism, based on its regime's interests. Since Prussia had no colonies in the Americas, that region must be made to seem a worthless distraction and even dangerous in order to discourage the growing emigration of Germans to America, where they would become British subjects and enrich that rival country.

According to De Pauw, Europe's discovery of America was the most disastrous event in the history of civilization. Useful European products—such as wheat, clothing, and wine—were shipped off to the colonies in return for useless luxuries like gold and tobacco. Not only were animals in America smaller than in Europe, he explained, but they were also "badly formed." Those brought over from Europe became "stunted; their height shrank and their instinct and character were diminished by half."[18] Indeed, everything in America was "either degenerate or monstrous." The natives were cowardly and impotent. "In a fight the weakest European could crush them with ease." Women quickly became infertile and their children, despite an early precociousness, lost all interest and ability to learn.[19]

Initiating another key anti-American theme of later times, De Pauw was the first European to insist also on the innate inferiority of American culture. In 1776, on the verge of the American Revolution, De Pauw wrote another book explaining that there was not a single American philosopher, doctor, physicist, or scholar of note. He described Americans as stupid, indolent, lazy, drunken, physically weak, and therefore—not surprisingly—incapable of making progress.[20]

Writing in similar terms, Abbé Guillaume Thomas François Raynal, a Jesuit priest, teacher, economist, and philosopher, was another key person setting the tone for French thinking about America. His history of the Western hemisphere appeared in the 1770s and eventually went through twenty authorized editions and another twenty pirated ones. Benjamin Franklin and Thomas Jefferson read with horror its accusations that they were part of an inferior people.

"Nature," explained Raynal, "seems to have strangely neglected the New World." English settlers in America "visibly degenerated" in their new environment. They were less strong and less courageous, but also incapable of prolonged thought.[21] America failed to produce a single good poet, mathematician, or any person superior in art or science whatsoever. Granted, he explained, Americans were precocious, but then they soon slowed down and fell far behind their European counterparts.[22]

In addition to all this, Raynal could also be called the first leftist anti-American. The European conquest of America had brought death, disease, slavery, and destruction to the innocent natives there, he wrote. Since America was the child of such evil imperialism, Raynal insisted, nothing good could come of it.[23]

Anti-American ideas became so predominant in Germany as to be repeated by that country's four greatest philosophers of the era. All agreed that America was fatally cursed. Immanuel Kant wrote in 1775 that Americans are "a not yet properly formed (or half degenerated) sub-race" with a "frigidity and insensibility of temperament."[24] Climate made these people "too weak for hard work, too indifferent to pursue anything carefully, incapable of all culture, in fact lower even than the Negro."[25]

Kant's colleague, G. W. F. Hegel, like many later ideologues, had to dismiss America because it did not fit into the simplistic linear model he constructed for the development of states and civilizations. Rather than revise his categories, he had to distort the American reality to prove them. In the 1820s, Hegel argued that civilization could only develop in temperate climates, whereas in North America surviving the "glowing rays of the sun" and "icy frost" took most of people's energy. As a result, the New World's animals were smaller, weaker, and more cowardly; their meat was neither tasty nor nourishing; and the birds had unpleasant voices. America lacked such basic requirements of civilization as the presence of iron or the horse.[26]

Hegel combined the degeneration theory with a newer view of America as a failed society. The United States was held back because it had too much geography and not enough history to attain the population concentrations and traditions necessary for real civilization. It had produced nothing original and was of no real interest for Europeans.[27] There was little room in his worldview for a workable democracy, which he thought trespassed on two of his main values by putting individualism ahead of community and weakening the state for the sake of private property.[28]

A third influential German philosopher, Friedrich von Schlegel, wrote of America in 1828 that "many of the noblest and most beautiful species of animals did not exist there originally and others were found most unseemly in form and most degenerate in nature."[29] And Arthur Schopenhauer claimed in 1859 that the inferiority of American mammals went hand in hand with the country's ignorance, conceit, brutal vulgarity, and idiotic veneration of women.[30]

Even in England, which had more experience than any other European country with what would become the United States, similar thinking prevailed. The leading American expert there during the first years of U.S. independence was William Robertson, a historian, Presbyterian minister, and politician who, in his *History of America* published in 1777, repeated all the familiar arguments about the cold climate, impoverished nature, "rude and indolent people," and inferior animals.[31] The climate that had "stunted the growth and enfeebled the spirits of its native animals proved pernicious to such as have migrated into it voluntarily."[32] His book became a huge success and was translated into many languages.

As one can well imagine, these prejudices drove Americans crazy. Knowing their experience totally refuted such claims, Benjamin Franklin and Thomas Jefferson felt angry and frustrated in trying to prove that their inevitable inferiority was a myth, especially when this problem became a vital issue during the independence struggle. If America was ever to be a country instead of a colony ruled by Britain, it had to convince other Europeans to give financial and military help by showing that a viable state and economy could be created in the North American wilderness. This is why Americans so passionately welcomed Europeans like the Marquis de Lafayette or Alexis de Tocqueville, who saw America not as the permanent victim of its past but as the wave of the future.

In 1755, Franklin published a work showing that America's population was thriving, not decaying. For example, he pointed out that there were twice as many marriages in America than in Europe, each resulting in eight births compared to four in Europe, and that the population was doubling every twenty years.[33] As the patriots strove to persuade Europe to back independence for the United States, they sent Franklin to Paris as an ambassador to mobilize support.

At a banquet he held at his home there in February 1778, Franklin asked all the guests to stand against a wall in order to see who had really "degenerated." All of the eighteen Americans were taller than the eighteen Europeans there. And, as the most delicious conceivable irony, the shortest of them all—"a mere shrimp," in Franklin's words—was Raynal himself, the main champion of the claim that Europeans were physically superior![34]

Jefferson was equally obsessed with proving anti-Americanism wrong. He wrote a book, *Notes on the State of Virginia*, in part to disprove the degeneracy concept. Jefferson compiled records of the weather to prove that America was not so cold and wet. He also reported about animals that were not so tiny as detractors had claimed. He pointed out that the American bear was twice as big as its European counterpart and that fossil elephants discovered in America were gigantic. Of fourteen animals common to both continents, he concluded, seven were actually larger in America while seven more were of equal size. He compiled statistics to demonstrate how rapidly the population grew, disproving the idea that Americans were sickly and relatively infertile.[35]

After the revolution, Jefferson took Franklin's old job as the American ambassador to France, where he continued his predecessor's efforts to combat anti-American ideas. In 1787, he had the remains of a New Hampshire moose shipped to France and had it displayed in the lobby of the hotel where he lived to show that American animals were big.[36] In response to Raynal's claim that there were no distinguished Americans, Jefferson cited Washington for his military achievements, Franklin as a genius in physics, and David Rittenhouse, a Pennsylvanian who would succeed Franklin as president of the American Philosophical Society, as an astronomer and artist.[37]

Along with Jefferson's and Franklin's great efforts, the American victory over Britain in the revolution had some effect in modifying European views. After hearing Franklin describe America's growth and prosperity, Buffon in 1777 publicly rejected the degeneration theory, conceding, "In a country in which Europeans multiply so readily, where the natives live longer than elsewhere, it is hardly possible that men degenerate."[38]

Even Raynal, impressed by Franklin, admitted that education was spreading in America, children were well brought up, and Americans had more leisure time to develop their intellects than did Europeans. Indeed, reflecting his own new uncertainty about the issue, Raynal personally underwrote an essay contest on whether America was a blessing or a curse to mankind.[39]

While after 1783, America was no longer so easily criticized as a formless continent whose climate made it inferior, the degeneracy theory was still repeated by many Europeans. Alongside it, however, new claims arose about the inferiority of the American system and society. The random mixing of different immigrant groups and a democratic system, it was said, undermined any possibility for the development of good manners, fine morals, and high culture.

The revolution's triumph and the founding of the United States as a republic also encouraged European liberals, who praised America because they wanted to see more freedom and representative government in their own countries. But indeed, as so often was to happen thereafter, institutions and policies that made friends also inspired enemies, especially among conservatives or those soured by the excesses of the French Revolution who wanted to blame America as its model. Thus, the creation of the United States as a democratic republic gave birth to the idea that such a system could work elsewhere and thus encouraged those opposing that idea to prove that America was a bad role model.

Thomas Moore, an Irish romantic poet who traveled through America in 1803 and 1804, merged the old and new schools of anti-Americanism in what might have been the first anti-American poems. Despite his Irish nationalism and satires on the British, Moore was horrified at a new society he saw as miserly, quarrelsome, and uncouth. "The rude familiarity of the lower orders" and low level of society might be acceptable if they came from a new and inexperienced people. But Americans were not merely passing through a temporary youthful stage but were already so full of vice and corruption as to destroy hope that the country would be great in the future.[40]

In a series of poems on America, Moore wrote that a combined degenerate environment of "infertile strife" and a rabble of immigrants created a:

Half-organized, half-minded race
Of weak barbarians swarming o'er its breast
Like vermin gendered on the lion's crest.

Americans were "the motley dregs of every distant clime" who reeked "of anarchy and taint of crime." Like anti-Americans of two centuries later, Moore concluded that the United States had no future but was already on the decline, a dying empire.[41]

Coming from the opposite end of the political spectrum, Thomas Hamilton, a British conservative, agreed with the rebellious poet. During his visit in the 1830s, he concluded that America was plagued by a wretched climate including extreme temperature changes and emanations from swamps that blighted life.[42] Even Charles Darwin, the great British naturalist, could still suggest in the 1830s that Buffon was largely correct. If fossil evidence showed that large animals had once lived there, this only proved that any vigor or creative force America once possessed "had lost its power." Thus, America was an example of evolution heading in the wrong direction.[43]

The greatest influence in preserving the theory of degeneracy into the

1830s, as well as spreading anti-Americanism generally during that era, was a young, German-speaking, Hungarian poet named Nikolas Lenau. Famous for his melancholy moods, Lenau said he hoped that going to America would cure him. As a liberal, Lenau had considered the United States to be the beacon of liberty and regarded Europe, caught in the toils of monarchist repression, as a lost cause. This, he claimed, motivated him to emigrate to the United States in 1831.

Instead, the experience banished his political ideals. His first year seemed hopeful, but then things started going wrong. Lenau became ill and was injured in a fall from a sled. He never learned much English and lost money on a property he bought in Ohio. With his enthusiasm waning, Lenau poured his anger into letters to friends back home, which were later published in a book and also inspired a best-selling 1855 novel by the Austrian Ferdinand Kurnberger. It depicts the travels in America of a gradually disillusioned German poet who finds people there to be egotistical, materialistic, vulgar, and immature braggarts who lack civilization, religion, freedom, or equality.[44]

Lenau attributed much of his growing dislike for America to the inferiority of nature there. The idea of degeneration, he concluded, was literally true, and he claimed to see it in the moral and mental decline of German immigrants who had lost their energy and even sanity. How could such a fate be avoided in a benighted land where nature "has no feelings or imagination," being itself so monotonous that it destroyed the personalities of those dwelling there?[45]

The absence of songbirds was for Lenau a symbol of this spiritual poverty. Lenau had captured birds in Europe and kept them as pets. But in America, he wrote his brother-in-law, "There are no nightingales, indeed there are no real songbirds at all." He also could not find "a courageous dog, a fiery horse, or a man full of passion. Nature is terribly languid."[46]

This and other themes of Lenau would become staples for the critique of America in later eras. "These Americans," he wrote, "are shopkeepers with souls that stink towards heaven. They are dead for all spiritual life, completely dead. The nightingale is right when he does not want to come to these louts."[47]

Sounding like many European leftists and rightists of later generations, Lenau found America to be hopelessly materialistic. Everything was based on the almighty dollar and the rational calculation of personal interest rather than some organic connection as in an antique and traditional society. "What we call Fatherland is here merely a property insurance scheme. The American knows nothing, he seeks nothing but money. He has no ideas," and so neither state nor society had any spiritual values.[48] Lenau returned to Europe "cured . . . of the chimera of freedom and independence that I had longed for with youthful enthusiasm." The New World represented not liberty but alienation, power, numbers, and money.[49]

There was, however, one terribly ironic detail of his life that Lenau kept from his readers. He had never intended to emigrate to America but merely went there to invest in property he could lease out. The critic who had castigated America for being in the toils of an avaricious materialism had gone there to cash in for himself.[50]

But it is impossible to overestimate the impact in Europe of Lenau's vision of America. The lack of nightingales became an international symbol of everything wrong with America. Already the British poet John Keats, who had never been in America and whose chronic illness and early death did not prove the superiority of European climes, had called America "that most hateful" and "monstrous" land because, the author of "Ode to a Nightingale" complained, it had flowers without scent and birds without song.[51] The 1843 lines of the German poet Hoffmann von Fallersleben also touched on the subject:

And so no grapes hang from your vine
Nor do your flowers have a scent,
No bird can even sing a line,
And poetry its life is spent.

But the problem was not just a natural one:

It is a land with dreams deceptive filled
O'er which the concept freedom, passing by,
Enchanting, lets its shadows flutter down.[52]

It is striking that such criticism came from Fallersleben, an outspoken political liberal who supported the growing unrest in the various German lands and was eventually deported from Prussia. He had never visited America and knew it only secondhand through friends who corresponded with German immigrants in Texas. He even wrote several songs honoring that state and, unlike Lenau's approach, refused an offer of land if he emigrated there.[53] But like other rebels and romantics of the day, Lenau dreamed of a very different sort of paradise from the American experiment.

Alongside the new political and cultural complaints—which grew louder throughout the nineteenth century—the idea that the United States was a hopeless enterprise doomed by nature lived on, especially in France.[54] Some French scientists continued to insist that the degeneracy theory was right and that Americans aged faster while horses, dogs, and bulls there showed less vigor and courage than in Europe.[55]

Indeed, criticism about America based on its environmental conditions, reminiscent of the degeneracy theory, survived well into the twentieth century. In 1929, the Frenchman Régis Michaud, who taught French literature for twelve years at U.S. universities and wrote a critical book on America, described, among many other vices, the United States as "a geographic mass without harmony, a country of contrasts and disparities on a grande scale with a violent climate."[56]

In 1933, the French diplomat and poet Paul Claudel wrote in his journal, while serving in Washington, that the early American statesman Alexander Hamilton had admitted that America's inferior climate stopped dogs from barking. In fact, this was one of De Pauw's claims that Hamilton had ridiculed.[57] Shortly thereafter, the liberal British poet W. H. Auden bemoaned the excesses of America's climate, including vast numbers of insects, snakes, and poison ivy. "The truth is," he wrote, "nature never intended human beings to live here and her hostility" forced its original inhabitants to a nomadic existence and continued to plague their successors.[58]

During anti-Americanism's first epoch, the cause of that country's inevitable failure was placed on the innately inferior nature of the land. After America's independence, though, this blame was increasingly transferred to a degraded people who lived in a badly structured society. By the 1830s, fear grew in Europe that ideas embodied in the United States—republicanism, materialism, the leveling of classes, and a rejection of aristocratic high culture—would spread back across the Atlantic Ocean.

In the reactionary climate following the French Revolution's turn toward terror and dictatorship, Napoleon's aggressive wars, and the challenge posed by democratic movements, the Old World's existing system seemed far more welcome to much of the political and intellectual elite there. It was thought better by those in the most privileged groups to stick with the status quo of monarchy, high culture, a strong class system, a traditional economy, and aristocratic-dominated politics than to make risky changes that threatened their interests and were obviously not going to work. Ironically, many of the antidemocratic ideas developed by the European right at this time would later become staples of the leftist critique of America.

Of course, all peoples like to see their innate superiority asserted and "proven." Americans themselves would certainly be no exception to this rule. Yet once the United States was established as a living challenge to the European monarchies, anti-Americanism came to serve a specific political function. While anti-Americanism still incorporated aspects of the degeneracy theory, it increasingly focused on the claim that the American democratic experiment was a failure leading to a degraded society and culture. As degeneracy theory declined throughout the nineteenth century, in the new version of anti-Americanism the Americans were still judged uncivilized and degenerate. But now they had no one to blame but themselves for this sorry state of affairs.

THE DISTASTEFUL REPUBLIC

The United States was a revolutionary experiment, a new type of country without a monarch, an aristocracy, strong traditions, an official religion, or a rigid class system. As the British journalist Henry Fairlie later wrote of this era, "One thing was agreed. For good or ill, America was the omen of something new that was happening in the world."[1] If the United States succeeded in proving itself a better way of organizing a society, the status quo in every other existing polity would be questioned and might well be jeopardized.

In the American republic's early years, this potential threat was handled largely through ridicule. By portraying America as an obvious and inevitable failure, European critics hoped that no one would follow its example and thus the danger would be averted.

The idea that civilization could never arise in America, the degeneracy theory, had been the first stage of anti-Americanism. The second stage was the claim that the Americans' efforts to create a civilization had failed. This view generally dominated the anti-American critique in the years between the creation of the U.S. system in 1783 until roughly the end of the Civil War in 1865.

Of course, some Europeans did think that the United States was offering a vision of something new and fresh that they wanted for their own countries. The popular German writer Johann Wolfgang von Goethe, for example, penned an ode to the United States embodying that view:

America, thy happy lot
above old Europe's I exalt:
Thou hast no castle ruin hoar
No giant columns of basalt.
Thy soul is not troubled
In living light of day
By useless traditions,
vain strife and array.[2]

With reform- and revolution-minded Europeans being inspired by the American precedent, their political adversaries had all the more reason to despise and discredit it. Nineteenth-century history proved just how subversive was the American example, the appeal of its ideas and institutions. Following the establishment of the United States, a series of struggles convulsed Europe that included the French Revolution, the rise of a British reform movement, continent-wide upheavals in 1848, and many more skirmishes in the conflict between aristocratic and democratic rule.

While the United States did not directly sponsor foreign democratic movements, its revolution was as inspirational for the nineteenth century as the Russian Communist revolution was for the twentieth: the resulting political system was an alternative to all existing societies that entranced some, repelled others, and could be ignored by no one.

The founders and early leaders of the United States were aware of their unique role as a democratic revolution confronting countries with a different system. "The Royalists everywhere detest and despise us as republicans," wrote John Quincy Adams shortly after the triumph of European reaction at the 1815 Congress of Vienna. America's political principles "make the throne of every European monarch rock under him as with the throes of an earthquake." America's growth and prosperity would naturally arouse jealousy and antagonism abroad because of its role as an alternative model.[3]

In a July 4, 1821, speech in Washington before an audience including the European diplomatic corps, then-President John Quincy Adams explained that America represented a new type of government "destined to cover the surface of the globe. It demolished at a stroke the lawfulness of all governments founded upon conquest. It swept away all the rubbish of accumulated centuries of servitude."[4]

For those viewing the United States as a threat to all existing Western civilization, destructive of order and an enemy of traditional values, discrediting it became a matter of life and death. Such was literally the case for Simon Linguet, a French lawyer, who warned in the 1780s that a rabble of adventurers would use the continent's rich resources to make the United States a great economic power. Eventually, he predicted, America's armies would cross the Atlantic, subjugate Europe, and destroy civilization.[5] Linguet did not have to wait long to see the society he revered destroyed by new ideas paralleling those in America. He was guillotined by the French revolutionaries in 1794.

In Britain, for the majority of the upper class seeking to limit democracy, the French Revolution's terror and disorder confirmed their fear that the kind of liberty and equality existing in America was dangerous. "Britain . . . has naught to learn from the present state of American democracy," wrote a clergyman named George Lewis in 1845 after spending several years in America, "except to thank God for the more compact and secure fabric of British freedom."[6]

Most Europeans visiting America to write about it—as opposed to those who went there as immigrants—were wealthy, conservative, and not predisposed to sympathy with the new country. Only the rich could afford the cost and time required for such a voyage. Most of them were repelled by that nation's basic precepts, democratic political institutions, and primitive cultural level.

Yet even when accurately noting the new country's problems, critics often wrongly insisted that these faults were innate in the American system rather than correctable over time. Of course, America was still very much a society in development, but many of its symptoms were those of youth that experience and experiment would solve. At the same time, it was also true that there was a spirit of America different from that of Europe. Many of the characteristics Europeans disliked—such as classlessness, secularism, and informality—derived from broader trends of modernity, which, though few realized it in the early nineteenth century, would come to characterize Western society in general.

Equally, the emerging American society was the global prophet of a pragmatic worldview not to European taste, especially outside of Britain. This worldview, so thoroughly integrated into their life and culture as to be taken for granted by Americans, can simply be described as judging any system, institution, or idea on how well it works in practice and showing a readiness to discard whatever fails that test. In contrast, European civilization up to that time—and, to a large extent, since then—judged everything on how well it accorded to past practices. Change was viewed as dangerous and destabilizing; the benefit of the doubt rested with the status quo. Innovations were often judged not on their own merit but rather on whether they fit with some preexisting doctrine or theory of how things should work.

Obviously, a pragmatic approach can mean jettisoning much that is good. Anti-Americans saw it as a general assault on tradition, high cultural standards, intellectual life, and all the good things of the past they cherished. They were blind to the benefits of that powerful American optimism and readiness for change that kept the door open to beneficial innovations while facilitating the correction of faults. Moreover, pragmatism was the basis for modernization and for challenging all the past's bad, nonfunctional aspects. Pragmatism was America's great philosophical and practical innovation. All the specific aspects of its model—equality, free enterprise, democracy, human rights, industrialization, and so on—related to this worldview.

While all the negative claims about America did not discourage many thousands of immigrants from going to America, they certainly shaped the views of future Europeans: those left behind who had never been there. It often seems, too, as if Europe's rejection of many factors at the root of future American success were reasons why it would fall behind in many arenas. Indeed, it was a mistake for the German philosopher Arthur Schopenhauer to couple in his condemnation of America "the most vile [pragmatism] combined with its inevitable companion, ignorance."[7] Ultimately, it was precisely American practicality that inspired battles against ignorance.

One of the most disconcerting notions emerging from the U.S. system was the advocacy of equality, not as some abstract ideal but as a reality of daily life. The assumption was that the best way to maximize human potential was to give the largest number of people the best possible chance of contributing to society. And if this goal was far from fully realized at the start of the United States, U.S. society continued to evolve toward implementing that principle.

Of course, people did not remain equal in practice. Some factor would determine the rise and fall of individuals' status. The nineteenth-century American measure of success, still a key theme today despite many changes in emphasis, was that worldly achievement would be largely the result of ability and hard work. This was a reaction against a Europe that Americans saw as bound by an aristocratic system that rewarded people simply for the good fortune of their birth. Most Europeans argued in contrast that by giving primacy to those who were literally noble, their system set a high standard of manners and culture. Underneath its democratic facade, they saw America as simply giving first place to those who attained wealth.

Though surface aspects of these arguments would shift over two centuries as Europe in some ways came to resemble America more closely, the essential difference between the viewpoints would remain. Europe would see itself as the repository of a high-quality culture, spiritual values, and intellectual merit. America was seen by them as a society in which an unbridled capitalism determined everything on the basis of profit and market rather than quality, ideas, or values. And if their own societies were moving in this wrong direction—in Europe and elsewhere—the blame was often put on the local imitation or external influence of America.

While many of these ideas developed among European conservatives in the early nineteenth century, the seeds of the left's parallel critique could already be seen in the European romantic movement's anti-Americanism. A country extolling materialistic pragmatism did not appeal to those extolling the transcendental glory of a society emphasizing high aesthetic values. America, then, was equally distasteful to the aristocrat who revered the European status quo and to the romantic rebel who hoped for spiritual transcendence, just as their right- and left-wing descendants would often agree only on the idea that America was not what they wanted.

As a result of their personal predilections, then, European critics often ignored the new society's practical accomplishments and reduced the United States to a country that merely permitted and encouraged money-making as its ideal. To make matters worse, European intellectuals and artists could never forgive the United States for denying their class the exalted or central role that they claimed to hold in Europe.

Such achievements as freedom from the restraints of Europe's class order, human rights, or the chance for individual betterment were discounted as dangerous illusions by the European critics. The United States was portrayed as merely an artificial creation with no animating spirit. As the Norwegian-born scientist and poet Henrik Steffens put it, America was "a classical statue, cold, motionless, it did not raise its eyes nor move its limbs and there was no living heart beating in its breast."[8] Its freedom was actually an insidious form of slavery. Steffens mixed his science with romantic philosophy. He was convinced that social progress could bring greater individual development. Instead, like others, he found America to be dominated by conformity and the enslavement of individuals to material goods. Steffens found America to be especially repugnant since, like others who would become harsh critics, he thought it contradicted his cherished theory.

The argument that the United States was soulless gained a virtual consensus among European critics. Americans, wrote the French novelist Marie-Henri Beyle, best known as Stendhal, "seem to have done away with a part of themselves. The wells of feeling appear to have dried up; they are just, they have common sense and they are unhappy."[9] The French diplomat Charles Maurice de Talleyrand, who visited the United States in the 1790s, determined that "the American people are perhaps the people least acquainted with passion in the whole world."[10] Victor Jacquemont, a friend of Lafayette and a naturalist, concluded after one night in New York in 1827 that the minds of Americans were "generally merely cold, platitudinous and vulgar."[11] Kant echoed this theme a few years later in explaining that Americans were incapable of civilization because they "had no passion, hardly speak at all, never caress one another, care about nothing, and are lazy."[12]

Even as the United States was being disrespected precisely in order to undercut its real and potential influence on Europe, its ingenious political structures and remarkably original revolution were being denied. When Europeans spoke of great revolutions, either to exalt or decry them, the French and not the American model was the standard for judgment.

For conservatives, the horrors of the French Revolution and the failed republic that followed showed the dangers of such experiments, a category in which they included the United States. They shuddered at its example, which gave them added incentive to find the American version a failure as well, one more proof that democracy didn't work or at best produced a dreadful society.

For Romantics as well as the political radicals who were starting to preach the revolutionary transformation of their own societies, the fact that the French Revolution had brought disaster to its own people and the continent—with its reign of terror, quick reversion to dictatorship, imperialist ambitions, and endless wars—was no proof that the American version was superior. For them, the American counterpart was too bland, bourgeois, and boring, insufficiently utopian or theoretical. In fact, before King Louis XVI was beheaded by them, some French radicals proposed it to be a sufficiently cruel punishment to exile him to Philadelphia,[13] then the capital of American society and culture, anticipating by 150 years the comedian W. C. Fields's famous joke that being in that city was preferable only to death.

Both sides often missed the point, viewing as shortcomings precisely the factors that made America succeed. Thus, in 1823, the Austrian diplomat Johann Georg Hulsemann denounced the country's "incoherence" in such institutions as the "separation of powers which, as well-known, is a theoretical error."[14] The word "theoretical" here is most significant. The great breakthrough of Franklin, Jefferson, James Madison, and their colleagues in devising a new and workable system of government based on federalism (a division of authority between central and state governments) and checks and balances (a division of power between the executive, legislative, and judicial branches of government) was of no importance.

Yet it was precisely this structure that was the centerpiece of the system's success. Gradually, European systems would move closer to an American-style model. But in the nineteenth century and afterward, the European left and right often extolled a centralization of power that would constantly produce failed regimes and repressive dictatorships in France, the USSR, and throughout the Third World. Ridiculed as purely practical, America was thought incapable of producing any valid political philosophy. The fact that its system worked so well in practice was thus irrelevant. The lack of guillotines and the absence of any decline into dictatorship were not counted to its credit.

Not everyone in Europe mocked the American system, but a remarkable number of people did so, including the leading philosophers and historians of the day. Often targeted for ridicule was the notion of giving the common people a voice in governing. It was, as one French observer, Abbé de Mably, wrote in his book about the government and laws of the United States in 1784, dangerous and impractical,[15] especially because as common people went, those of the United States were particularly unimpressive.

In the words of François Soules's 1787 history of the American revolution, "In America the wise are few indeed in comparison with the ignorant, the selfish, and those men who blindly allow themselves led."[16] American-style democracy was a step backward, wrote the German poet Ludwig Borne in 1830, into a "monstrous prison of freedom" whose "invisible chains" were more oppressive than the visible ones in Germany, for in the United States, "the most repulsive of all tyrants, the populace, hold vulgar sway."[17] Louis Marie Turreau de Linières, former French ambassador to the United States, agreed that it was "a fraud" to let common Americans influence public affairs since they were incapable of reasoning. The Bill of Rights would cause anarchy because it would paralyze government from acting effectively.[18]

Thus, the French novelist Stendhal, writing in 1830, concluded that American-style democracy was boring and banal because it let "the tyranny of opinion" of the small-minded masses control society.[19] Another French writer, Felix de Beaujour, consul-general in Washington from 1804 to 1811, was so critical of the United States that the British used his book as anti-American propaganda during the War of 1812, when they again fought the Americans.[20] Beaujour explained that unless the Senate was elected for life and the House of Representatives limited to big landowners, the U.S. government would collapse in despotism or disunion.[21]

An economy that bred rampant materialism was seen as the counterpart of a spiritually empty society and an unworkable political system. The country's obsession with greed combined with mob rule, Beaujour wrote, and ensured that American civilization would be "ugly and vulgar, with unpolished manners, indelicate feelings, primitive social life, and conversation entirely centered on money."[22] In 1783, the German historian A. L. von Schlozer wrote that as a "commercial country," the United States had replaced monarch and aristocracy with "the nobility of money, which is far more dangerous and tyrannical." The revolutionary German dramatist Karl Gutzkow expressed the same idea in the mid-nineteenth century: "It is unbelievable how easily the American can change ideas into money."[23]

This was a consensus view among much of the European elite and intelligentsia. Heinrich Heine, the romantic German poet, concluded, "Worldly utility is their true religion and money is their God, their once all-powerful God."[24] The stereotype of the grasping Yankee, who lived only to work and profit while neglecting all spiritual or cultural values, would remain unchanged over the decades.

As scores of European writers purveyed this image, it entered the world of fiction and in many forms passed down to the following generations. In the mid-nineteenth century, several German novels focused on the unfortunate experiences of immigrants in America: the violence, theft, and fraud practiced on newcomers, as well as American arrogance and greed. Some authors openly said their purpose for writing such things was to stop emigration to the United States.[25]

For example, in his 1841 German novel, Rulemann Friedrich Eylert writes of the unhappy experiences of a German immigrant, who discovers that "degraded thinking, lying, deception, and unlimited greed are the natural and inescapable consequences of the commercial spirit . . . that like a tidal wave inundates the highest and lowest elements of American society. Every harmless passion and all moral sentiments are blunted in the daily pursuit of money."[26]

This theme is illustrated by incidents that might easily have taken place in Germany. The hero breaks an oil lamp at a hotel and is sent to jail when he cannot pay for the damage. The hotelkeeper bribes his lawyer so that the poor man is sentenced to be a servant at the inn and has to work long hours. A fellow immigrant tells him the secret of success in America: work hard and deny oneself all pleasure, which the author called "the best and truest description of the whole American character" and quite different from the German spirit.[27]

Ferdinand Kurnberger, in his very popular 1855 tale of a similarly disillusioned German immigrant, agrees that American culture is impoverished.[28] Newsboys sell smutty literature, and a "Negro band" plays so badly that the German has to correct them. A student tells him, quoting Franklin, that "time is money"—a concept particularly repugnant to the author—and that man's purpose on earth is to produce wealth. A boarding house owner's dilution of his champagne with brandy is a symbol of decadence. In an art gallery, puritanical Americans put clothes on Greek statues. A German immigrant who tries to spread culture in America is hung. The hero remarks, "All men are equal. Does that mean all hogs are equal? What a sham this culture is."[29]

The basic cultural critique of America prevalent in twentieth- and twenty-first-century Europe was already in place by the 1830s, long before the onset of mass production, consumerism, Hollywood, or television. Materialism plus democracy made for a spiritual emptiness. The United States was a mass culture based on the lowest common denominator. Instead of standards being set by an aristocratic and privileged class of intellectuals and artists, its society catered to the vulgar mob with low values, bad manners, and a grubby materialistic outlook.

Perrin Du Lac, who visited the American frontier in the first years of the nineteenth century, turned an equally memorable phrase about how materialism destroyed any cultural or spiritual values: "A brook, were it worthy of the muse of Virgil . . . is nothing to them but so much pure water, so of no value." In general, Americans only cared for material things: "A good Havana cigar, a newspaper, and a bottle of Madeira— those are the joys of an American life."[30] Yet those who extolled the virtues of material deprivation for the masses' spiritual welfare rarely themselves shared in this supposedly beneficial lifestyle.

Nothing reveals the universality of this view of American materialism more than the fact that it was echoed by even one of the greatest European defenders of the United States, the French nobleman Alexis de Tocqueville. Americans, he explained, were so insensible to the wonders of nature that they only "perceive the mighty forests that surround them [when] they fall beneath the hatchet." In sum, he concluded, "Nothing conceivable is so petty, so insipid, so crowded with paltry interests—in one word, anti-poetic—as the life of a man in the United States."[31]

The story behind Tocqueville's trip to the United States gives important clues to the disdainful conclusions of so many European visitors. When Tocqueville wrote about America, he was heavily influenced by the current situation and recent experiences of his own country. In the 1830s, no place in the world had suffered more from the excesses of democracy. France's own revolution had been followed by a quarter-century of turmoil that ended in a devastating national defeat with Napoleon's fall in 1815.

Tocqueville decided to make his famous visit to America when the conservative Bourbon monarchy he served was overthrown in 1830 by a regime oriented toward middle-class demands. This was precisely the kind of regime that anti-Americans identified negatively with the United States. Unhappy with the transition, Tocqueville looked for a way to get out of Paris for a while, nominally to study the American prison system for the French Ministry of Justice. Instead, he produced his two-volume *Democracy in America*, published in 1834 and 1840.

While Tocqueville's praise of the United States is well-known to Americans, rarely noted is the fact that he shared most of the contemporary European criticisms of its state and society. He wrote: "Unlimited power is in itself a bad and dangerous thing. Human beings are not competent to exercise with discretion. . . . The main evil of the present democratic institutions of the United States does not arise, as it is often asserted in Europe, from their weakness, but from their irresistible strength. I am not so much alarmed at the excessive liberty which reigns in that country as at . . . the inadequate securities which one finds there against tyranny."[32]

Yet Tocqueville's words seem to relate more to the French Revolution's Reign of Terror, the guillotine, and Napoleon than to the rule of Washington, Jefferson, and Madison. When the author describes America, he is frightened not by dictatorship from above but about tyranny arising from below, by public opinion and such institutions as elected legislatures or juries drawn from common citizens. America's rulers, he complains, are only passive tools of the masses. Writing at a time when autocracy was ascendant in much of Europe, with rampant censorship and repression, he concludes, "I know of no country in which there is so little independence of mind and real freedom of discussion."[33] So great is this alleged majority tyranny that "freedom of opinion does not exist in America." The power of the majority "is so absolute and so irresistible" that dissent from it would bring ruin. Thus, no one dares to voice his own view.[34]

He writes that in the United States, "The power of the majority [far] surpasses all the powers with which we are acquainted in Europe."[35] In Europe, opposition views circulate in secret. But in America, he explains, discussion is open only until the majority decides, and once that happens, "Everyone is silent, and the friends as well as the opponents of the measure unite in assenting to its propriety." This type of repression explains why America stifles literary genius.[36] In effect, he makes the United States sound as if it practices the "democratic centralism" that was later a principle of Communist parties, in which discussion is only permitted before the party line is set, a mistaken view of America still being voiced by Europeans in the twenty-first century.

In a remarkable passage, Tocqueville foresees the type of "repressive tolerance" critique that would characterize the European post-Marxist left's critique of the United States. By instituting democracy and satisfying peoples' needs, he seems to say, America has created a terrible society because it undermines the desire to revolt against it:

> The Inquisition has never been able to prevent a vast number of anti-religious books from circulating in Spain. The empire of the majority succeeds much better in the United States, since it actually removes any wish to publish them. Unbelievers are to be met with in America, but there is no public organ of infidelity. Attempts have been made by some governments to protect morality by prohibiting licentious books. In the United States no one is punished for this sort of books, but no one is induced to write them; not because all the citizens are immaculate in conduct, but because the majority of the community is decent and orderly.[37]

If Tocqueville had been a romantic, he might have attributed this problem to the absence of spirit that would give rise to poetry and philosophy or at least have pointed to the weakness of an intellectual class in providing guidance and high culture. As a conservative, though, he concludes that the proper element missing in the society is the absence of guidance by an aristocratic class secure in its wealth and values.

As a result, Tocqueville is sure that pragmatism must lead to a mindless materialism. Americans, he writes, are tormented by a vague dread "lest they should not have chosen the shortest path which may lead to" their own welfare.[38] The American "clings to his world's goods as if he were certain never to die; and he is so hasty in grasping at all within his reach that one would suppose he was constantly afraid of not living long enough to enjoy them. He clutches everything, he holds nothing fast, but soon loosens his grasp to pursue fresh gratifications."[39]

While Tocqueville was a better reporter of what he saw than most of the other visiting writers, he shared the agenda of most to prove beyond any doubt that democracy was a bad system that should not be imitated by France or Europe in general. Virtually identical sentiments also dominated the British elite's perspective on the United States. It had watched with horror events in France and engaged in an all-out war to defeat the revolutionary regime there in addition to fighting two wars with the United States. Following the victory over Napoleon in 1815 came several decades of internal British struggles between reformers demanding more democracy and Tories fighting against change.

British conservatives focused on the same points as their French counterparts but with their own national flavor. G. D. Warburton took a vacation to New England in 1844 and concluded that the Constitution's authors had shown but "the ingenuity of the madman" and democracy meant the reign of the "oracle of the pot-house and the ignorant swineherd of the backwoods."[40]

One simple factor making the British believe that the American experiment had to be flawed was the fact that the colonists had rebelled against the mother country and then established a very different kind of society. And anything different from Britain, in British eyes—or, more broadly, anything different from Europe in European eyes—had to be inferior. Edward Wakefield, an influential writer in the 1830s and 1840s— one of his books was entitled the *Art of Colonization*—saw the problem as a failure to transfer to America the British social structure. Unchecked access to the frontier had created people who were too isolated and independent, bereft of the beneficial presence of aristocrats and gentleman capitalists.[41]

He derided Americans as a "new people" who increased in number but made "no progress in the art of living." In terms of wealth, knowledge, skill, taste, and civilization in general, they had "degenerated from their [British] ancestors." They lacked education, moved around too much, did not acquire a great enough wealth to be an elite (except the slave owners), and were too violent, vain, obstinate, intolerant, and aggressive. Their notion of equality was too extreme and against nature, favoring the vile over the noble. In short, they were "a people who become rotten before they are ripe." As the father of the colonization of New Zealand, Wakefield consciously tried to set up that society as an alternative that would avoid all the mistakes of America.[42]

Ironically, Wakefield came from a radical Quaker family, but as so often happened, anti-Americanism blended radicalism and conservativism. As one historian characterizes his thought, Wakefield viewed the proper colonial community as harkening "back to a legendary past, to the squire surrounded by his contented, cap-tipping yokels, in the good old days before industrialism and new ideas had upset the rural harmony."[43]

Equally blunt on this issue was Frederick Marryat, who was a former British government official as well as a former naval officer and author of popular sea tales. Marryat's agenda was to prove democracy, or at least what he considered to be the excessive democracy ruining the United States, dangerous.

Both Tocqueville and Marryat made their visits at a time when populism was at one of its highest points in U.S. history. The defeat of the austere President John Quincy Adams, about the closest thing to an American aristocrat, by Andrew Jackson in 1828 ushered in a period in which frontier regions held more influence and American culture became self-consciously more mass-oriented. It was an era certain to feed Europeans' worst fears, though they might well have reached the same conclusions anyway.

At the age of forty-five, in 1837, Marryat made a grand tour of America and produced a popular book about his travels. He concluded, "With all its imperfections, democracy is the form of government best suited to the present condition of America." Given Marryat's views, this was apparently not intended as a compliment.[44]

Compared to Tocqueville's literary elegance, however, Marryat was quite blunt. Political equality, he wrote, made "the scum . . . uppermost, and they do not see below it. The prudent, the enlightened, the wise, and the good, have all retired into the shade, preferring to pass a life of quiet retirement, rather than submit to the insolence and dictation of a mob."[45]

He concluded that the United States "has proven to the world that, with every advantage on her side, the attempt at a republic has been a miserable failure and that the time is not yet come when mankind can govern themselves. Will it ever come? In my opinion, never."[46] He added, "No people have as yet been sufficiently enlightened to govern themselves."[47]

Marryat's political prejudices were reinforced by events. In 1837, a rebellion against British rule broke out in Canada, and Americans sympathized with it. The media whipped up anti-British sentiment, and the U.S. government let anti-British insurgents operate from American territory in New York state until a group of British loyalists crossed the border and destroyed their base. Marryat, at that moment visiting Toronto, attended a dinner honoring the raiders and toasted them. When news of this behavior reached the United States, he was denounced in the press and burned in effigy.

As one might expect, this did not make Marryat fond of the American press, which he considered "licentious to the highest possible degree."[48] As a result, he wrote, mutual defamation was a pervasive disease in America, and everyone was "suspicious and cautious of his neighbor." The real cause of this internecine warfare was each citizen's relentless effort to maintain equality by pulling everyone down to his own level.[49]

Yet this kind of rot was said to pervade all aspects of American life. Giving the common people education, for example, and teaching them to read and write merely corrupted "those who might have been more virtuous and happy in their ignorance." Parents, Marryat wrote, did not control their children, who learned only what they wanted from a school curriculum that was largely republican propaganda teaching students to hate monarchies and glorify revolution. The schooling for the elite was inferior to Europe's, and there were few who could be called "a very highly educated man."[50]

Most European observers agreed with Marryat's conclusion that, at best, American society was "a chaotic mass" with little that was "valuable or interesting."[51] Jacquemont's assessment of Americans was: "Disgusting, disgusting! It is shameful to speak of them: these animals are below criticism. . . . No population is as anti-picturesque. . . . [The United States is a] free and boring country."[52]

It was hardly surprising, then, that Europeans thought that bad taste was king in America. Du Lac reported that liberalism was the enemy of politeness, for if everyone was equal, no one would give deference to others. On the contrary, they would be obnoxious in asserting their rights. In theatres, men kept their hats on, smoked smelly cigars, and did not give up their seats to ladies, who, for their part, were pretty enough at first but lost their teeth by the age of eighteen, lost their looks by age twenty, and were constantly wiping their noses.[53]

Talleyrand spoke of Americans as clumsy parvenus who wore hats "that a European peasant would not be caught dead in." Unsurprisingly, the Frenchman found the cuisine dreadful. It was a country of "32 religions and only one dish . . . and even that [is] inedible."[54]

Yet while America was seen as banal, passionless, and ruled by conformity, it was simultaneously—and not without reason—portrayed as an extraordinarily hot-headed and violent place. Before the cowboys existed as a stereotype, Americans were compared to the "Indians" in this respect. By 1785, a British dictionary was defining the word "gouge" as "to squeeze out a man's eye with the thumb, a cruel practice used by the Bostonians in America."[55] Certainly, there was great lawlessness, especially on the frontier. European visitors were able to catalogue a wide variety of murders, shootings, knifings, duels, and lynching. This problem, too, was ascribed to democracy. In Marryat's words, "Dueling always has been and always will be, one of the evils of democracy."[56] This was a strange distortion since that practice had long been a mainstay of European aristocrats. Still, the idea of Americans as excessively and irrationally violent people would become another of the enduring European stereotypes.

As the first half of the nineteenth century went by, some British visitors became more outspokenly critical of slavery.[57] But the personal habit that seemed to symbolize everything Europeans disliked about America was tobacco chewing. Alexander Mackay, a British journalist who wrote a travel book in 1849, described a veritable flood of tobacco juice squirting throughout railroad cars. Passengers spit between Mackay's feet and over his shoulders. One even took a piece of tobacco from his mouth and drew pictures on a window with it.[58]

Heine, who never visited the United States, wrote a poem about this vice in 1851:

I have sometimes thought to sail
To America the free
To that Freedom Stable where
All the boors live equally.
But I fear a land where men
Chew tobacco in platoons,
There's no king among the pins,
And they spit without spittoons.[59]

"I hardly know of any annoyance so deeply repugnant to English feelings, as the incessant remorseless spitting of Americans," said the

British writer Frances Trollope, who added that this habit had made the lips of male Americans "almost uniformly thin and compressed."[60]

Trollope might have been the single most influential person shaping European perceptions of America in the first half of the nineteenth century. Her book *Domestic Manners of the Americans*, published in 1832, enjoyed a phenomenal success and was translated into several languages. Within a few years, people were speaking of "to trollopise," meaning to criticize the Americans. To sit "legs à la trollope" referred to that rude allegedly American habit of putting one's feet on the table and slouching back in a chair.[61]

So much did she dislike the United States that the experience of visiting there transformed her from an optimistic liberal advocate for democracy to a reactionary opponent of change. A summary of her impressions may be gleaned by her conclusion that the main reason to visit America is "that we shall feel the more contented with our own country."[62] In retaliation, on display in New York was a waxwork of the author in the shape of a goblin.[63]

Trollope never set out to play such a historic role. In 1827 she arrived in Cincinnati with three small children, sent by her eccentric husband to open a department store there. The store went bankrupt, and Trollope was stranded with her ill offspring. Desperate for money, she hit on the novel idea of writing a best seller. Americans criticized her book but bought it anyway. Even British liberals condemned it as an exaggerated indictment. Still, it proved a most persuasive one.[64]

The focus of her attack was America's ascetic and cultural failings. Like other Europeans before her, she disliked American nature and people for being too wild compared to the highly domesticated ideal symbolized by the British garden. This simile was extended to American behavior, which she saw as equally untamed. Asked the greatest difference between England and the United States, Trollope pointed to the latter's "want of refinement." No one had an interest in high culture. In America, she explained, "that polish which removes the coarser and rougher parts of our nature is unknown and undreamed of."[65]

People ate too fast, had bad table manners, spoke poor English, talked too much about politics and religion (subjects not appropriate for public conversation), and rode roughshod over personal privacy. American gregariousness grated on her British sensibilities. When she wanted to take her meals at a Memphis hotel in a private room rather than with the rest of the guests, the landlady became angry. In Cincinnati, a hotel-keeper demanded that she drink her tea with the other guests or leave. People tried to engage her in conversation when she wanted to be left alone. She even complained that Americans, at least white ones, could not sing a song in tune. Women walked badly and their clothes, except in Philadelphia, were in terrible taste.

In this vein, a leading British journalist, G. S. Venables, wrote in November 1866: "Perhaps an American England may produce a higher average of happiness than the existing system, but it would not be a country for a gentleman, and I for one would be quite a stranger in it."[66] The essayist Matthew Arnold pointed out that in Europe, one was assigned a place in society at birth, while in the United States one must create it.[67] For those already at the top of society—in terms of privilege, power, or prestige—this was a frightening thought.

Always, the subtext was the ruinous nature of the American belief in equality, ranging from the low character of American political leaders to the difficulty of finding proper servants among such people. Indeed, Trollope wrote, "If refinement once creeps in among them, if they once learn to cling to the graces, the honors, the chivalry of life, then we shall say farewell to American equality, and welcome to European fellowship one of the finest countries on earth."[68]

This was a remarkable revelation of a major anti-American theme. Any positive effect of equality was more than cancelled out by the fact that it would undermine the social position of those shaping Europe's interpretation of America. The success of America and its imitation by their own countries would undermine—or, at least, they thought it would undermine—their personal interests. In short, anti-Americanism was a class interest, not of the masses—who were the ones most likely to emigrate—but of the elite.

Another negative consequence of America's emphasis on freedom and equality was said to be an excessively elevated status for women and children. This criticism was also intended to prove that the United States had rejected the natural order of society. Schopenhauer's list of American sins included a "foolish adoration of women."[69] Like others, Médéric Louis Elie Moreau de Saint-Méry, a Frenchman who owned a bookstore in Philadelphia in the 1790s, claimed that American women soon lost their beauty (due to the terrible climate) and never found good taste. He also thought their breasts excessively small. But most importantly, he and other Europeans thought they were not well-behaved, obedient, or affectionate.[70]

America was sarcastically nicknamed in some European writings a "paradise for women." In a classic statement of the German writer Rulemann Friedrich Eylert:

Woman! Do you want to see yourself restored to your aboriginal place of honor with your husband in the house as your slave and at your side in society? Do you want him to dance to your tune and early in the morning rush to buy meat, butter, vegetables and eggs, while you lie comfortably in bed and devote yourself to sweet morning dreams? . . . If you want to experience the full blessings of a pampered existence, then go to America, become naturalized, purchase an American husband, and you are emancipated.[71]

The underlying problem in this allegedly exalted status was that equality had gone too far, even in an age when no woman could vote.

Another German contemporary wrote of the "typical" American woman: "She always carried books, brochures, and newspapers on her memorandum book and pencil, with which to copy down fragments from books and conversations. Full of claims to nobility, she nevertheless played the part of an avowed republican. She combined information with misinformation, common sense with transcendental nonsense . . . one of those educated women who because of pretensions to equality with men have lost all the charm and advantages of their sex."[72]

A working-class Scotsman, James D. Burns, who visited the United States during the Civil War, in his book about the experience recorded, "In America, female notions of equality and personal independence have to a great extent reversed the old order of things in the relation of the sexes. . . . The woman has made up her mind not to be bossed by her husband, which means she will do as she likes irrespective of his will." This damaged marriage and led to more frequent divorces.[73]

Already, when Hollywood was still a howling wilderness, Americans were also said to be juvenile and obsessed with being youthful. The United States, as an immature society rejecting tradition, was a veritable never-land of Peter Pans determined to stay young forever. "In America," said one wit, "the young are always ready to give to those who are older than themselves the full benefits of their inexperience."[74] This was precisely what Europeans accused America of trying to do to them. As always, Oscar Wilde put it best and briefest: "The youth of America is their oldest tradition. It has been going on now for 300 years."[75]

Given the alleged exalted status of children attributed to American society, one could hardly blame Americans for wanting to stay young. According to James F. Muirhead, a British editor of guidebooks to the United States, children there "learn to throw off the restraints of parental authority" since they feel, according to the national credo, that they are "equal to everyone. I do not know of any task more difficult than for a father to keep his children well in hand."

Muirhead added: "Nowhere is the child so constantly in evidence; nowhere are his wishes so carefully consulted; nowhere is he allowed to make his mark so strongly on society in general. . . . The small American . . . interrupts the conversation of his elders, he has a voice in every matter, he eats and drinks what seems good to him, he (or at any rate she) wears finger-rings of price, he has no shyness or even modesty."[76]

Anthony Trollope, who as an adult wrote a book about the place where he spent time as a child with his mother, Frances Trollope, thought American babies, "eat and drink just as they please; they are never punished; they are never banished, snubbed and kept in the background as children are kept with us, and yet they are wretched and uncomfortable. . . . Can it be, I wonder, that the children are happier when they are made to obey orders."[77] Meanwhile, Marryat insisted that "there is little or no parental control," adding:

> Imagine a child of three years old in England behaving thus:
> "Johnny, my dear, come here," says his mama.
> "I won't," cries Johnny.
> "You must, my love, you are all wet, and you'll catch cold."
> "I won't," replies Johnny. And so forth.
> "A sturdy republican, sir," says his father to me, smiling at the boy's resolute disobedience.[78]

Given the fact that everyone in America was criticized for their spirit of equality, it is not surprising that later criticism would often come down to sneering at an insufficient elitism, an excessive emphasis on the lower common denominator. Even when those complaints came from leftist intellectuals who claimed to revere equality, the old aristocratic disdain for the masses was often barely concealed beneath the supposed love for all humanity. Naturally, the peasants and workers who flocked from Europe to America as immigrants did not share this attitude.

Moreover, the European visitors' view that materialism and democracy blocked the creation of a serious culture in the United States was already being disproven. Henry David Thoreau, Ralph Waldo Emerson, Walt Whitman, James Fenimore Cooper, Edgar Allan Poe, the Hudson River school of painting, and many others were doing important and original work. As in politics, a viable mass-oriented alternative to Europe's official aristocratic culture was possible.

Even the kindly British novelist Charles Dickens, least snobbish of his nation and defender of the downtrodden in his great novels, could not quite shake himself loose from European disdain. Dickens had some positive things to say about the United States in a book about his 1842 journey there, finding Americans "by nature, frank, brave, cordial, hospitable and affectionate." He also had good personal reasons for turning against America after being cheated by speculators in a canal company fraud and by publishers who stole his writings and never paid him royalties.

Nevertheless, his conclusion was that while the British suffer from being self-absorbed, inner-oriented characters, Americans are colorless because they are obsessed with what their fellows think of them, a result of that dreaded equality that makes them want to be like everyone else. And, at times, even Dickens was overcome by the American disease that so often affected European travelers. Its main symptom was an angry feverish hatred toward America in general that made otherwise sane people almost froth at the mouth.

Traveling from Cincinnati downstream to Cairo, Illinois, he wrote of "the hateful Mississippi circling and eddying before it, and turning off upon its southern course a slimy monster hideous to behold; a hotbed of disease, an ugly sepulcher, a grave uncheered by any gleam of promise: a place without one single quality, in earth or air or water, to commend it: such is this dismal Cairo."[79]

Ironically, this was the very material that Mark Twain would render so unforgettably as a writer exemplifying a distinctly American worldview. At any rate, in Dickens's rendition, the United States was a land of sleazy business ethics, rampant lawlessness and violence, crass materialism, insufferable and undereducated boors, and gluttony. It is a list quite familiar a century later. Instead of an eagle as its national symbol, Dickens proposes choosing a more appropriate animal for America's emblem: a bat "for its short-sightedness, [a rooster] for its bragging," a magpie "for its [dis]honesty," a peacock "for its vanity," or an ostrich for its desire to avoid reality.[80]

Dickens's novel, *Martin Chuzzlewit*, published in 1866, is certainly the funniest nineteenth-century anti-American satire. His poor hero, who makes the mistake of immigrating to America, suffers the entire repertoire of American ills, ranging from terrible climate to cultural barbarism to predatory swindlers who sell him land in a malaria-infested frontier town where he becomes seriously ill.

When Martin is invited to dinner, he hears a bell "ringing violently" and is convinced the house is afire as a series of agitated gentlemen rush in. The alarm turns out to be only the dinner bell. American gluttony was a favorite theme of nineteenth-century European writers, perhaps because the average American ate far better than his European counterpart. In the dining room, Martin sees: "All the knives and forks were working away at a rate that was quite alarming; very few words were spoken; and everybody seemed to eat his utmost in self-defense, as if a famine were expected to set in before breakfast time tomorrow morning."[81]

And when he finally returns to England, according to one of the book's running jokes, every time the word "America" is mentioned, he becomes ill.

Obviously, the reactions to America of each country's nationals reflected the priorities and problems of their native lands. The British put a little more emphasis on excessive equality, the French on intellectual and cultural poverty, and the Germans spoke much of spiritual barrenness. Yet all these themes are found in the ideas of each of them. It is telling, too, how much of this criticism came out of a combination of aristocratic and romantic spirit, of leftist and rightist ideas intertwined.

Both aristocrats and romantics, conservatives and radicals, looked down on a middle-class republic that was certainly not their idea of utopia. Conservative Germans, who had a horror of republicanism, easily classified America as unpalatable. But so did German romantics who had an equal horror of materialism and the masses.

During the first half of the nineteenth century, European anti-Americans concluded that the United States was to be ridiculed, not feared. Its ludicrous political system was a clear failure and might well collapse of its own weight. If the United States posed any threat, it arose from bad example rather than global ambitions. The word "model" sneeringly appeared most often in anti-American literature to discredit the idea that this country might provide an example to emulate. This concept would later be expressed as the rejection of "Americanization."

The second stage of anti-Americanism then was to insist that the United States was a failure. But contrary to these predictions of early-nineteenth-century anti-Americans—who would see the Civil War as the doom they had been expecting—the United States did not collapse. On the contrary, it grew steadily stronger and more visibly successful. Only when the American experiment had clearly worked—around the 1880s, when American industrialization began to lead the world, or after 1898, when the U.S. victory over Spain made it an incipient world power— was it no longer possible to insist that it had failed. But the anti-Americans would find the threat of American success to be an even more serious matter. And this would lead to the third stage of anti-Americanism.

THE FEAR OF AN AMERICAN FUTURE

By the late nineteenth century, America was emerging as a great in-dustrial country. While it was still far behind Britain, France, or Germany in military might or political influence, far-sighted people were starting to see what would become so apparent later: the rise of the United States to global preeminence as it pioneered in the development of big industries and assembly-line methods. By 1924, it produced 38 percent of the world's coal, 70 percent of its petroleum, 38 percent of electric power, 54 percent of copper, 40 percent of lead, 33 percent of iron ore, 75 percent of corn, 25 percent of wheat, 30 percent of cereals other than wheat, 55 percent of cotton, 53 percent of timber, and 22 percent of tobacco.[1]

Culturally, America was becoming known as the land of jazz, movies, and advertising. It was becoming easier to speak of a distinctive American worldview, style, and way of life. In some ways, the modernization of Europe seemed to parallel what already existed in America: it became more secular, democratic, urban, faster paced, mass-oriented, geographically mobile, classless, questioning of tradition, deifying change, and many other such characteristics.

This prospect, however, while embraced by many Europeans, horrified others who identified it with, among other things, the influence of America's baleful example. This reaction gave rise to the third era of anti-Americanism. "For some reason or other," the American writer James Russell Lowell wrote in 1869, "the European has rarely been able to see America except in caricature."[2] Yet this caricature evolved over time. The idea that America was a failure, widely held in the first half of the nineteenth century, had proved wrong. Anti-Americans had discouraged taking that country as a role model by ridiculing it as politically unviable, culturally impoverished, and socially failed.

Now, however, as the French economist Paul de Rousiers aptly wrote in 1892, "America ceased to be an object of curiosity to become an object of dread."[3] If America was no longer a joke to be laughed at or an inferior to be sneered at, if it actually was going to be the prototype of their own future, the United States might really be a danger to the entire world. If America was going to be a great power, it might impose itself on others. And if Europeans were persuaded to copy voluntarily its alleged spirit of relentless, soulless industrialization, and modernization, they, too, would sink into social, political, and cultural barbarity.

Thus, in 1901, Goldsworthy Lowes Dickinson, a British writer, said in a letter from the United States to his friend, the novelist E. M. Forster: "The things that rubbed into me in this country are 1) that the future of the world lies with America, and 2) that radically and essentially America is a barbarous country. The life of the spirit . . . is, not accidentally or temporarily, but inevitably and eternally killed in this country."[4]

Ironically, then, as the United States proved wrong its historic anti-American critics who said it could never succeed, this very success only inspired more anti-Americanism. One could well believe it was headed for world economic domination and that others must copy its methods or fall far behind. The anti-Americans believed that while the United States had became highly productive, its progress had come at a significant cost to cultural and spiritual values. The cost of the enterprise seemed too high for these critics, who felt that it had literally sold its soul to attain material riches.

One clear expression of this attitude came in 1926 from Johan Huizinga, a Dutch historian of the Middle Ages, a time that European conservatives might find preferable to the new age. Huizinga wrote that his group of Europeans traveling together through America constantly felt, "We all have something that you lack; we admire your strength but we do not envy you. Your instrument of civilization and progress, your big cities and your perfect organization, only makes us nostalgic for what is old and quiet, and sometimes your life seems hardly to be worth living, not to speak of your future."[5]

But was it the future of only the United States itself that was at stake? Perhaps that country's success would allow it to dominate the whole world. Or perhaps that same success would convince others to copy the American model. In his 1926 novel, *The Plumed Serpent*, the British novelist D. H. Lawrence records the thoughts of his protagonist Kate Leslie on encountering America: "Was it the great continent that destroyed again what the other continents had built up, the continent whose spirit of place fought purely to pick the eyes out of the face of God?" Was America the place "where the human will declares itself 'free' to pull down the soul of the world?" Was America merely a negation of all that existed, "the life-breath of materialism? And would the great negative pull of the Americans at last break the heart of the world?"[6]

This was the fear in Europe. The United States would break the heart of the world by becoming the wellspring of a new and very destructive type of society in which everything was subjected to efficiency, organization, and material gain. This new theme of anti-Americanism began to be apparent during the Civil War. The British and French governments were hostile to the Union partly because they saw it as the embodiment of America's terrible society, as opposed to the more "European-style" agricultural and aristocratic South. The French government was on the verge of recognizing and aiding the Confederacy as an independent country. Despite its own antislavery policy, the British government only awaited a decisive Confederate victory to provide an occasion for doing the same thing.

Ironically, the widespread sympathy for the Confederacy in England and France also rested on the fact that a Southern victory would restart the flow of cotton to their textile mills.[7] Thus, on the one hand, the Europeans opposed the Union as a competing industrial power while, on the other hand, in anti-American terms, they condemned it as inferior to themselves because it was an industrial society.

Many Europeans, both conservatives and romantics, thus defended the Southerners as victims of Yankee imperialists who wanted to seize their wealth. The Europeans claimed that the drive to eradicate slavery was just a smokescreen for imperialism, just as a century later their spiritual descendants portrayed the U.S. role in promoting freedom and democracy in the world as an excuse to conquer the globe. In part, Europeans failed to understand that American policies in the Civil War, Cold War, or 2003 Iraq War were motivated in large part—if by no means completely—by moral considerations beyond pure realpolitik. And equally, in all three wars, beyond an alleged humanitarian intention, Europeans were concerned that a U.S. victory would leave the United States too powerful, a threat to their own interests.

European liberals and reformers—like John Bright, Richard Cobden, and John Stuart Mill in England, and even the more leftist Karl Marx[8]—supported the Union precisely because they saw it as a role model. But most of the ruling classes and intellectuals in Britain and France denounced the United States during the Civil War as a country so dreadful that it should not be allowed to survive. The French newspaper, Le Pays, called the U.S. government, "one of the most barbarous, most nefarious, and most inept which has ever been seen." While the South was a European-style, homogeneous, integrated society, the North was no more than a collection "of turbulent immigrants."[9]

A Spanish newspaper, El Pensamiento Español, made the comprehensive anti-American case in September 1862: "The history of this model republic can be summed up in a few words. It came into being by rebellion. It was founded on atheism. It was populated by the dregs of all the nations in the world. It has lived without law of God or man. Within a hundred years, greed has ruined it. Now it is fighting like a cannibal, and it will die in a flood of blood and mire."[10]

Similar sentiments were voiced by the London Times, the newspaper of the British establishment, in hardly less restrained language: "We ought to give our moral weight to our English kith and kin [Southern whites], who have gallantly striven so long for their liberties against a mongrel race of plunderers and oppressors." The breakup of the United States, it concluded, would be good "riddance of a nightmare."[11]

So deep did the hostility of the Union's critics run that they even refused to be swayed by President Abraham Lincoln's 1862 decision to free the slaves, though they had attacked his failure to do so earlier. The British ambassador in Washington, Lord Russell, denounced this step as "cold, vindictive, and entirely political," a vile encouragement to "acts of plunder, of [arson], and of revenge."[12] The *Times* claimed that Lincoln was appealing "to the black blood of the African; he will whisper of the pleasures of spoil and of the gratification of yet fiercer instincts and when the blood begins to flow and shrieks come piercing through the darkness, Mr. Lincoln will wait till the rising flames tell that all is consummated, and then he will rub his hands and think that revenge is sweet."[13]

Disgusted by the hypocrisy of those for whom the United States could never be in the right, the liberal philosopher John Stuart Mill sat down on October 27, 1862, and wrote a letter to an American friend, noting that "the proclamation [freeing the slaves] has only increased the venom of those who after taunting you for so long with caring nothing for abolition [of slavery], now reproach you for your abolitionism as the worst of your crimes." And then he added a memorable thought that still rings fresh today, denouncing those who claimed to be objecting only to American policies but "who so hate your democratic institutions that they would be sure to inveigh against you whatever you did, and are enraged at no longer being able to taunt you with being false to your own principles."[14]

When Mill wrote the phrase "your democratic institutions," he was quite aware that these critics did not necessarily hate the United States because they opposed democracy as such. The most ferocious British anti-Americans were staunch defenders of parliamentary democracy. What they hated was the specific American version of such institutions, its purported soulless, narrowly capitalist, anti-intellectual, mob-ruled, and culturally inferior society.

Even in France, there were sympathizers with America who thought along the same lines as Mill. In 1865, several liberal French intellectuals met to celebrate the Union victory, the triumph of American democracy, and the abolition of slavery. Their leader was Edouard René Lefebvre de Laboulaye, a legal scholar. Opposed to their own dictator, Napoleon III, they wanted to establish a French republican government modeled on America's constitution. They toasted the two countries' historic ties and mutual love of liberty, which made them like "two sisters." At one point in the evening, Leboulaye remarked, "Wouldn't it be wonderful if people in France gave the United States a great memorial to independence" to show their mutual dedication to the cause of mutual liberty? And this began the movement that twenty-one years later, when France had indeed reestablished a republic, resulted in it presenting the Statue of Liberty to New York.[15]

These were legitimate sentiments and an important part of the historic French view of the United States as well. But they never silenced the alternative and powerful anti-American attitudes of some very vocal sectors. Indeed, even as the Statue of Liberty was being presented, there were grumblings in Paris of American ingratitude for all France had done for it.[16] Increasingly after the Civil War, as America began to outproduce Europe in the making of so many manufactured products, it came to represent not so much liberty but rather freedom's restriction and hollowness in the archetypal modern capitalist commercial society.

What could be more significant in this regard than the context of the first French use of the word "Americanization," in *Le Journal* on January 16, 1867, proclaiming how a recent French fair, the Universal Exhibition, constituted "the latest blow in what amounts to the Americanization of France—Industry outdoing Art, steam threshing machines in place of paintings."[17] The peculiar but powerful idea that the growth of technology as such would jeopardize culture derived in large part from the European conception that this is what had happened in the United States.

One after the other, France's most celebrated nineteenth-century writers brought their pens down on the head of America. Honoré de Balzac portrayed the United States as excessively materialistic, greedy, and insensitive. Stendhal said America's democracy was merely the appeasement of shopkeepers. In 1873, the poet Charles Baudelaire was complaining that humanity was almost hopelessly Americanized because of the triumph of the "physical" over the "moral" element in life.[18]

In his preface to a translation of Edgar Allan Poe's *More Tales of the Grotesque and Arabesque* in 1875, Baudelaire concluded that nothing could be more grotesque than the fact that "Americanmania has virtually become a socially acceptable fad."[19] He described the United States, in a phrase echoed by many contemporaries, as gaslight barbarism, the alliance of technology with primitiveness.[20] Baudelaire thought the real ruler of America was far more cruel and inflexible than any monarch: the tyranny of public opinion.[21]

One uniquely French argument for America's march toward world domination was that it was part of an Anglo-Saxon, English-speaking alignment with the world's most powerful country, Great Britain. True, the colonists had made common cause with France to win their independence, but they had then revived their loyalty toward England. Many echoed Talleyrand's complaint: "I have not found a single Englishman who did not feel at home among Americans and not a single Frenchman who did not feel a stranger."[22] To some extent, French antagonism of America was displaced from its historic rivalry toward Britain, which the United States gradually replaced in French thinking as the leading English-speaking power and alternative society.

Certainly, reactions against America in Britain were much milder than in France. True, in the House of Commons, a resolution was introduced in 1900 denouncing the demoralizing effect of American plays on the London stage, but it did not pass.[23] Teachers briefly protested the alleged rise of Americanisms in the English language, yet, contrary to what later happened in France, this did not become a national obsession.

At about this time, negative assessments from the new socialist left began to appear, like one by a British journalist in the 1890s, who claimed that America had disappointed British progressives because of its machine politics ruled by party bosses and because of the growing gap between rich and poor. There was, of course, a strong basis for a critique of American society based on its very real ills of that era, one of the most corrupt in the country's history, during which robber barons held sway and corporations bought and looted governments. Indeed, Europeans learned about such matters mainly from the books of American authors who skewered the corruption and injustice of that period. Upton Sinclair's *The Jungle* and Jack London's *The Iron Heel* were widely read in England during those years.[24]

It is surprising, though, how small a part the problems that most concerned Americans played in mainstream anti-Americanism. In part, this was because the American critics focused on the decline of what previously had been considered a better, more democratic society, while the anti-Americans saw the country as innately rather than temporarily in disrepute. Instead, most of the criticisms continued to be those of the past, more conservative and antidemocratic in nature.

For example, again and again, especially among British writers, America was deemed to be a badly organized society because people there did not know their place. For example, James Bryce, a historian, member of parliament, Liberal Party leader, and frequent visitor to America whose three-volume work on the country, *American Commonwealth*, was published in 1889, believed that America's problem was an excess of democracy. Among the evils of democracy were a "commonness of mind and tone, want of dignity and prevalent in and about conduct of public affairs, insensibility to nobler aspects and finer responsibilities of national life; apathy among luxurious classes and fastidious minds because they are no more important than ordinary voters, and because they're disgusted by vulgarities of public life; lack of knowledge, tact and judgment in legislature."[25]

As was often true, America might well deserve criticism, but anti-Americans' claims had little to do with the actual problems the country faced. Two of Bryce's most positive remarks—that Americans were law-abiding and there was little conflict between the privileged and under-privileged—were also wrong. Equally, Bryce thought that the upper classes and best minds did not deign to intervene in public life because they were disgusted by the vulgarities of a system dominated by the masses. Rather than "magnifying his office and making it honorable," the national leader panders to the people instead of adhering to an aristocratic sense of duty to higher principles.[26] The real problem was quite different: politicians were ignoring the people's interests and catering to those of corporations that enriched them.

In a remarkable passage, Bryce charged that ordinary people were too uppity for their own good, and suffered because they tried to defend their interests rather than accept the rule of a proper elite. If only the average American was "less educated, less shrewd, less actively interested in public affairs, less independent in spirit [he] might be disposed, like the masses in Europe, to look up to the classes which have hitherto done the work."[27]

The dangers of liberalism and equality were also seen as spreading to religion. Some insisted that America was a godless country, while many Catholics thought the United States was dangerously Protestant, which amounted to the same thing. Those on the left, or cultural romantics, considered the United States to be saturated with a narrow Puritanism. But when a liberal reform movement—emphasizing education and social reform—arose in the American Catholic church late in the nineteenth century, it was denounced by French Catholic traditionalists as the heresy of "Americanism," a dangerous infection of democratic ideas that would be condemned by Pope Leo XIII in 1897. As in other areas, America was condemned as a dangerous hotbed of excessive democracy and disrespect for tradition. One conservative leader, Abbé Henry Delassus, wrote a book entitled *Americanism and the Anti-Christian Conspiracy*, which posited the existence of an alliance of Jews, Masons, and Americans to destroy Christianity.[28]

Mixing all the traditional themes, the *Paris Review* warned that Americanism was "not only an attack of heresy; it is an invasion of barbarism. It is . . . the assault of a new power against Christian society. . . . It is money against honor, bold brutality against delicateness . . . machinery against philosophy. . . . The purchase of all, the theft of all, joyous rapine supplanting justice and the demands of duty. . . . Religious Americanism is only one of the assaults of pan-Americanism."[29]

One of the most bizarre anti-American incidents, which showed some Europeans' readiness to believe anything bad about America, was the Diana Vaughn affair. A Frenchman named Leo Taxil claimed that the imaginary Vaughn was born among Native Americans and, at a secret ceremony in Charleston, South Carolina, was personally commissioned by Satan to destroy Christianity. She was sponsored by the Masonic order and even went to Mars at times to consort with devils. But after arriving in France, she supposedly changed sides and began exposing Satanists on both sides of the Atlantic.

In the 1880s and 1890s, Taxil wrote a dozen long books on the subject—including a fictitious "autobiography" of Vaughn, which focused on an American-based conspiracy to seize control of the world. Finally, in 1897, he promised that Vaughn would make a public appearance but instead, before a crowd of 300 people, Taxil admitted he had made up the whole story. Many conservative European Catholics continued to believe, however, that the devil was in league with America.[30]

If anti-American intellectuals of the day did not accept the notion that the devil was literally backing America, they still thought that the threat from the United States amounted to just about the same thing. Such people evinced a growing sense of fighting a losing battle against a tidal wave of globalizing American evil. This is not to deny the admiration of America by some or the adoption of its cultural and technological products by many more. Yet it was precisely a readiness to import American technology or signs that Europeans were copying its ways that set off the anti-American alarm bells.

That is also why anti-Americanism usually came from conservatives, leftists, and cultural aesthetes rather than from liberals, who were more likely to think American institutions were invitingly democratic and American innovations socially useful. As a result, much anti-Americanism combined both aesthetic and intellectual, leftist and conservative critiques. The left would gradually come to view the United States as capitalism in its purest, most distasteful form, which would seduce others and prevent the creation of a socialist utopia. To conservatives, American capitalism was equally objectionable since it rejected the notion of an elite based on breeding, which conservatives favored, or refined taste, which aesthetes advocated.

For example, John Ruskin, a popular British aesthete, who refused an invitation to visit the United States because it had no castles, was nonetheless able to condemn that country in 1863 for its "lust of wealth, and trust in it; vulgar faith in magnitude and multitude, instead of nobleness; . . . perpetual self-contemplation [resulting] in passionate vanity; [and] total ignorance of the finer and higher arts."[31] For the French aesthete Philippe B. J. Buchez, writing in 1885, America was the materialist threat to human destiny, merely "a nation of ignorant shopkeepers and narrow-minded industrialists whose entire vast continent contains not one single work of art or scientific work that they made."[32]

The British poet and aesthete Matthew Arnold complained that America's better treatment of the poor was less important than the fact that it degraded the aristocracy of those who could distinguish "that which is elevated and beautiful."[33] Arnold's friend, Lepel Henry Griffin, put the same idea more crudely. In his 1884 book, sarcastically entitled *The Great Republic*, he dubbed the United States "the country of disillusion and disappointment." In the entire civilized world, only Russia could compete with it in sordidness, meanness, and ugliness. Griffin explained that America was far worse than British-ruled India because it had a government in which "the educated, the cultured, the honest, and even the wealthy, weigh as nothing in the balance against the scum of Europe which the Atlantic has washed up on the shores of the New World."[34]

Similar views were expressed by the right-wing German philosopher Oswald Spengler, author of *The Decline of the West* and a precursor of fascism, who saw the United States as a major cause of that decline. Not only did its people think only of "economic advantages," but lesser races had also seized control from Anglo-Saxons and dragged the country to ruin.[35]

Aside from any political or cultural ideology, America often reduced otherwise intelligent people to a state of sputtering indignation because it was simply different from their familiar world. After his visit to America in 1909, Sigmund Freud, a cultural conservative despite the revolutionary nature of his ideas, succumbed to a severe case of Americaphobia. He even blamed his chronic intestinal trouble on its cooking, though he suffered from this ailment before his trip.[36] On hearing an American ask another to repeat something he had said, Freud remarked in contempt, "These people cannot even understand each other." His biographer, Ernest Jones, said that Freud found it hard to adapt himself to the "free and easy manners of the New World. He was a good European with a sense of dignity and a respect for learning which at that time was less prominent in America." After his trip, he told Jones, "America is a mistake; a gigantic mistake."[37]

No matter what the ideology, interest group, or psychological cause of anti-Americanism, that idea's presence often told more about its perpetrators than about the United States itself. This was especially so in regard to one powerful personal issue that was rarely addressed directly. Everyone in Europe had the option of emigrating to America, and anyone who thought about that alternative—or perhaps about America at all—had to deal, consciously or subconsciously, with the question of whether or not he or she should do so.

This was a major decision. To stay in Europe implied that one was happier, too thoroughly wedded to that way of life, too fearful, or too well-off to benefit from such a dramatic change. Having a negative view of that potential destination was an easy way to solve the problem and justify one's choice. Looking down at America allowed one to rationalize that decision as being based on a preference for precious traditions and lofty culture rather than, say, fear, self-interest, or a smug satisfaction with the status quo.

Rejecting America as a destination for oneself was, in effect, a decision to decide that it was inferior. The temptation had been virtuously resisted in the name of fatherland, pride, and spirituality, as well as a hundred other superior features. In contrast, the lure could be denounced as a work of the devil, the siren call of purely material wealth that entailed a loss of individuality or, say, intellectual and cultural stature.

For example, the British historian Thomas Carlyle talked a brother out of emigrating to escape his poor and unhappy life by saying, "That is a miserable fate for any one, at best. Never dream of it. Could you banish yourself from all that is interesting to your mind, forget the history, the glorious institutions, the noble principles of old Scotland that you might eat a better dinner, perhaps?"[38]

Similarly, the French novelist Stendhal had the hero of one novel ask himself the question: To go or not to go? He takes a long walk and concludes the answer must be "No" because, "I would be bored in America, among men perfectly just and reasonable, maybe, but coarse, but only thinking about the dollars. . . . The American morality seems to me of an appalling vulgarity, and reading the works of their distinguished men, I only have one desire: never to meet them in this world. This model country seems to me the triumph of silly and egoist mediocrity."[39]

And what would be the issue that would most obsess writers, intellectuals, and the others who wrote down their opinions and shaped public opinion about this choice? That in America they would be unimportant, not only because they were on unfamiliar ground but also because their "class" as a whole was less appreciated there. As a result, they romanticized how elevated was their fate at home. Since most of these opinion makers were either aristocrats (or aspired to that status), artists, or intellectuals, they fixated on the low status of these groups as America's true sin.

Later, as the United States became a cultural superpower and could bestow great rewards upon artists, creative figures, and writers, many did emigrate, often fleeing persecution. Some of them achieved their greatest success there. All the more reason, then, for those who stayed behind— or who quickly returned because they did not like America or failed there—to justify themselves by making even angrier critiques.

One of the first such people was the Norwegian writer Knut Hamsun, who spent some miserable years in the American Midwest during the 1880s working as a farmhand, store clerk, railroad laborer, itinerant lecturer, and church secretary. After returning home, Hamsun turned his experiences into a lecture series and later into a book, *The Cultural Life of Modern America*, published in 1889, a scathing account of a country with "too little culture and not enough intelligence."[40]

In particular, like Stendhal, he disliked American pride. "American patriotism never tries to avoid a flare-up, and it is fearless about the consequences of its hot-headed impetuosity."[41] The alleged eagerness of Americans for conflict, contrasting to the supposedly more pacific European nature, was a constant theme of anti-Americans down to the present day, and is made more ironic in this case given Hamsun's later support for fascism. Similarly, like many other European anti-Americans, Hamsun concluded that the country was characterized by a "despotism of freedom . . . all the more intolerable because it is exercised by a self-righteous, unintelligent people."[42]

Another theme that was gathering impetus in the 1880s, though its roots went back a century, was that the United States was a society that had surrendered to technology and become its slave. This futuristic United States was a Frankenstein's monster of wild, inferior, and anti-human ways that might escape to ravage the countryside. Typically, the German philosopher Richard Muller-Freienfels wrote of America in his 1927 work, *The Mysteries of the Soul* that a "chief characteristic of Americanism is the technicalization or mechanization of life. In Europe it is a servant—at least in theory—but in America it is the almost undisputed despot of life."[43]

Anti-Americanism, however, was not an inevitable response even for the most fervent aesthetes, including those discussing the question of industrialization and mechanization. Oscar Wilde, who made a long lecture tour of America in 1882, emerged with a reasonably balanced view despite a sometimes hostile reception in the United States. When Wilde urged the locals to love beauty and art, American newspapers had a field day making fun of his languid poses and costume of velvet jacket, knee breeches, and black silk stockings. Given his views, Wilde could have been most critical of America and indifferent to its success in raising the common people's living standards. Instead, he was a reasonably fair observer, telling his British lecture audiences in 1883, "The first thing that struck me on landing in America was that if the Americans are not the most well-dressed people in the world, they are the most comfortably dressed." They might not wear the latest fashions, he recounted, but had decent garments, unlike England where so many people were clad in rags.[44]

Wilde also perceptively noted America's eagerness to fix its problems and improve the quality of life. In England, he explained, an innovator was regarded as a crazy man who often ends in disappointment and poverty. In America, an inventor was honored, helped, and rewarded with wealth. Foreseeing new approaches to art, Wilde even found American machinery beautiful, an ideal combination of strength and beauty, and described one waterworks as "the most beautifully rhythmic thing I have ever seen."[45]

Of course, Wilde was known for his cutting wit, and he did not disappoint his listeners. Back home, his most famous joke was that the American knowledge of art, especially in the West, was so limited that a wealthy miner turned art patron successfully sued a railroad company for damages when his plaster cast of the Venus de Milo arrived without arms.[46]

While humorous, Wilde's critique also gives still another vision of the European fear of what an industrialized-defined society would do to culture. Everyone in America, he explained, was always running, hurrying to catch a train, "a state of things which is not favorable to poetry or romance." One can only imagine, he added, how the story of Romeo and Juliet would have lost all its charm if they had been racing to jump on trains all the time. He found America to be "the noisiest country that ever existed." One awoke to the sounds of steam whistles, not nightingales. Since "all Art depends upon exquisite and delicate sensibility . . . such continual turmoil must ultimately be destructive of the musical faculty."[47] Of course, the United States would come to excel in the production of popular music, though some European critics would agree that the results only proved that American musical faculty had indeed been destroyed.

Less charitable was the American-born émigré writer Henry James, who lived in London and identified with the European critique. A book based on his grand return visit to the United States was essentially the work of a hostile British traveler. Indeed, it is dreadfully unreadable largely because James wrote in a style seemingly intended to make him sound like an exceptionally jaded and effete British aristocrat.

When a kindly lady trying to help James asked him what kind of people he would like to meet in America, he thought to reply, "Why, my dear madam, have you more than one kind?" For in what he called this "vast crude democracy of trade," he insisted, only "the new, the simple, the cheap, the common, the commercial, the immediate, and, all too often, the ugly" could be found.[48] Change and practicality were America's worst sins. Unlike holy London, James's new home, the cities contained only buildings without any history or value aside from the crassly commercial. Skyscrapers lack "the authority of permanence or . . . long duration" and were simply "the last word of economic ingenuity only till another word be written."[49]

For a moment, James does ask himself why New York's inevitably dirty port area should offend him when he would find a similar scene in Naples or somewhere else in Europe to be picturesque.[50] But soon he is off again on the perpetual American ugliness due to the "complete abolition of forms."[51]

In short, America was accused of being so terrible because it was simultaneously too homogeneous and yet too varied, too democratic and not democratic enough, too amoral and yet too puritanical. If the same yardsticks were applied to other countries, they might also be found wanting. Yet the anti-Americans never asked why squalor, for example, should be a sign of respectable age or local color in one place and of degradation in another.

Of course, America did lack the seasoning that Europe possessed. By definition, any new society will lack that quality. But America was able to use European achievements as its past while constructing its own future. In addition, as many European writers noted, the United States had the youthful qualities of vigor and adaptability. The Europeans had a different problem, which examining the United States highlighted for them: whether they would be able to build a future different from that of America.

Many of the realities neglected by Europeans in general and anti-Americans in particular showed that this was the true issue. For example, the cultural apex and creativity of which Europeans boasted was largely monopolized in each country by a single capital city and by the upper classes alone. The greatness of opera, ballet, chamber music, or poetry was enjoyed by a tiny minority of society. It was all very well to say that Europe had a high culture and Americans had a low one, but how many Europeans actually had access to or preferred those exalted artistic heights?

In bragging about their lofty intellectual level and exalted tastes, anti-Americans were comparing the average American to the top 10 percent of their own society, while ignoring the other 90 percent. Local mass culture was beneath notice in Europe. Only after being challenged by a popular culture exported from America to fill the vacuum would European intellectuals claim that their own people were being deprived of the classics in exchange for imported junk.

In addition, the anti-American idea initiated in this period—that its modernization was innately inimical to culture—would be proven wrong. The United States would excel in new forms of creative endeavor (jazz, film, photography, dance, and new literary schools) that took as their inspiration the industrialized modernism it pioneered. The United States would produce a high-quality culture of its own using new media and themes, based on a society whose distinctive attributes were not roadblocks but an occasion for originality.

Moreover, while American techniques of mass production could be said to debase culture, they were also the greatest tools ever created for spreading its benefits. The common people came to be exposed to the finest artistic works—though only they could decide whether or not to like them—through a mass educational system, records, film, radio, television, and other innovations developed primarily in the United States.

To this kind of familiar condemnation of American society in terms of its internal functioning, however, in the late nineteenth century was added a growing fear about the United States becoming a (perhaps the) main global power. As America's growing economy combined with the insecurities or outright decline of their own states and empires, there were more patriotic reasons for Europeans to denounce the United States. It was the alleged American combination of being so "ethically primitive and technologically advanced" and its growing strength, in the words of historian Simon Schama, that petrified them.[52] In this vein, the United States seemed the power of the future, and its rise would seemingly come at the expense of Britain, Germany, France, and other European countries.

Such warnings had been issued by Frenchmen as far back as the 1790s, but they reached the level of obsession by the 1890s. Either the U.S. empire would be one of armed conquest or of economic and cultural domination—or both, as increasingly seemed possible and later appeared to be obvious. In the words of one Frenchman backing the former theory, the United States "aspires to nothing less than having the entire humanity in its orbit. Today Mexico, tomorrow the world! Such is the real, only maxim of this imperialist and merchant republic." Americans are only united, the author added, by "the ambition they have to extend their empire far beyond the present limits."[53]

This alarm bell was set off not only by growing American economic power but also by four defeats of European states in their own imperialistic struggles around the turn of the century: Italy by Ethiopia in 1896, Spain by the United States in 1898, Britain by the South African Boers, and Russia by Japan in 1905. These were unsettling omens of, to paraphrase Spengler, the decline of most of the West. The French poet Paul Valéry called these events "symptoms" of a possibly fatal European illness and predicted that America would be the dying continent's unwelcome heir.[54] The U.S. victory over Spain in 1898, Valéry explained, was the moment he felt a loyalty to Europe as a whole, for which America was an alien rival.[55]

Strangely, the man who most symbolized this new American world role and who seemed to embody many of the negative stereotypes about Americans, Theodore Roosevelt, was rather popular among his European colleagues for his intellectual scope, although he was patronized for his typical American youthfulness and vigor.[56] Yet the policies he represented were a different matter. When Roosevelt advocated that America speak softly and carry a big stick, originally an African saying, Europeans exaggerated the size of the stick and could not possibly imagine any American capable of speaking softly.

While a military threat remained a future and hypothetical concern, American cultural and spiritual aggression was already seen as a clear and present danger. The United States, warned Edmund Mandat-Grancey, a French nobleman writing in 1891, was like a disease that would infect Europe. Even if Americans could live with their dreadful institutions, they were the carriers of a cultural plague that would kill European civilization.[57] Two years later, in *Voyage to the Land of Dollars*, Emile Barbier warned that the United States was invading Europe with its commodities—locomotives, coal, silk, fruit, cotton, and even wine.[58]

Yet much of this hysteria and antagonism took place before the United States was even active on the world scene. By the time it actually defeated Spain in 1898, easily capturing Cuba and the Philippines, the event simply confirmed the already formulated theory about the American threat. The Spanish-American War was nonetheless a pivotal event that European critics saw as the start of an American advance on their continent. To make matters worse, many observers in France and Germany feared that the English-speaking nations, the United States and Britain, would combine forces to dominate the world.

In the words of Philippe Roger, the foremost historian of French anti-Americanism, "The idea was that the daughter of Europe—America—had turned against Europe and was now a potential enemy." That year, 1898, was also the peak of conflict between liberal and conservative forces in France. One issue alone brought French people together: hatred of

America. A visiting Cuban, who himself welcomed Spain's defeat, re-marked, "Weird spectacle indeed. . . . Republican and anticlerical France joins with the France of the manor houses (restored thanks to the rich American marriages [made by French aristocrats]) to shout down the United States and heap praise upon the Spanish monarchy!"[59]

America's second big action on the world stage was its intervention in World War I, and this, too, provoked an anti-American reaction, even from the countries that it helped as an ally. Arriving in France, the U.S. forces thought that they would be popular. General John Pershing marched his troops directly to the tomb of the Frenchman who had done so much to help America become independent and who had praised George Washington as the father of liberty. "Lafayette," an-nounced the American general proudly, "We are here!"

But the earlier bitterness and suspicion of the United States remained unvanquished in many French and some British hearts. Once victory was attained, warm feelings declined toward the Yanks despite their blood sacrifice on behalf of their European allies. There was much envy for a society so relatively wealthy and unscathed by war, secure enough, in a later British writer's words, to have "ignored so many problems" and "professed to believe itself immune from most human ills [and] to have conquered most human problems." To those who had suffered so much, American "optimism seemed indecent."[60]

The conservative British magazine, *The Spectator*, which had looked at the United States as the world's savior during the war, was complain-ing by 1921, "We are too proud to be helped by the daughter country." And a year later, it published an article under the title "Mother's Eldest Daughter," which said that the United States was wealthy, energetic, and powerful but quite immature. "Its resources were physical, like a youth's, and like a youth it did not know what to do with them."[61]

In Britain, though, anti-Americanism remained more a matter of snobbishness and nasty journalistic remarks than of any political impor-tance. Like a British comedic rhyme of the 1920s, making fun of imported American literature, "Our children need these refining books/About gangsters, bootleggers, thugs and crooks."[62] A 1936–1937 survey of British schoolchildren found they thought that the United States was a place to get rich quickly and produced good athletes but that Americans were boastful, were unable to speak English correctly, and made inferior prod-ucts. Nevertheless, British leaders could simply view America as a junior ally and protégé merely in need of proper tutoring. Still, old stereotypes endured.[63]

But the two countries had too much in common culturally and politically for serious antagonism to develop. There were proportionately more pro-Americans in Britain than anywhere else in Europe. The relative good feeling in Britain was expressed by such well-known figures as H. G. Wells, the visionary writer, who was not only impressed by American cities and living standards but also thought the universities "far more alive to the thinking and knowledge-making function of universities than [those of] Great Britain." He did not fear rising American power, concluding that "by sheer virtue of its size, its free traditions, and the . . . initiative in its people, the leadership of progress must ultimately rest [in American hands]."[64]

The British politician most committed to close friendship with America was the greatest of his generation. Winston Churchill, himself half-American, undertook his four-volume *History of the English-Speaking Peoples* in 1932 to promote friendship and alliance between the two countries. Churchill foresaw that this partnership would one day literally save the world. He had to delay completion of the book in order to put his idea into practice as Britain's prime minister during World War II.

France was a totally different matter. Indeed, while the United States had saved France during World War I, the reaction in many circles was not exactly one of gratitude. President Woodrow Wilson, like several of his well-meaning successors, thought his efforts to fight dictators and ensure peace would be appreciated. Instead, he was detested in France as being self-righteous and too soft on the defeated Germans. Wilson was seen as a wooly-minded idealist and a religious fanatic, stereotypes that would also be applied to other American leaders. When he failed to persuade Congress to ratify the Treaty of Versailles and America withdrew into isolationism, French critics added weakness to their indictment of him.

Two more developments particularly enraged the French: the U.S. attempt to be paid for its wartime loans and the dramatic postwar increase of American cultural exports to France. What followed was a high point in the long history of French anti-Americanism. Unnoticed in America, whose news from Paris was mostly about American writers living there, the 1920s in France was characterized by a remarkable degree of anti-Americanism.

In tremendously influential books published throughout the 1920s and into the 1930s—like Robert Aron's and Arnaud Dandieu's *The American Cancer*, J.-L. Chastanet's *Uncle Shylock*, and Charles Pomaret's *America's Conquest of Europe*, and many other works—every American action was put in the worst possible light. The United States only entered the war in 1917 because it wanted to profit from European suffering as long as possible and then dominate that continent at the lowest possible cost. Chastanet predicted that the future belonged to American imperialism: "You will practice usury on a lot of nations and you will dominate them."[65]

These authors, as others in the past, all denounced American society as being hypnotized by technology and obsessed with moneymaking to the point where human spiritual life was destroyed. This was a country that wanted to impose its system on the whole world. Imperialism was at the core of its nature. They portrayed America as the main threat to Europe—and to France above all—a notion that took some awesome blindness in an era when Adolf Hitler, Benito Mussolini, and Joseph Stalin were among that continent's rulers.

French anti-Americanism was a unanimous nonpartisan affair. The left and right could agree on one thing: the United States was the land of a harsh and brutal "absolute capitalism." Conservatives stressed its spiritual poverty and destruction of tradition; leftists claimed it was dominated by monopolies that exploited workers. Both saw it as a threat to the kind of France they preferred. Charles Maurras, the French right's leading philosopher, painted America as a society shaped by the impersonal requirements of an uncaring market to the exclusion of all humane concerns. The left made the same argument by citing the repression of strikes, the weakness of the American left, and the tendency of mechanization to destroy jobs.

Yet both sides were also reacting against the greatest threat of all. The 1920s was a period of great prosperity in the United States. Economic growth was accompanied by the spread internationally of such American innovations as jazz, films, and automobiles. The pilot-author Antoine de Saint-Exupéry argued that the material productivity of American industrial society was not a significant benefit because it was cancelled out by the spiritual emptiness that accompanied it. This was a common characteristic that meant that there was no difference between German Nazism, Soviet Communism, and Americanism. Of these, however,

Americanism was the most dangerous of all because France would find its version of the "industrial disease," the "American cancer," most attractive.[66]

Similarly, the Spanish philosopher José Ortega y Gasset, in his lectures and writings during the 1920s, warned that the elite best qualified to lead and govern was being crushed by the masses. In this sense, American society was a brutal one with "a primitive people camouflaged behind the latest inventions." There, "The masses crushes [sic] beneath it everything that is different, everything that is excellent, individual, qualified and select. Anybody who is not like everybody, who does not think like everybody, runs the risk of being eliminated."[67]

In some cases, however, anti-Americans were concluding that these faceless masses did indeed have a sinister and secret elite as its leader. Increasingly, both French and German[68] anti-Americans in the 1920s closely linked their doctrine with anti-Semitism. Jews and Americans became twin symbols of blame for those who hated modern society and rapid change. Earlier contempt for the new immigrants to America, as expressed by Griffin, Spengler, and others, was generalized. But this hatred increasingly focused on the Jews as the authors of the problem, an idea echoed by such anti-American American expatriates as James, T. S. Eliot, and Ezra Pound. The negative stereotypes of Jews and Americans had developed in parallel. Both groups were said to be money-grubbing enemies of tradition who conspired to foist a new system on humanity to serve their own interests. The intertwining of these hatreds grew with fascism in the 1930s and 1940s.

In France during the 1920s, Maurras portrayed American Jews as blocking U.S. entry into World War I because they allegedly favored Germany. Later, when he and likeminded people became favorable toward Nazi Germany, they developed conspiracy theories about anti-German American Jews pushing the United States into World War II. There was a strong, albeit false, belief in France that Jews ran the U.S. financial system and thus were to blame for France's large debts to America and for the U.S. economic threat to that country. The choice of the nickname "Uncle Shylock" for the United States was not accidental. Robert Brasillach, a right-wing French intellectual who collaborated with the Nazis, explained that there were three reasons for Frenchmen to hate America: its dollars, hypocrisy, and control by international Jewry.[69]

In novels, essays, films, plays, and travel books during the 1920s,

America was also denounced by the French intellectual class as threatening to engulf the world with its malformed society. A 1924 play warned that in the United States the Americans had already infiltrated France. Parisians learned how mechanized American farming threatened the pastoral idyll of the French countryside. The surrealist, soon to be Communist, writer Louis Aragon quipped in 1925 a prophecy of a September 11 far in the future: "Let faraway America and its white buildings come crashing down."[70] The United States was portrayed as monotonous and provincial, a nightmare of identical boxlike houses, standardized products, and narrow minds.[71] While there were grains of truth in many such ideas, they were so exaggerated and stereotyped as to be rendered meaningless.

It was America, far more than the Soviet Union—which supposedly respected and honored intellectuals—that frightened the French intellectual class as a model. Emmanuel Berl neatly coupled these themes in a sentence: "America is multiplying its territory, where the values of the West risk finding their grave."[72]

While 1927 was the year in which the American aviator Charles Lindbergh was toasted in Paris for his solo flight across the Atlantic, a wave of books and articles argued that America and Europe were growing apart culturally. In *Who Will Be Master: Europe or America?*, Lucien Romier said that although no American held such ideas, "Europe and America no longer represent the same type of civilization."[73]

That, too, was the year that André Siegfried wrote his book, *The United States Today*, which presented the all-too-common thesis that the United States represented a bad society with the power to impose itself on others, long before it had any such influence, at least outside of the smallest Latin American states. "America can do anything," he warned, to "strangle men and governments, help them in situations she chooses, watch over them and finally—the things she likes above all— judge them from the heights of moral superiority and impose her lessons on them."[74]

Siegfried explained that "the chief contrast between Europe and America is not so much one of geography as a fundamental difference between two epochs in the history of mankind." The American model was based on an assembly line that reduced people to automatons, as slaves to machines. "We Westerners must each firmly denounce whatever is American in his house, his clothes, his soul." Otherwise, technology would conquer all, becoming an end in itself, as had already happened in the United States.[75]

In every way, America continued to be portrayed as inferior to Europe, even when these differences were largely imaginery. For example, American cities were said not to be like French cities. Régis Michaud, in the 1928 book *What's Needed to Understand the American Soul*, explained that "neither art nor harmony preceded their birth. One can hardly believe that civilized beings have been able to pile up so many dreadful spectacles." Anything attractive in American landscape was European.[76]

The French woman, Siegfried explained, "doesn't lose sight of [her] purpose, which is the preparation of pleasant meals."[77] In contrast, the American woman, described in earlier decades as too bossy and independent, continued to be denounced, as one French traveler summarized it earlier, for her "brutality . . . autonomy, egoism and excessive independence . . . practical intelligence, trivial materialism and a self-interested mind. . . . She seems to us ignorant and pretentious, unable to follow a conversation, so cold she freezes us . . . mute, sour-tempered, prudish. . . . Do they have domestic qualities? Even less. The American woman is laziness personified."[78]

Similarly, Octave Noël of Paris's prestigious L'École des Hautes Études explained in his book, *The American Peril*, the difference between good European chauvinism, derived from "an excess of patriotic sentiment," and bad American jingoism, which arose from a "ferocious[ness] dictated by the appetites or aspirations of a people whose . . . efforts have been directed over the past century toward the endless increase of wealth and material goods, and the achievement of comfort."[79] In other words, Europeans genuinely loved their countries while Americans only supported their nation out of greed.

Americans prided themselves on their individualism, rejecting social controls to an extent almost unprecedented in the world. Yet French anti-Americanism insisted that the United States was a mass society that imposed an unacceptable standardization on each person. A century after Europeans first accused the United States of lacking any culture, French critics saw no reason to change this verdict. "North America," wrote one of them, "has inspired no painters, kindled no sculptors, brought forth no songs from its musicians, except for the monotone Negroes." And whatever poets and writers it had produced could not wait to leave for Europe, to "turn from their native soil with bitterness."[80]

As a result of this outpouring of indoctrination, in 1931, sixty years after Baudelaire warned that Americanization was triumphing, Paul Morand concluded, "It is fashionable for the intelligentsia to detest America."[81] In that year, *The American Cancer* and *Decadence of the French Nation* (because it was being influenced by the United States) were published as anti-American, anti-industrialization books.

While there were Frenchmen who liked the United States, what they had to say only further inflamed the anti-Americans by seeming to show that the cultural and intellectual invasion was gaining momentum. Morand's well-intentioned praise for America was like waving a red cape in front of an already enraged bull. Americans, he wrote, are

> the strongest race in the world—the only one which has succeeded in organizing itself since [World War I]; the only one which is not living on a past reputation. . . . A sporting instinct makes the pupils in any history class long to be Spaniards in the sixteenth century, Englishmen in the eighteenth, Frenchman in the days of [Napoleon]. And that same enthusiasm makes us now desire, momentarily at least, to be Americans. Who does not worship victory?[82]

To demand that Frenchmen protect themselves against American culture, Morand concluded, "is simply to refuse that preestablished order which is called the future. [I go to America] to apply to Europe such things as I saw there."[83]

But when Georges Duhamel saw this future, he shuddered and became one of France's leading anti-American thinkers. Duhamel had been an army doctor during World War I who achieved success thereafter as a novelist, but he also wrote essays and travel literature. His *Scenes of Future Life*, published in 1930, came out just after the Wall Street crash, when stories about America's failures were more credible than they had been at any time since the Civil War. The title of the book tells all, for, Duhamel fears, the "future life" of Europe will be lowered to the level of America. Ask not for whom the bell tolls, he warns his countrymen; it tolls for the civilized way of life.

Yet in this ferocious attack, he presents no statistics, interviews with real people, quotes from actual Americans, or evidence of any kind. America is condemned because of its effect on his psyche. Facts, he seems to be saying, are for the kind of mass-produced, standardized minds produced by a decadent industrial civilization. Long live subjectivity! And yet, partly due to this approach, if the same book was reissued as a new volume penned by a French intellectual in reaction to the September 11, 2001, attacks or the U.S. war on Iraq, it would require only a little updating for the specific fads and technologies being harpooned by the author.

After a preface emphasizing France's vulnerability to the American disease, Duhamel tells his story in the form of dialogues with his fictional interlocutor, the well-educated—for an American—Parker P. Pitkin. Pitkin is understandably baffled by Duhamel's unrelenting view of America as the world's most dangerous anti-utopia. For the author, America represented the machine versus art and vulgarity versus refinement. The United States was "a deviation" from Western civilization. Europe was the land of the spirit, while America destroyed the spirit.

Duhamel called American dance music the "triumph of barbaric silliness." For him, jazz "seems to have been dreamt up to arouse the reflexes of a sedentary mollusk." The noise of the railway had killed music, he said, failing to understand—or determined not to appreciate—how the rhythm of the American city would lead to George Gershwin's miraculous melodies. His "American in Paris" would no doubt have been for Duhamel the ultimate work of the devil.[84]

He found the American people to be "miserable, care-worn creatures stupefied by drudgery." Everything is identical, the result of mass production, a claim he makes even regarding the legs of American women, which he describes as being beautiful but only because they looked "as if they had come off an assembly line." The country's bureaucracy was worse than that of Soviet Russia. His horror is limitless. America is the "belly of the monster" and "the abyss of perfect falseness."[85]

Filmmaking, an area where France would soon excel, was to Duhamel a characteristically American "pastime of illiterates . . . a spectacle which demands no effort, which assumes no continuity in ideas, raises no questions, and deals seriously with no problems." He predicted that a steady diet of films would destroy the American people's intellect in a half-century and so subvert the French as to make them unable to govern themselves.[86]

In every aspect of its existence, America embodied the effacement, the destruction of the individual. Its civilization was an even greater threat than any foreign military invasion, he warned. People reject what is imposed on them by a tyrant or by foreign domination, but they might eagerly accept the rule of a different kind of dictatorship, "a false civilization." He feared it might already be too late, as American civilization was already ruling the world. But he bade the citizens of France to take up arms, to form their battalions and rise to the defense of their 100 kinds of cheese, 50 types of plum, and beloved cafés against the ruthless standardization represented by American technology. He called on each fellow citizen to "denounce the American items which he finds in his house, in his wardrobe, and in his soul."[87]

It is hard to overstate either the ludicrous caricature of America in Duhamel's writing or the influence that these kinds of arguments had on French society and, to a lesser extent, on other Europeans. Many of these ideas sank into the psychological bedrock, shaping attitudes at times of future international tension or apparently advancing Americanization. Like his fellow anti-Americans, Duhamel loves France, traditional France as he sees it, and fears modern society as likely to destroy all its good features. America is the epitome of this destructive alternative, and so he hates and must discredit it. The resulting passion carries away any possibility for even a balanced critical approach that points out the real shortcomings of America, as well as the forces that limit or can be used to remedy them.

What is especially noteworthy is how anti-Americanism was, in the work of Duhamel as elsewhere, so easily able to embrace totally contradictory complaints about the United States without any of its proponents—or even opponents—noticing.

For example, Duhamel ridicules Americans for counting calories and worrying about whether their food was healthy, a barbaric introduction of science into the mysteries of cuisine.[88] Yet his successors would later complain that unhealthy American food was being forced on them. He condemned the movie theatre as the "temple of the images that move," yet it was in France that the cinema would be most deified and American films would be decried for defiling this superb art form.[89]

He and others spoke passionately in defense of an old culture they portrayed as permanent and naturally superior, yet his successors would condemn America by using a postmodernism that portrayed all cultures as artificial and ridiculed the United States for adhering to allegedly oppressive standards of high culture. And while Duhamel did not concern himself with foreign policy, his compatriots made fun of American ideas of morality and democracy in diplomacy, defending the obvious primacy of realpolitik and raison d'état—even the very words are French—in any proper nation's conduct of its affairs. Yet their successors would condemn America as being self-seeking and insufficiently moralistic in its international involvements.

Of course, in claiming that their views were accurate, anti-American critics could always cite American writers who said similar things, though on which side of the Atlantic the ideas originated was not always clear. Henry Miller, for example, reflected French-style anti-Americanism just as James earlier had imitated the British version. Miller's account of his travels through the United States in 1940 and 1941, after his long residence in Paris, repeated the three favorite themes of the French anti-Americans: American arrogance, absence of culture, and ruthless conformity.

According to Miller, "We are not peaceful souls; we are smug, timid, queasy and quaky." America was "a fruit which rotted before it had a chance to ripen," the most monotonous country in the world, lacking any honest publishers, artistic film company, decent theatre, music other than that created by African-Americans, museums with anything but junk, or more than a "handful" of writers with any creativity. Anyone with talent is "doomed to have it crushed one way or another," bribed into being a hack or ignored until starved into submission. Living in a country of such "spiritual gorillas" would tempt anyone to commit suicide.[90]

Miller, like Henry James before him, was an American whose hostility to his native country had become that of a defector rather than a domestic critic, though Miller later chose to return to living in the United States. Beginning with a rejection of real faults, he had simply, though sincerely, adopted the foreign anti-American perspective on America as a means for asserting his own superiority. The effect of his writing in both reflecting and shaping French and other European views of America can only be understood if he is quoted at length:

We are a vulgar, pushing mob whose passions are easily mobilized by demagogues, newspaper men, religious quacks, agitators and such like. To this a society of free peoples is blasphemous. What have we to offer the world beside the superabundant loot which we recklessly plunder from the earth under the maniacal delusion that this insane activity represents progress and enlightenment?[91]

It is a world suited for monomaniacs obsessed with the idea of progress—but a false progress, a progress which stinks. It is a world cluttered with useless objects. . . . The dreamer whose dreams are non-utilitarian has no place in this world. Whatever does not lend itself to being bought and sold, whether in the realm of things, ideas, principles, dreams or hopes, is debarred. In this world the poet is anathema, the thinker a fool, the artist an escapist, the man of vision a criminal.[92]

Yet at the same time, as Duhamel had warned, Europe was evolving in ways paralleling or pursuing the path pioneered by America. Some Europeans idolized American music and film while being introduced to the dubious pleasures of American-invented advertising. Aristocracies declined and democracy developed, bringing to Europe institutions that had once been American novelties. Modern factories, too, came to Europe, as did large corporations. In general, then, Europe, especially the masses, ignored the anti-Americans' warnings while embracing a degree of Americanization, at least in the way critics had defined it.

In distinction to the conservatives, pro-Americans embraced or at least did not fear change. They had confidence in their societies' ability to pick and choose what it wanted. Unlike romantics and leftists, pro-Americans also, out of self-interest or realism, wanted to limit change, seeking improvement rather than utopia. That is why the political locus of those favorable to the United States was among moderate socialists, liberals, and moderate conservatives. They also included average people who wanted to improve their living standards. In contrast, intellectuals in general were the class enemy of America as a model because it challenged the ideas of tradition or revolution for which they saw themselves as guardians. It also represented a society that lowered their status and pushed aside the things they most treasured.

Thus, while America had a tremendous influence because many in Europe wanted this outcome, the negative associations with the United States and institutionalized hostility to it also remained. And this was most true in France, where all the anti-American forces were present and relatively strong. Outside of Communist Russia and Nazi Germany during the 1930s, France had by far the most anti-American intelligentsia in Europe, but this pattern also continued in other countries. Obviously, criticisms of America could be valid, but many leading European intellectuals held views based on the most puerile stereotypes, the same ones that had been circulating since the American revolution.

By the late 1930s and well into the 1940s, though, outspoken anti-Americanism became increasingly, if temporarily, restricted to pro-Communist and pro-fascist circles. These were the movements that sought to remake the world in their own, not an American, image. Liberals and moderate conservatives increasingly looked to the United States as a necessary ally in their struggles to save themselves, first from Nazi Germany and then from the Communist USSR.

But the problem of Americanization and anti-Americanism would not go away. For while French and other European cultures survived quite nicely the depression of the 1930s, the Nazi era, the war and occupation, and even the Communist challenge, the anti-Americans' worst nightmare did seem to come true. The United States became more powerful and influential, saving Europe in another world war and a cold war while finding even more ways to spread its culture. For a time, the non-Communist varieties of anti-Americanism would recede, though French and other European intellectual life was deeply influenced by Soviet propaganda and Marxist or semi-Marxist thinking. Yet all the old anti-American concepts further developed during this period would remain very much alive, waiting to be revived on numerous occasions thereafter.

AMERICA AS A HORRIBLE FATE

While earlier nineteenth-century anti-Americanism had ridiculed that country as a failure and unattractive model, by the 1880s its success and potential power were undeniable. Anti-Americanism adjusted to these changes by using the same basic critique but now recoiling in horror at the prospect of America being the model for the future of humanity and, in particular, their own societies.

This was an era in the United States that combined the dynamic of rapid growth and change through industrialization with terrible social problems. Economic booms alternated with busts, levels of corruption reached their highest, and city slums proliferated. New immigrants poured into the country, changing its face as they underwent the throes of adjustment to a very different society. Workers were often exploited; farmers had to cope with many hard times.

Europeans, like Americans, observed all these developments. Yet while there was much to criticize, a fair assessment would have taken into account three factors. There was much positive as well as negative in what was happening in America during that era. Equally, there was much evidence of the hard work taken to make things better and of the transitory nature of many problems. Finally, equal, sometimes parallel, and often worse difficulties were being suffered in Europe. Many foreign observers did note these points.

At the same time, though, there was a strong factor of anti-American bias in the evaluation of more than a few Europeans, applying earlier prejudices about the United States to the new situation. There were two aspects of this critique. First, the American social, cultural, and political system was portrayed as terrible in its own right, as the embodiment of soulless industrialization and all-powerful capitalism. Europeans feared that this model would spread to their own and other countries. Second, there was a belief that the United States was becoming more powerful and thus posed a direct threat of being able to impose its control on others and transform them in its despicable image.

Both left- and right-wing ideologues gave such warnings, with their ideas soon being taken up by mass movements. Beyond avoiding the danger of imitating America, they sought to use its alleged threat and bad example to mobilize supporters for their own plans to revolutionize society. Thus, for both Communists and fascists, the United States was a prime competitor—first as a rival model for organizing society, later as a great power that opposed their designs. The United States represented one potential future, but they had a better alternative to offer. American democracy must be shown as a sham, its higher living standards exposed as a myth.

The far left and right each had its own particular emphasis. The extreme right argued that America had changed European society too much, while the leftists claimed that it had not gone far enough. Marxists said that America was racist, while fascists insisted it was a mongrel society based on race mixing. Rightists focused more often on America as a threat to their tradition, society, and culture. Leftists wanted to portray America as a false utopia, not a paradise for the common man but a hell dominated by a ruthless ruling class whose apparent success only strengthened its real oppressiveness.

Yet in ridiculing its democratic pretensions and questioning its economic successes, the political spectrum's two extremes also shared a surprising amount in common regarding their critique of the United States. Each saw the United States as a real direct threat to its own global triumph. Both used similar themes—sometimes in virtually identical words—built on previous European anti-Americanism of both the aristocratic and romantic varieties.

Precisely because America was attractive to the earlier nineteenth-century European left and to so many liberals and reformers, radicals were all the more determined to destroy any such "illusions." Take Russia, for example. The Decembrist reformers of the 1820s, whose coup attempt against the czar failed, based much of their proposed constitution on that of America. Leaders of the following generation of Russian oppositionists thought in similar terms. Michael Bakunin, the great theorist of anarchism, saw the United States as the "classic land of political liberty," while his liberal counterpart Alexander Herzen believed that the United States was the only country that might become the ideal state for promoting human welfare.[1]

In contrast, the conservative arch-opponent of Russian liberals and leftists, Fyodor Dostoyevsky, in his 1871 novel, *The Devils*, retells the familiar tale of America being so horrible as to turn a revolutionary into a reactionary. The character closest to Dostoyevsky's political standpoint is a Russian who went to America to discover how American workers fared and concluded that it was there that men "live under the worst possible social conditions." When a Russian liberal laughingly responds that their own country better fits that description, the conservative protagonist claimed that workers in America are routinely beaten, robbed, and cheated at every turn. Two years there taught him that Russians—not Americans—were the people destined to "regenerate and save the world."[2]

Ironically, it was the reactionary Russian view of America rather than the progressive one that would prevail under the Soviet regime. But until the Communist takeover in 1917, Russian liberals and socialists continued to see the United States in a positive light.[3]

Karl Marx, too, had many good things to say about the United States, albeit because he saw it as being a step ahead of contemporary Europe rather than as the embodiment of his own ideal society. After Lincoln's 1864 reelection, Marx even wrote the president: "From the commencement of the [Civil War] the workingmen of Europe felt instinctively that the star-spangled banner carried the destiny of their class." America was the place that "the idea of [a] great Democratic Republic had first sprung up . . . the [Bill of Rights] was issued, and the first impulse given to the European revolution of the eighteenth century." The South's secession was nothing more than "a crusade of property against labor," and the interests of European workers required that the Union would win.[4]

Remarkably, Marx added, "The workingmen of Europe feel sure that, as the American War of Independence initiated a new era of ascendancy for the middle class, so the American Antislavery War will do for the working classes." He called Lincoln the "single-minded son of the working class," who would lead his country through the "struggle for the rescue of an enchained race and the reconstruction of a social world."[5]

Yet such attitudes did not always characterize the main cultural figures of the left or its politicians as they neared power. Even Marx's daughter, Eleanor, who came with her lover, Edward Aveling, to the United States in 1886 to raise money for the cause, was not enchanted. They wrote a book entitled *The Working-Class Movement in America* but didn't find much of one, claiming nevertheless that capitalist exploitation had created greater extremes of wealth and poverty than in Europe.[6] They especially sought to debunk the romantic image of the quintessentially American figure of the free-spirited cowboy, portraying him simply as a low-paid proletarian "as much at the mercy of the capitalist" as any factory slave.[7]

The younger Marx's writing tried to deal with the central problem that the United States posed for Marxists. Their doctrine claimed that the workers' impoverishment, inability to escape from servitude, and absence of any better alternative system would inevitably force the proletariat to wage a socialist revolution. Thus, the idea that America could provide a better future for its workers must be quashed. Many immigrants to the United States discovered that they could dramatically improve their personal conditions and change classes in a way that was impossible in contemporary Europe. Eventually, American workers achieved heights of prosperity unimagined in the Old Country. Many Europeans suspected that this was so and that they should thus emigrate or seek to install a similar system at home. The left, like the ruling establishment, needed to convince them otherwise.

Ironically, another source for the future left's style of anti-Americanism was the same kind of anti-industrialization, antimodernist romanticism that was supposedly alien to its ideology but that had so long prevailed among European artists. The novelist Maxim Gorky, whose admirer Lenin would soon begin the task of modernizing and industrializing Russia, expressed well the notions that would come to dominate Western pro-Communist circles and those in the Soviet Union.

Gorky's 1906 book, *The City of the Yellow Devil* was an anti-ode to New York, a place "lacking in any desire to be beautiful" whose buildings "tower gloomily and drearily.... The city seems like a vast jaw, with uneven black teeth. It breathes clouds of black smoke into the sky and puffs like a glutton suffering from his obesity.... The street is a slippery, greedy throat, in the depths of which float dark bits of the city's food— living people." Each resident is a victim as the city "strangles him, sucks his blood and brain, devours his muscles and nerves, and grows and grows.... Inner freedom, the freedom of the spirit does not shine in these people's eyes."[8]

And yet even Gorky admits that these people are not miserable but rather "tragically satisfied with themselves." Like later European cultural critics, Gorky had to find a way to explain why Americans were not unhappy given the alleged awfulness of their lives. And he used a rationale employed by many such successors: they are kept happy only since they "buy rubbish they do not need and watch shows that only dull their wits."[9]

This argument required, however, the self-proclaimed tribunes of the people to ignore the expressed preferences of the American masses, who generally supported their democratic system while rejecting the left's ideology and proposed solution. This analysis of Americans as paralyzed by false consciousness failed to understand the blessings of stability, relative prosperity, and an opportunity for advancement that often were within reach.

Gorky's writings also show how much of the European left's condescension to America was in reality based on a snobbishness and European chauvinism shared with their reactionary counterparts. In a letter he wrote while visiting America in 1906, Gorky declared, "Everything beautiful comes from Europe."[10] Long after the Communist revolution in Russia, he told an American magazine that the United States "is the most deformed civilization on our planet," for whatever Europe's faults, these had been "magnified to monstrous proportions" there.[11]

Once the Soviet Union had been established, Communist views of the United States were no longer a matter of individual choice but were determined by the regime's policy. The USSR was the first country to impose mandatory anti-Americanism on its citizens and all aspects of its educational and media system. Since the USSR was to be the masses' hope and humanity's future, it must be made clear to all citizens and followers in the Communist movement that the United States could not play that role. And if the new Soviet regime needed imported American technology or products—as many other radical rulers would in the future—this made discrediting America even more urgent. No one could be allowed to think that America's scientific or technical achievements were proof of that system's superiority.

As Soviet leaders focused on the threat of America's international power, they ordered propagandists, journalists, and cultural workers to emphasize the failings of America as a society. According to Lenin, who wanted to counter the appeal of Wilson's advocacy of freedom for other nations, the United States embodied "the most rabid imperialism" and "the most shameless oppression and suppression of weak and small nationalities." Democracy in America "provided the most perfect mask for the most horrible policies."[12] While President Wilson saw World War I as a battle to promote democracy and end future conflicts, Lenin insisted that U.S. participation in the war was only due to "the interests of the New York Stock Exchange."[13] Lenin's USSR thus saw America as also being engaged in a drive for world domination that only one side could win.

Lenin's "Letter to American Workers" of August 1918 proclaimed that America was one of the worst countries in the world regarding the gap "between the handful of arrogant multimillionaires who wallow in filth and luxury and the millions of working people who constantly live on the verge of pauperism." Rather than a country of relative democracy and equality, the United States was merely "the latest, capitalist stage of wage-slavery."[14]

Stalin, Lenin's successor, viewed America as his main rival. As early as 1929, he highlighted America's role as the great Satan of global evil. "When a revolutionary crisis has developed" there, he said, "that will be the beginning of the end of all world capitalism."[15]

Thus, from the 1920s until the USSR's collapse seventy years later, anti-American propaganda there—and from foreign Communist parties—was quite consistent since it derived from a centrally dictated political line based on Moscow's interests. At times, it focused on specific U.S. policies, but the details never affected the overall message. Nothing positive could ever be said about the United States. Aside from direct clashes on the international stage, it was the existence of the United States as a visibly more successful alternative model for human society that made discrediting it so important for the Soviet Union's masters.

Yet once one gets beyond the rhetorical flourishes about capitalism and the frequent claims of America's economic failure (by no means fantasies, of course, during the Great Depression of the 1930s), the content of most of that domestic critique was strikingly like pre-Soviet and contemporary non-Marxist European complaints. When degrading American culture and society, pro-Communist intellectuals and those influenced by them in the West often sounded like both their romantic or conservative anti-American ancestors. On these two issues as well as on America's role in the world, their claims were also virtually identical to those of their successors in the early twenty-first century.

In earlier years, however, the Communists' two main themes were about America as an economic failure and as a phony democracy. The United States was portrayed as a plutocracy ruled by a handful of ruthless monopolists, who held the vast majority of the population imprisoned in poverty. Thus, a 1931 Soviet primer on its own economic progress contrasts the anarchy, waste, exploitation, and economic insecurity rampant in America with the USSR's system: "In America the machine is not a helper to the worker . . . but an enemy. Every new machine, every new invention throws out upon the street thousands of workers." But in Russia, "We build factories in order that there may be no poverty, no filth, no sickness, no unemployment, no exhausting labor."[16]

A Soviet engineer even authored a poem to explain this idea:

We have a plan.
In America they work without a plan.
We have a seeding campaign.
In America they destroy crops.
We increase production.
In America they reduce production and increase unemployment.
We make what is essential.
In America hundreds of factories consume raw materials and energy in order to make what is altogether unnecessary.[17]

Thus, Soviet peasants starving from the disasters wrought by collectivization or urban workers facing terrible conditions could rest secure in the belief that their American counterparts were worse off. At the same time, of course, the Soviet regime controlled all the means of communication and information—down to letters from relatives abroad or conversations with visiting Americans—to ensure that only negative images rather than more balanced ones reached its people.

The state-approved image of the United States was represented by a picture in a 1938 textbook in which unemployed American workers, clad in shabby clothes and without coats, stamp their feet on the pavement to get warm, while a passing "elegantly dressed lady" offers half a bar of chocolate to one man as a way to alleviate his starvation. American society consisted of millionaires swallowing up feebler folk and helpless proletarians. Yet a brighter future was already visible in the form of black and white workers uniting to bring a Communist revolution and, no doubt, raise America to the dizzy heights achieved by Stalin's regime.[18]

Social decadence was said to undercut any technological achievement that America could claim. The silhouette chosen for the cover of Alexander Hamadan's *American Silhouettes*, published in 1936, was that of a hobo against the backdrop of a New York City skyline. In the 1930s, the truth of poverty and racial prejudice was bad enough, but Soviet propagandists had to embellish it. Thus, the 1941 Soviet *Handbook for Elementary School Teachers* told them to instruct Soviet youth that their counterparts in the United States "are deprived of real knowledge," taught only the essentials of reading, writing, and arithmetic "because in the opinion of the American bourgeoisie this is enough for the children of the toilers." A 1934 novel has a Soviet thief dreamily comparing the advantages of forced labor on the White Sea–Baltic Canal to the far more terrible conditions of American prisons.[19]

When the Soviets loosened up beyond the barest clichés about America, though, they quickly returned to all the usual European charges against the United States, as in the satirical travel book, *Little Golden America*, published in 1937 by the comic writers Ilya Ilf and Evgeni Petrov at the moment Ilf was dying of tuberculosis contracted on the trip. Like their Western European predecessors of a century earlier, they found American life annoyingly homogeneous and sadly "colorless and depersonalized."[20]

They also made fun of the rapid pace of life ("we were constantly racing somewhere at top speed"), the obsession with both religion and financial success (on examining the Bibles found in American hotel rooms, they noted that the pages referenced "for success in business" were "greasy" with use), the horrors of American cuisine ("quite tasteless"), and yet the gluttony of the people (Americans "do not eat; they fill up on food, just as an automobile is filled with gasoline.").[21] But while they were ostensibly condemning capitalism, they were actually arguing America's inferiority to Europe.

Sounding precisely like the aristocratic travelers of the early nineteenth century, the authors explained that Americans are simply unintellectual, lazy creatures who are inferior: "The average American, despite his outward show of activity, is really a passive person by nature. He must have everything presented to him in a finished form, like a spoiled husband."[22]

While Americans did have "many splendid and appealing traits," including being good workers, neat, accurate, and honest, "They simply did not possess . . . curiosity."[23] Americans, the authors added, "cannot endure abstract conversations [but are] interested only in what is directly connected with his house, his automobile, or his nearest neighbors."[24] Mistaking pragmatism for a lack of intelligence or intellectual ability was a common European error about America.

Sounding like the romantics of a century earlier—and, ironically, at a time when Russian patriotism was still condemned in the USSR—they wrote that while Russians have a powerful love of their native land down to the level of its soil, an American only asks of his country to "let him alone" and "not to interfere with his listening to the radio or going to the movies."[25] Since, of course, Soviet citizens' slightest deviation from the party line would have landed them in a slave labor camp, perhaps being left alone by one's government did not sound so bad.

Similarly, like earlier critics of America, many of their complaints resulted from the fact that a modernization process—despite all the Soviet talk of progress and industrialization—was simply not understood in Moscow or other places. At least the nineteenth-century aristocratic and romantic critics knew they did not want a mass society, even if it did provide a better life for the masses. But the leftist anti-Americans could never admit that.

Ilf and Petrov, for example, said that American food was of poor quality because it was more profitable to ship meat (frozen chickens) and produce (unripe tomatoes) longer distances than to grow fresher foods near cities.[26] Yet any culinary loss was mitigated by the fact that this technique allowed for a much greater quantity of relatively better quality food and at far lower prices than would otherwise have been the case.

In other words, while American workers might eat imperfect tomatoes, they did at least have—unlike in the USSR—tomatoes to eat at affordable prices. American farmers generally also made more money from this system. In contrast, seventy-five years after the Communist regime came to power, Russia still had a huge number of impoverished peasants who could not provide its workers a decent diet. For its city people, no tomatoes or chicken of any kind were on the menu.

Similarly, the authors concluded in orthodox Marxist fashion that while American technology and industry produce "ideal things which make life easier, social conditions do not let the American earn enough money to buy these things."[27] There is much talk about other mainstays of the anti-American social critique: the horrors of commercialism, advertising everywhere, and the sale of products that consumers might not really need.

Yet despite the negative attributes of advertising that produced consumer demand, the production of a wide range of consumer goods did provide workers with the money to buy things. This was a central aspect of American success that Marxists mistakenly ignored because it contradicted their idea that the workers would be inevitably impoverished. Advertising might be annoying and demeaning, but it also paid the bills for those on the automobile assembly lines. Only people who already had the basic necessities of life could think of buying frivolous things.

The American political system also had to be thoroughly discredited. It was not enough to please their masters for Ilf and Petrov to write— whatever they personally believed, of course, is another matter in all these cases—that American democracy was a sham. They had to insist that the system required its people be constrained and unhappy. Americans might be fooled into thinking they had a right to liberty and the pursuit of happiness, "but the possibility of actually enjoying [these things] is exceedingly dubious. This right is in too dangerous proximity with the money vaults of Wall Street."[28]

Ilf and Petrov predicted that America would soon collapse. It was "capable of feeding a billion people, but cannot feed its own population. ... It has everything needed to create a peaceful life for its people, yet ... the entire population is in a state of unrest." The end was, no doubt, near.[29]

During World War II, when the United States was the Soviet Union's ally and main supplier of aid, it was the USSR, however, that was in danger of collapse and badly in need of all the American productivity it had earlier ridiculed. Even then, though, the theme of Soviet propaganda was still anti-American, stressing the need to remember that America was not a real friend and there should be no gratitude for its help. In 1942, Stalin reminded his subjects that no Soviet citizen should ever forget that America was a capitalist country, and thus hostile and decadent.[30]

As would be so often true at other places and times, the basis of anti-Americanism in the USSR was not a hurt or outraged response to U.S. policy but an attempt to benefit the sponsoring regime or movement. Not only did anti-Americanism mobilize the people around their own dictators but it also discouraged them from seeing the very American achievements they might want to emulate at home. As Winston Churchill so wisely said in March 1949, the "Kremlin fears the friendship of the West more than its enmity."[31]

Once the Cold War began, of course, these themes of suspicion and hostility were greatly simplified. The USSR, the Communists, and their supporters insisted that one bloc led by the USSR represented everything good, and the other headed by the United States promoted everything bad. As so often happened, the only world power in history that did not seek global conquest was the one most often accused of that sin. Nevertheless, this claim about America's ambitions was accepted by many Western and Third World intellectuals. Even such productive and well-intentioned policies as the post–World War II rebuilding and democratic reform of Europe and Japan were portrayed as a cynical attempt to turn those countries into colonies. This was at the same time that the USSR was unleashing a reign of terror and demanding total subservience in Eastern Europe, where it was the dominant power.

In somewhat modified form, other anti-Americans simply put the two sides on an equal basis, accepting Soviet claims about the United States without necessarily liking the USSR. A good example of this was a letter written by the British philosopher Bertrand Russell to an American acquaintance in 1956 in the midst of the Cold War: "Mankind is divided into two classes: those who object to infringements to civil liberties in Russia, but not in the United States; and those who object to them in the United States, but not in Russia. . . . The fundamental fallacy . . . is this: "A and B hate each other, therefore one is good and the other is bad." From the evidence of history, it seems much more likely that both are bad."[32]

Alongside the Soviet Union's anti-American condemnations regarding U.S. foreign policy was its offensive against American culture, whose rising influence seemed to threaten bringing global political influence in its wake. It was the first battle in what would decades later become the struggle over "globalization."

The Soviet state and the many parties, front groups, cultural organizations, and intellectuals that it controlled or influenced went on the offensive beginning in 1947 to block the advance of American culture. The effort had so much appeal to many European intellectuals because it blended perfectly with the older ideas they held regarding American culture as alien, inferior, and mass-oriented. An endless stream of Communist-influenced articles, speeches, and resolutions warned against the subversive onslaught, which in the USSR itself extended to the dangers of American capitalist architecture, jazz, and ballroom dancing.[33] In 1947, Soviet artists were mobilized for the most systematically coordinated anti-American campaign in history.

At times of more "normal" hostility, Soviet propaganda would sometimes distinguish between "progressive" and "reactionary" aspects of American culture, while at times of extreme hostility—as in the early Cold War years—all American writers, including non-Communist leftists, were seen as evil. If the socialist Upton Sinclair was merely a man without honor and the independent leftist John Dos Passos a renegade, Thornton Wilder was an outright fascist and John Steinbeck a Wall Street lackey.[34]

In an article, charmingly entitled, "Dealers in Spiritual Poison," the USSR's greatest film director, Serge Eisenstein, wrote that while he liked Americans personally, their movies—like *Going My Way* and *Anna and the King of Siam*—made attractive the poison of indifference and the delusions of class harmony in a sugar coating of patriotism, sentimentality, and humor, a sure proof that bourgeois culture was opium for the masses.[35]

Of course, Eisenstein's own analysis requires analysis. Eisenstein had directed great films, but his own talent had been stymied by Stalin and the system he had to uphold if he was to survive. Hollywood has been accused of many sins, but executing directors or sending them to forced labor camps is not one of them. In addition, of course, he selected films that could be portrayed as mere froth. But even Hollywood could send worthwhile messages. *Going My Way* was a moving rendition of the spiritual comforts of religion and a plea for tolerance toward Catholics in a largely Protestant America, while the story of the tutor for the Thai king's children might have caricatured Third World cultures but also taught respect for them and the belief that they could achieve progress.

Such products of American mass culture can be easily ridiculed—and far sillier examples are easily found. From the point of view of Soviet or Western European critics, however, even songs and dances transmitted American culture that, in turn, carried a set of values and attitudes toward life deemed objectionable. Moreover, the popularity of such products with the masses was the very point that made these books, films, or songs so dangerous politically and so horrifying for people who, despite their leftist ideologies, were elitist and patriotic on cultural issues.

In general, then, the USSR portrayed American culture as a tool for world conquest. Thus, *Soviet Music* magazine warned that the American music industry not only was dominated by greedy capitalists (which was true) but also culturally deprived its listeners (which was arguable). "All attempts to engulf the world with the scanty products of the venal American muse are nothing but frontier ideological expansion of American imperialism, propaganda for reactionary-obscurantist misanthropic ideas," it maintained.[36]

The powerful international appeal of American culture made it the equivalent of the atomic bomb as a Cold War asset for gaining influence and winning admiration. Its power was enhanced by the fact that, unlike the atomic bomb, Soviet scientists could not discover—or steal—the secrets of duplicating it. After all, it was much easier to find rhymes for "love" than it was for "tractor."

Rather than compete with far less attractive alternative cultural products, the USSR focused on warning about the American ones. In fulfilling the regime's orders during this 1940s campaign, Konstantin Simonov wrote a play, *The Russian Question*, which was later made into a film. The story is about two naïve Soviet scientists, who are devoted to humanism and international scientific cooperation. American spies who pretend to have similar values steal their medical breakthroughs and sell them to a large company for a big profit. When the Soviet scientists go on trial, one recants and is forgiven by Stalin, and the other refuses and is only punished by losing his job.[37]

Soviet writers over the following decades were urged to produce similar works. Viktor Konetskii, in his 1977 novel about Soviet sailors, shows them repelled by America's "polluted environment" and domination by the Mafia. In a revival of the degeneracy theory, even American trees are dirty and shabby. The author was so enthusiastic that he described the German luxury car Mercedes-Benz as a cheap, poorly built American-made auto.[38]

Analyses of American literature were also used to serve this purpose. In a 1980 meeting of the Union of Soviet Writers, for example, the literary critic Leonid Novichenko appealed to his colleagues to combat professionally "American imperialism's aggressive militaristic designs."[39] One of many such studies concluded that Mario Puzo's novel about the Mafia, *The Godfather*, showed that this criminal organization was just imitating other U.S. institutions, a form of fascism backed by the country's government. A Soviet critic concluded that American novels proved that the United States "is directed at the suppression and subjugation of the individual to the interests of the state [and] the anti-human interests of business and profits."[40]

Occasionally, as Soviet Communism lost its self-confidence in the post-Stalin era, the picture of the United States was sometimes tempered—at least inside the ruling elite—by admissions of American success. After his 1959 visit to the United States, Soviet dictator Nikita Khrushchev told a top-level meeting of the Communist Party Central Committee, "In America, communism has already been built. There everyone lives well. Everyone has his home, car, bank savings, etc." Subsequently, Khrushchev insisted on including the famous slogan "Catch up to and surpass America" in the 1961 party program.[41]

In its international propaganda, however, there was no change from the 1930s up to the time when the Soviet Union collapsed. The Soviets perfected, for example, the art of systematic anti-American propaganda based on disinformation. An item of Western origin (perhaps planted originally by Soviet agents, inaccurately quoted, or from a marginal source) would provide "credible" evidence of some American misdeed. The United States was blamed for every dastardly act, and the motives for its policies were portrayed as devious or disreputable.[42]

The United States was said to be escalating the arms race, provoking conflict, introducing sinister new weapons, forcing allies to buy expensive weapons, using foreign aid as blackmail to gain concessions, and spreading lies about the USSR. It was constantly accused of interfering against progressive movements or subverting other countries.[43] There were, of course, times when these charges were true. But whatever wrongs the United States committed were greatly multiplied, deepened, and portrayed as more deliberate, while any good actions were ignored or distorted.

Whole fleets of completely false allegations were continually launched. One series of Soviet articles, "Bosses without Masks," depicted America as controlled by money-hungry billionaires who engineered the assassination of President John Kennedy.[44] Other campaigns charged that the AIDS disease was developed by the Pentagon as a "killer virus . . . in order to obtain military superiority."[45]

The United States was portrayed in the Cold War's last decade as being as ugly in its policies at home as it was abroad. It was a vicious, exploitative society whose main features included high unemployment, racial discrimination, abject poverty and excessive wealth, demoralization and material deprivation among the poor, unaffordable education and health care, rampant crime, antisocial behavior involving drugs and pornography, mistreatment of workers, large numbers of political prisoners, and no real democracy. To discourage defections, Soviet emigrants there were portrayed as miserable and unsuccessful, a tactic identical to that employed by Prussia two centuries earlier to reduce emigration or by Dostoyevsky a century before to defend the czarist regime.[46]

Despite its overlay of Marxist rhetoric—full of talk about "imperialism" and "capitalism"—the themes and complaints of official Soviet anti-Americanism continued to be quite close to that purveyed by far more conservative Europeans. For example, it was often claimed, as one anti-American book put it, "The important thing in America is money, regardless of how it was come by."[47] Despite fitting the Communist view of "capitalist" society, this statement reflects the consensus nineteenth-century anti-American view as well.

Geopolitical competition between the United States and the USSR, largely fictional in earlier years but quite real during the Cold War, brought criticism of many specific American policies in the world, yet that sense of rivalry had also been a common theme in British, French, and German anti-American writings for decades.

The main difference between the USSR's version of anti-Americanism and earlier anti-Americanism elsewhere was that the Soviet variety was officially dictated, not just the individual attempts of people to express themselves or inform fellow citizens. Moreover, these works had to be purely anti-American. Unlike in Western Europe, they could not be balanced by other, favorable accounts or even by minor positive statements within a largely critical work. Another distinction is that Soviet anti-Americanism was a product manufactured for export to convince people in other countries to believe negative things about the United States in order to further the Soviet regime's interests.

The goal, as a U.S. government study put it, was to show the United States as a "doomed, decadent, inherently evil society opposing all progressive change . . . to persuade others that it is not a model for their own countries."[48] This denial of the United States as being a good example for other countries was the oldest anti-American theme of all.

Of course, this propaganda ran up against a largely favorable view of the United States among many Europeans, especially the masses. Ironically, a great deal of positive sentiment and the diminution of anti-Americanism during the Cold War was due to the fact that Europeans saw the United States as defending them from the USSR's aggression and an unpleasant future living in a Soviet-style state. Occasionally, even Soviet propaganda admitted that most people believed living standards were higher in the United States. As one book written at the height of state-sponsored Soviet anti-Americanism put it: "The common conception of American life among Europeans [is a belief] that in the United States everyone lives in a state of economic security and confidence of the future [and] that American youth grows up carefree and happy."[49]

It is easy to laugh at the extremes of Communist propaganda about the United States or view it as totally ineffective. Nevertheless, it did have a tremendous agenda-setting influence on the European and Third World left, which meant a large proportion of the intellectual and cultural elite that shapes other people's views. The main claims made by the Soviets, though also featured in earlier European anti-Americanism— that America was seeking global political and cultural domination and that America was responsible for many global problems—became far more widely accepted around the world a decade after the USSR's collapse. This was the Soviet Union's posthumous revenge on the Cold War's victor. Obviously, U.S. foreign actions and domestic situations contributed to this perception, but it was the way these events were interpreted and distorted that broadened hostility from specific complaints to a more general condemnation of the United States.

Another important feature of Soviet anti-Americanism was that it showed how useful a tool this was for a regime or for an opposition seeking to gain power. Anti-Americanism was a demagogic gold mine for mobilizing people behind a nationalist dictator or revolutionary cause. As a result, anti-Americanism was transformed from a matter of largely intellectual interest into being one of the world's most important political tactics.

Fascism made a parallel, though less important, contribution to all these aspects of anti-Americanism. It, too, sought to offer Europe an alternative future to the "American" one feared by so many. Despite a greater emphasis on racism and anti-Semitism, the Nazis and their sympathizers drew many of their ideas from past European aristocratic and romantic anti-Americanism. For example, German fascist anti-Americanism focused on the usual claims that America was characterized by excessive materialism, a low cultural level, soullessness, degenerate pragmatism, and excessive power for women. In short, America represented everything negative in "modern" life and, even worse, was seeking to remake the world in its own dreadful image.

While fascist ideology in its explicit form was mostly discredited after 1945 and never had the global reach of its Soviet rival, it would be wrong to underestimate its lasting impact. Equally, despite fascism's special features and ultimate defeat, its ideas about America—even if on no other issue—would also be echoed in the later views of many in Europe and the Middle East who seem to be of a totally different political hue.

Although racialist thinking was common in nineteenth-century Europe, the originator of this doctrine as a systematic ideology was the Frenchman Arthur de Gobineau, who lived from 1816 to 1882. He applied this idea to the United States in his *Essay on the Inequality of the Human Races*. Originally, Gobineau wrote, Anglo-Saxon Aryans had controlled America, but the admission of so many immigrants, who Gobineau called "a mixed assortment of the most degenerate races of olden-day Europe," had destroyed the country. Among these inferior peoples, he included the Irish, Italians, and—ironically—lower-class Germans. "It is quite unimaginable that anything could result from such horrible confusion but an incoherent juxtaposition of the most decadent kinds of people."[50]

America was not a new or young nation that created its own people, Gobineau wrote, but simply the refuge for Europe's human dregs, who took advantage of the greater freedom there to behave worse. Its ethnic eclecticism and rootless population ensured that it would be a violent, unstable society dominated by mob rule.[51] This was almost word for word identical to an idea put forward by the French lawyer Simon Linguet a century earlier, as well as a reflection of many other early critics of the United States.[52] Alfred Rosenberg, National Socialism's official philosopher, would write similarly in 1933 that by giving rights to all—and especially by extending them to African-Americans after the Civil War—the United States doomed itself to be without a coherent people (*volk*) such as existed in Germany.[53]

Yet while racialism seemed to be fascism's most obvious contribution to the anti-American cause, it also developed a far more lasting, though less totally original, idea. Gobineau argued that the United States was the unrestrained "monster" that Europe created from its own modernist vision. True, Gobineau agreed with a thousand precursors that immigrants to America who sought "the temple of virtue and happiness were sorely disappointed." He realized that America represented the logical development of potential European trends. It was, as one author summarized his work, Europe on fast forward.[54]

As we have seen, this belief that the American example was actually transforming the world became the most important new development in late-nineteenth-century anti-Americanism. The United States was not merely a joke or a disappointment but by its example and power actually threatened the way of life of everyone else. Like the classical monster, Cerberus, America had three heads: it was a sinisterly successful example that invited imitation, a seductively attractive culture that indirectly spread its poison everywhere, and a powerful state that could take over other countries directly through military and economic means. The official optimism of Communism—which maintained its own victory was inevitable—prevented it from fully accepting the implications of this idea.

The gloomier conservatives were much more worried about this American danger because they were also readier to believe that the United States would succeed in ruining the world. Moeller van den Bruck, the German rightist who coined the phrase "Third Reich," felt that the rise of America was transforming the West in the wrong direction.[55] Such ideas would later influence a large portion of the left, as it lost its own faith in the triumph of socialism, and of the Third World, which had a better sense of its own weaknesses.

A clear and comprehensive sense of this menace was provided by the profascist German philosopher Martin Heidegger. He warned that America represented humanity's greatest crisis in that it represented alienation, a loss of authenticity, and an impediment to spiritual reawakening.[56] In lectures given in 1935 and published in 1953, he claimed that America was rotting German society from within, reshaping its whole use of language and worldview into a materialistic, alienated, inhuman one. Implicitly, this was a critique of American pragmatism, which was said to restrict knowledge to mastering reality and turning people into objects.

Precisely like the German and French romantic critics of America a century earlier, Heidegger declared that American society rejects history and nationhood. It is the dictatorship of pragmatism, technology, and mass society, a monstrous nonbeing, thoughtlessly stumbling about and trying to annihilate what it cannot understand. America represents homelessness, uprootedness, and the absence of the poetic. In contrast, Germany was a rooted society with a coherent people, connected to the poetic in life. The historic confrontation between these two countries, he predicted, would be nothing less than a struggle over the soul of humanity.[57]

This paralleled Soviet views on the subject. The Communist-fascist debate was in no small part about which ideology and country—the USSR or Germany—was better able to provide an alternative future to the dreadful one offered by America.

Heidegger, like people of very different political views in other decades, defined America as the embodiment of the type of modern society that Europe—and, in their own ways, the Middle East and Latin America—wanted to reject. It is characterized by "dreary technological frenzy" and the "unrestricted organization of the average man." There is too much change. It is a place where "a boxer is regarded as a nation's great man; when mass meetings attended by millions are looked on as a triumph."[58]

Yet perhaps boxers didn't make such bad heroes compared with the one who Heidegger thought was Germany's "great man" in 1935, Adolf Hitler. It was that dictator who addressed mass meetings attended by many thousands, where he was hailed as the solution to Germany's problems. And it was the Nazi regime Heidegger supported that carried out an "unrestricted organization of the average man" far beyond anything Americans could conceive. By 1953—or 2003—though, Heidegger's anti-American sentiments could be passed off as rather mainstream European critiques of American consumer culture.

While aspects of Heidegger's criticism come from romantic antecedents, others were virtual transcriptions of nineteenth-century conservative complaints. Thus, it is not only the corruption of the masses but also the devaluation of the elite that makes him disapprove of America. In the United States, he wrote, "Intelligence no longer meant a wealth of talent . . . but only what could be learned by everyone, the practice of a routine, always associated with a certain amount of sweat and a certain amount of show." The mediocre masses rule and enforce conformity, reveling in the destruction of everything creative. "This is the onslaught of what we call the demonic (in the sense of destructive evil)."[59]

Just as the Communists often called America fascist, Heidegger and other profascists viewed America as being akin to the USSR. But to him, the United States was worse, and more dangerous, "because it appears in the form of a democratic middle class way of life mixed with Christianity."[60] Thus, while Communism could never win the allegiance of the masses and transform the world, America might succeed in doing so. Indeed, this idea that America was remaking the world in its image would be the basis of post-Communist, twenty-first-century anti-Americanism.

Of course, German fascists did not forget to mix the hatred of America with the hatred of Jews, another feature of anti-Americanism that would reappear—and on the left, no less—a half-century after the German Reich's collapse. Who else but the Jews would prosper in and promote such a destructive, rootless, and even demonic society? And who else but the Jews would be the masterminds behind the U.S. drive for world conquest?

In his 1927 book, *Jewish World Domination?*, Otto Bonhard promoted a theory that America was merely a Jewish front. Alfred Graf Brockdorff said America was degenerating as a result of the Jews, who were best able to exploit the corruption engendered by its democratic institutions.[61] In a best-selling book on the subject in the 1920s, the pro-Nazi Adolf Halfeld sounded identical to a leftist critic of America in tracing its ethos to a combination of "Puritan ethic" and "crafty business practices," typified by "the preacher who is an entrepreneur" and "the businessman with God and ideals on his lips." The apparent high morality of Wilson's foreign policy was actually "world peace with Wall Street's seal of approval."[62]

At the same time, Halfeld added, America was a country dedicated to blind "efficiency" so that "everyone wears the same suit, boots, colors, and collars; they all read the same magazines and propaganda, which knows no limits." The Jew, best able to adapt to a society so profoundly based on alienation and modernization, was "the sum of all American civic virtues."[63]

Once in power, the Nazis would put this idea into even cruder terms, as in a 1943 declaration that behind everything in America stands the "grotesque face of the wandering Jew, who sees it as nothing less than a precursor to the implementation of his ancient and never-abandoned plans to rule the world." Yet when Giselher Wirsing, in his 1942 book about America, *Der maßlose Kontinent* (The Excessive Continent), wrote that "Uncle Sam has been transformed into Uncle Shylock,"[64] he was only stealing a phrase employed as the title of a popular French book more than a decade earlier. The anti-Semitic element of anti-Americanism neither began nor ended with the German fascists.

Equally, there was much more to the fascist critique of America than hatred of the Jews. The same Nazi text that spoke of wandering Jews who controlled the United States also accused America of imperialism in phrases indistinguishable from those of Marxists. The United States had "robbed other states of their rightful possessions with lies and deceptions, violence and war" and "murdered hundreds of thousands of Indians." Wirsing, who spoke of Uncle Shylock, also said that America was ruled by a Puritan-Calvinistic plutocracy that sought world conquest out of greed.[65] As many later Europeans would agree, he claimed that Europe was only acting in self-defense in opposing American interests and ambitions.

The dangerous yet seductive decadence of American culture was another theme that fascists shared with the Communists and other European anti-Americans. In a brochure on the evils of Americanism published in 1944 by the elite Nazi SS organization, jazz was seen as a Jewish weapon to level "all national and racial differences, as liberalism has done throughout the world."[66]

Another cultural theme taken from the nineteenth century was the

European attribution of American decadence to the belief that women were too powerful there. Rosenberg said that the "conspicuously low level of culture" was a "consequence of women's rule in America."[67] Females were said to foster excessive materialism because they encouraged men to earn and spend money. The loss of masculinity was linked to the replacement of aristocratic by bourgeois values. Halfeld said that American men seriously believed that women have a "moral, aesthetic, and intellectual advantage." The resulting system made American men weak and cowardly. It damaged their "creative intelligence" and offered a model that threatened to spread to the rest of the world with dangerous results.

Of course, the final authority on the German fascist view of America was Hitler himself, and he had strong views on the subject. While earlier in his career he had admired American technological development and its supposed domination by Aryans, Hitler reversed these views very strongly. Like Stalin, he believed that the United States was on the verge of collapse in the 1930s, weakened by democracy and a loss of racial pride.

Most of his ideas seemed to be taken from a century of European anti-American stereotypes. "What is America," Hitler told a friend, "but millionaires, beauty queens, stupid records and Hollywood?" Its corrosive appeal was so great that even Germans would succumb to America's decadence if they lived there: "Transfer [a German] to Miami and you make a degenerate out of him—in other words—an American." The idea of immigrant degeneration was, of course, the main theme of German anti-Americans a century earlier. Americans, Hitler continued, were spoiled and weakened by luxury, living "like sows though in a most luxurious sty," under the grip of "the most grasping materialism," and indifferent to "any of the loftiest expressions of the human spirit such as music."[68]

At a 1933 dinner party in his home, when a guest suggested that he seek America's friendship, Hitler responded that "a corrupt and outworn" American system was on its deathbed. It was Americans' greed and materialism that had brought about their failure. He defined the problem in virtually Marxist terms, arguing, as Lenin had, that since the Civil War, "A moneyed clique . . . under the fiction of a democracy" ruled the country. As a result of the crisis of the Depression, Hitler, like Stalin, claimed that the United States was on the verge of revolution that, in his version, would result in German Americans seizing power.[69] The main difference was the Nazi substitution of race for class as their category of analysis.

At the dinner party, Hitler's Propaganda Minister Joseph Goebbels chimed in to agree with his boss: "Nothing will be easier than to produce a bloody revolution in . . . America. No other country has so many social and racial tensions. . . . [It] is a medley of races. The ferment goes on under a cover of democracy, but it will not lead to a new form of freedom and leadership, but to a process of decay containing all the disintegrating forces of Europe."[70]

But whether or not America collapsed, Hitler thought that the United States would be no threat in a war because Americans were cowards and military incompetents who during World War I had "behaved like clumsy boys. They ran straight into the line of fire like young rabbits."[71] Even in the midst of World War II, as U.S. military and industrial might was beginning to destroy his empire, Hitler did not acknowledge that mistake. In 1942, he called America "a decayed country, with problems of race and social inequality, of no ideas. . . . My feelings against America are those of hatred and repugnance." It was "half-Judaized, half-Negrified. . . . How can one expect a state like that to hold together—a state where 80 per cent of the revenue is drained away from the public purse—a country where everything is built on the dollar?"[72]

This underestimation of America's internal coherence and external strength was a mistake that not only Stalin and Hitler but also many later dictators would make, often to their own detriment. It is important to understand that whatever their different thoughts on the subject, Hitler's and Stalin's views on America were fairly typical of those which had been conveyed by mainstream European anti-Americans for a century.

Of course, their disdain was focused to some degree on all Western democratic countries, yet the United States was portrayed as the worst, most extreme case of the malady to be combated. For example, Hitler could say—even as he made war on Britain and France—"I feel myself more akin to any European country, no matter which. . . . I consider the British state very much superior [to America]."[73] When his deputy, Martin Bormann, gave him a translated copy of a 1931 book satirizing the United States, *Juan in America* by the Scotsman Eric Linklater, Hitler said, "When one reads a book like this about them, one sees that they have the brains of a hen!"[74] Sounding like a left-wing French intellectual,

Hitler added of the Americans: "I grant you that our standard of living is lower. But the German Reich has two hundred and seventy opera houses—a standard of cultural existence of which they . . . have no conception. They have clothes, food, cars and a badly constructed house—but with a refrigerator. This sort of thing does not impress us. I might, with as much reason, judge the cultural level of the sixteenth century by the appearance of [indoor bathrooms]."[75]

His Italian fascist counterparts had strikingly similar views, seeing America as a machine-centered, urbanized society with lax moral attitudes and a low level of culture. During the 1930s, most of the fifty-one books on America published in Italy portrayed life there in the usual anti-American terms. People lived in hellish cities under the thumb of machines, a parody on European civilization. In 1938 and 1939, Emilio Cecchi, a leading journalist and sympathizer with fascism, wrote a series of articles collected as *Bitter America* that threw in all the contradictory clichés about American life, simultaneously said to be puritanical and conformist but also pagan, individualistic, and respecting no taboos, and said to be violent but putting security before anything else. Americans were compared in their behavior to sheep and machines.[76]

Like Hitler and many other anti-Americans, Italian fascist dictator Benito Mussolini explained that he had great sympathy for America's people but not for its government. "Under the guise of democracy it was really just a capitalistic oligarchy, a plutocracy." As for American culture, he criticized, "awful cocktails, feet on the tables [and] chewing gum." Regarding U.S. foreign policy, it was the worst form of imperialism ever, not merely wanting to gain power over others but to change the existing societies into one that would lower "human intelligence and dignity all over the world."[77]

Communist and fascist anti-Americanism were distinctive from earlier approaches by being so systematic and state-sponsored, while they were also different from each other in certain emphases.[78] Yet their definite continuity with historic European anti-American ideas and themes was remarkably strong.

Moreover, they posthumously helped shape the anti-American views held by many in Europe and the Third World into the twenty-first century. Communism and fascism saw America as the main external threat to their societies, as culturally subversive, as a rival to their ambitions, and as the main alternative system they must battle for directing the world's future. Later, European leftists and Middle Eastern Arab nationalists or Islamists would take over these basic concepts and copy that style of propaganda, often without realizing it.

Originally, anti-American ideology had suggested that America could never produce an advanced society or that the United States had already failed. Later, it raised the alarm that this deplorable and degenerate country represented something threatening and evil. But now the transition had been made to the highest stage of anti-Americanism: that the United States was indeed responsible for most of the world's evil and was trying to take it over entirely.

YANKEE GO HOME!

While Europe was the area of the world where anti-Americanism was most comprehensively developed, South America was the place more identified with that doctrine, especially between the 1950s and 1980s.[1]

Indeed, Latin Americans did have a far more negative encounter with U.S. policies than did Europe, but many of the key elements of anti-Americanism there were often identical. Like their European counterparts, Latin American intellectuals—the group that was always the main propagator of anti-Americanism—saw the United States as an inferior society, were skeptical about its democracy, and were concerned that it would be a bad role model for their own countries.

Of course, the difference was that Latin America, not Europe, was the area most exposed to American power. In both Europe and Latin America, there was a belief that the United States might dominate the world politically and culturally. In Latin America, unlike Europe, there was a material basis for that fear and anger.

Both the United States and Latin American states shared the experience of waging independence wars against European colonialism from Britain and Spain, respectively. Yet almost from the start, Latin Americans reestablished their identification with Spain and shared much of the European anti-American critique. They did not welcome U.S.-style liberal democracy or its antitraditional approach. Their society was based on big estates, oligarchy, centralization, and a very strong church. But while they rejected the mass industrialized society built in the United States, they were also envious of that country and all too conscious of their own failure to make dramatic progress.

Two themes intertwined in the long history of anti-Americanism there. First, Latin America believed itself to be culturally and morally superior to the United States, which made its relative weakness all the more frustrating and hard to explain. Second, the failure to catch up or surpass the United States was blamed on American policy.

Conservatives in the ruling oligarchies and army shared the sentiments of the European right, including a suspicion of America as too secular, soulless, modernist, and Protestant. The left's emphasis was that U.S. imperialism was the source of all their problems. Yet each side used all of these themes. A sense of superiority coupled with one of victimization would always characterize Latin American anti-Americanism across the political spectrum.

Still, American behavior toward Latin America would often be of an imperialistic nature and constituted an important factor in anti-Americanism. Arguably, no anti-Americanism in the world was more rational than that arising in Latin America. Yet even this objective situation left much room for interpretation. The distinction most important regarding anti-Americanism was between those who criticized specific U.S. policies and those who made a blanket condemnation of that country.

As many Latin Americans recognized, American power and progress were more humiliating reminders or scapegoats than causes for the fact that the region was often bogged down in military juntas, bitter factionalism, repression, instability, weak economies, and social repression. At the most basic level, the roots of anti-Americanism in Latin America arose from the encounter between a united, successful, and powerful country with two dozen divided, weak, and frustrated ones. The anti-American standpoint, especially among intellectuals, however, would reflexively interpret events and American actions in the most hostile sense possible.

From the very start, Latin America was at pains to distinguish its identity and strategy for progress as being different from that of the United States. Símon Bólivar, the general who did the most to lead South American armies to victory in the independence wars, was called the "George Washington of South America." But, unlike Washington, he favored highly centralized political systems with strong presidents, perhaps chosen for life, and he seriously considered establishing a monarchy. So antagonistic to the United States was Bólivar that he sarcastically remarked that it would be better for South America to adopt the Muslim holy book, the Qu'ran, rather than U.S.-style institutions. As early as August 5, 1829, in a letter to a British diplomat about the unsuitability of the American system, Bólivar asked whether the United States was destined to plague South America with misery in the name of liberty.[2]

Indeed, the old colonial power, Spain specifically, and Europe generally would remain the role model for Latin American politicians and intellectuals. In 1845, for example, former president Joaquin Pinto of Chile said: "We will never use the methods of democracy as practiced in the United States of America, but rather the political principles of Spain."[3] Yet Spanish institutions were antidemocratic, highly centralized, and monarchist, and they inhibited progress, helping to ensure that the country fell steadily further behind the rest of Europe.

When Latin Americans remarked on visits to the United States in their writings, they sounded quite similar to their European counterparts. The conservative Mexican writer Lucas Alamán was quite sarcastic about any U.S. claim "to be in the vanguard of nineteenth-century civilization." After all, that country lacked morality, order, and good customs. Even American diversity provoked his scorn: "We are not a people of merchants and adventurers . . . and refuse of all countries whose only mission is to usurp the property of the miserable Indians, and later to rob the fertile lands opened to civilization by the Spanish race. . . . We are a nation formed three centuries ago, not an aggregation of peoples of differing customs."[4]

Like Europeans, South Americans saw the United States as merely materialistic while they occupied a higher spiritual plane. Benjamin Vicuna MacKenna, the Chilean statesman and writer, thought Americans put too much emphasis on making everything the biggest and best. MacKenna's 1856 travel book duplicated many European criticisms with only slight variations. Thus, while Europeans were scandalized by tobacco spitting, he was dismayed by the way Americans ate apples.[5]

As in Europe, though slightly earlier, the fear of a threatening United States also arose. The first dangerous omens were seen in the revolt of American settlers to win Texas's independence from Mexico in the 1830s, followed by its incorporation into the United States, and the U.S. defeat of Mexico in the 1848 war, leading to the annexation of California and other territories from that country.

Francisco Bilbao, a Chilean, wrote *America in Danger* in 1856, in which he included a remarkable prophecy that the two great future empires would be Russia and the United States, with the latter trying "to secure the domination of Yankee individualism throughout the world." Their proximity made the Yankees most dangerous for South America. Already, it "extends its talons . . . against the south. Already we see fragments of America falling into the jaws of the Saxon boa . . . as it unfolds its tortuous coils. Yesterday it was Texas then it was northern Mexico and the Pacific that greets a new master."[6]

Bilbao's proposed solution was to imitate the secrets of U.S. success: "Let us not scorn, let us rather incorporate in ourselves all that shines in the genius and life of North America. We should not despise under the pretext of individualism all that forms the strength of the races."[7] A similar point was made by a Guatemalan leader: "It's curious that in the heart of the United States, the source of our pain is also where our remedy is."[8] But few Latin Americans agreed with that assessment.

Not surprisingly, it was in Mexico, the only Latin American country bordering the United States, where the greatest suspicions developed toward the United States. It was Porfirio Díaz, Mexico's dictator during most of the nineteenth century's second half, who supposedly coined the famous lament, "Poor Mexico, so far from God, and so close to the United States."[9] In 1877, the Mexican poet Guillermo Prieto, after a visit there, rejected the idea that anything good could come from the United States. He wrote bitterly,

They can do everything;
they can change the shreds
of my unhappy country
into splendid nations,

booty of deceit,
victims of outrage!¹⁰

But Mexico was not the only country that saw itself as a victim. Already by 1893, the Brazilian Eduardo Prado claimed, quite inaccurately, "There is no Latin American nation that has not suffered in its relations with the United States."¹¹ The Spanish-American War of 1898 marked a decisive escalation of such sentiments. American forces defeated Spain and gave Cuba independence, though bypassing the Cuban nationalist movement already fighting for that cause. The defeat of the oppressive mother country, Spain, however, stirred more sympathy in Latin America than the however imperfect liberation by the United States.

Immediately after the war, a spate of novels attacking the United States was published throughout the region. One of them, *El Problema*, by a Guatemalan, Máximo Soto-Hall, defined Latin America's problem as the penetration of North American companies anxious to grab its oil, mineral resources, or fruit. Those responsible were heartless Yankee businessmen or managers who worked with servile local overseers. They seduced maidens while colluding with politicians to steal the nation's resources. At the same time, they represented a cultural invasion armed with whiskey, aspirin, their strange language, and immoral ways.¹²

One of the most outspoken critics of the United States and supporters of Spain in this period was José Santos Chocano. Born in Peru in 1875, Chocano was a poet who so expressed continental sentiments that he was hailed as the "Poet of America." He wrote of the glories of the Incas and the Spanish race, ignoring the fact that the latter had committed genocide on the former. "My blood is Spanish and Inca is my pulse," he wrote in one poem. On two occasions, in 1894 in Peru and 1920 in Guatemala, Chocano's involvement in failed revolutions ended with imprisonment. The second time, he was saved from execution only by the intervention of the king of Spain, among others.

Latin America's most popular poet viewed the conflict with the United States in racialist terms, as a battle for dominance between Anglo-Saxons and Latins. He wrote in his poem "The Epic of the Pacific (Yankee Style)":

[Latin] America must, since it longs to be free,
imitate them first and equal them later....

Let us not trust the man with blue eyes,
when he wishes to steal the warmth of our homes. . . .
Our Andes ignore the importance of being white,
Our rivers disdain the worth of a Saxon. . . .[13]

Chocano had predicted that the North Americans, "the race with blonde hair," would not succeed in building the Panama Canal. Only Latin Americans "with dark heads" could do so.[14] But he was wrong. The U.S. building of the Panama Canal showed that the gap in effective organization and institutions could not be banished by poetry. Even the idea of racial solidarity was disproved as Panamanians used U.S. backing to seize independence in their own interest against a Colombian regime that had so long neglected their isolated province.

Both Bilbao, who was basically a liberal democrat, and Chocano, a romantic nationalist, agreed very much on one point. To maintain their sovereignty and ward off the U.S. threat, their people would have to learn from what their rival had done, certainly through technological progress, possibly by social modernization. Yet it was Latin America's failure to do so, its inability to stamp out chaos and put its own house in order, which invited U.S. intervention. In that sense, Latin America in the late nineteenth and early twentieth centuries would most resemble the Middle East in the late twentieth and early twenty-first centuries. Also, in both cases, the frustration of local failure produced a high level of anti-Americanism and the notion that—in addition to all its other sins—it was actually the United States' fault that they had not succeeded.

One of the earliest and best-known of such arguments came from Rubén Darío, the Nicaraguan poet, journalist, and diplomat who re-peatedly expressed his distaste for civilization North American style. After an 1893 visit to New York, he called that city "the gory, the cyclopean, the monstrous capital of the banknote." Five years later, he wrote that Americans were "red-faced, heavy and gross . . . like animals in their hunt for the dollar."[15]

Responding to the canal issue, Darío composed a 1904 poem, "To Roosevelt," which became one of the best-known works of Latin American literature and was assigned to generations of students to memorize. Indeed, it stands as the clearest statement of the Latin American critique of the United States. The United States is "the future invader" of the innocent America that has Indian blood, speaks Spanish, and practices

Christianity. True, the United States is powerful as a lion and rich, too, but this is merely crudeness. In contrast, Latin America was heir to the great ancient cultures and a mass producer of poets. It was a place of light, fire, perfume, and love. In comparison, the people of the United States were "men of Saxon eyes and barbarous soul" who "lack one thing: God!"[16]

But, like some other anti-Americans, Darío would change his mind about the country he initially so reviled. Only two years later, in 1906, Darío would write another poem urging his brothers to learn "constancy, vigor and character" from the Yankees. On a later visit to New York, he described it as a city of happy laughing boys and bright girls.[17] Darío even wrote a friendly tribute to the United States and called for a union of all the American republics.[18] These lesser-known statements show that, despite objections to U.S. policy and fear of future American intentions, the Latin American response was far from exclusively one of resentment. But, even more significantly, these were not the images that would dominate the anti-American side of the Latin American intellectual tradition.

Joining the wars of 1848 and 1898 and the canal issue as anti-American grievances was the growing U.S. power in the area. American involvement and control over the region's economics and politics were proportionately greater than they have ever been in any other area of the world. United States Marines intervened more than a dozen times in Caribbean states from 1905 through the 1920s at times of civil war or social disorder.[19] American companies owned large tracts of land in some countries, controlling the key products for export and even determining—in the case of the United Fruit Company—who governed such states as Honduras and Guatemala.

The anger of Latin American intellectuals at U.S. economic power was most clearly expressed by Pablo Neruda, the Chilean poet, diplomat, and Communist who won the Nobel Prize for his poetry and the Stalin prize for his politics. In "The United Fruit Company," he sarcastically suggested that the corporation had benefited from God's partition of the universe among big American corporations. There, the company killed the heroes who harassed it, chose the dictators, carried off booty, and oppressed the workers.[20] The United States turned these countries into "Banana Republics" whose "farcical society" was built over the bodies of the great heroes of liberty. The United States "abolished free will/gave out imperial crowns," and created "the dictatorship of flies."[21] In a similar poem, "The Standard Oil Company," Neruda wrote that the "obese emperors" of Latin America—"suave and smiling assassins"—lived in New York buying the continent's products, land, governments, and whole countries at will.[22]

There were valid complaints about the brutal behavior of these powerful companies, which often enjoyed U.S. government backing. But they also contained the basis of an idea that both radical and conservative Latin American intellectuals often accepted: that American influence was to blame for everything, that dictators and injustice would not have existed if there had been no such U.S. presence, and that such behavior was innate in the U.S. system.

Yet while such sentiments were incorporated into the rhetoric of Latin American anti-Americanism, they took a place alongside such other factors as the idea that the United States was inferior on racial and religious grounds or that its system, apparently so successful, was evil in itself. This kind of thinking was manifested in a belief that Latin Americans had been endowed by the culture of the pre-Columbian inhabitants and Spain with qualities superior to the materialistic, vulgar culture of America, which disrupted family, tradition, religion, and all the things that made Latin America unique.[23]

As in Europe, such ideas were embraced by both leftists and rightists. Many of the region's greatest intellectuals and cultural figures expressed such concepts endlessly throughout the nineteenth and twentieth centuries: "If there is real poetry in our America, it is to be found in things refined . . . in the legendary Indian, in the subtle and sensual Inca, in the great [Aztec Emperor] Montezuma of the Golden Throne. The rest I leave to you, Oh Democratic Walt Whitman," wrote the Nicaraguan poet Darío in 1896.[24]

One of the most important such anti-American works in Latin America was *Ariel*, by the Uruguayan critic, essayist, and philosopher José Enrique Rodó. Its publication in 1900 was hailed as the continent's definitive manifesto, as it called on Latin Americans to reject the materialistic values represented by America and hold true to their own superior civilization. The book's similarities to European anti-Americanism are striking but not accidental since Rodó, like many of his compatriots, combined a mystical celebration of the pre-Columbian heritage with an impassioned admiration of French culture.

In his prologue to a later edition of *Ariel*, Carlos Fuentes, an important anti-American writer in his own right, made this connection clear. France "gave us culture without strings and a sense, furthermore, of elegance, disinterestedness, aristocracy, and links to the culture of the classics solely lacking in the vagabond, unrooted, homogenizing pioneer culture of the United States."[25] No Frenchmen could have more elegantly put the case for French superiority and American inferiority.

In *Ariel*, Rodó identifies the spirit of Latin America with Ariel, who symbolizes the "noble, soaring aspect of the human spirit. He represents the superiority of reason and feeling over the base impulses of irrationality. He is generous enthusiasm, elevated and unselfish motivation in all actions, spirituality in culture, vivacity and grace in intelligence . . . the ideal toward which human selection ascends."[26]

In contrast, the United States is the brutish Caliban, a "spirit of vulgarity" who cannot "distinguish the delicate from the vulgar, the ugly from the beautiful," and certainly could not tell "good from evil." These traits arise inevitably in a democratic society like the United States, which enthrones a "code of conduct by utilitarianism in which our every action is determined by the immediate ends of self-interest." In short, Rodó concluded, basing his case on quotations from French philosophers, "Democracy is the . . . dominance of a mediocre individualism."[27] The American has achieved wealth, "but good taste has eluded him."[28]

While the United States appeared to be winning as it accumulated money and won wars, these triumphs were meaningless. Latin America represented a highly cultured Athens, while North America was merely the incarnation of materialistic Phoenicia and militaristic Sparta. It would fail and leave no heritage.[29]

Rodó warned that "left to itself—without the constant correction of a strong moral authority to refine and channel its inclinations in the direction of exaltation of life—democracy will gradually extinguish any superiority that does not translate into sharper and more ruthless skills in the struggles of self-interest, the self-interest that then becomes the most ignoble and brutal form of strength."[30] America merely represented an empty pursuit of well-being as an end in itself.[31]

The complaint of most anti-American intellectuals during the nineteenth century and well into the twentieth century was not that the Yankees inhibited democracy or progress in Latin America—as later leftists would suggest—but rather that they were offering a bad model of excessive democracy and too much change, a system that neither worked well nor fit with the continent's own heritage.

An interesting detail about Rodó's work was his use as the story's hero of Ariel, a character from William Shakespeare's play, *The Tempest*. In Shakespeare's tale, Prospero, an Italian ruler fleeing a coup, and his daughter are washed ashore on an island. There they meet Ariel, a spirit with magical powers, and Caliban, an ignoble savage who Prospero makes his servant. Prospero uses Ariel to rule the island.[32]

Rodó identifies the spirit of Latin America with the noble Ariel and that of the United States with the brutish Caliban. Democracy in the United States is no more than the "enthronement of Caliban."[33] Yet, a century later, Latin American and European anti-Americans had completely reversed this metaphor. Now the evil United States was portrayed as a symbolic Prospero in its insatiable thirst for domination, while Latin America—or the Third World, or the entire world—was embodied in the unjustly repressed, falsely slandered Caliban. Ariel was merely a dupe of imperialism, a collaborator with imperialist domination.

The contradictory use of these images shows well the mixed strands that merged under the banner of anti-Americanism. Conservative and romantic thinking viewed Latin America and Europe (and later the Middle East) as superior, aristocratic cultures dragged down by racially inferior and crude American upstarts who represented a decadent democracy and a society with too much freedom. In short, America was too radical and modern. From the leftist perspective, though, Europe and Latin America (and later the Middle East) were portrayed as weaker, oppressed societies facing domination by a reactionary, antidemocratic United States, which allegedly considered them inferior and inhibited them from changing. These conflicting ideas often existed in the same thinkers or movements with no sense of their opposite origins or implications.

This theme of Latin American superiority proved persistent as the message of countless Latin American literary and nonfiction works, like the 1917 prose-poem of José Vargas Vilz, a Colombian novelist, who branded North Americans as "barbarians," "drunken mobs," and "a voracious, unfriendly, disdainful race," committed to the "doctrine of plundering, robbery, and conquest." The United States was no more than "a burly bandit" cutting the throats of other nations.[34]

One of the best embodiments of the European–Latin American link and superior-victim themes for anti-Americanism was Manuel Ugarte. Born in Buenos Aires in 1878, he went to Paris after graduating college and became a noted cultural figure there. On visiting the United States and Mexico in 1900 and 1901, he became convinced that the United States was seeking to dominate Latin America. He began a campaign of writings and lectures, supported by French and Spanish intellectuals, in Europe and Latin America to rouse people against the Yankee peril.[35]

His 1923 book, *Destiny of a Continent*, was part travelogue, part anti-American indictment, coupling anti-imperialist rhetoric with the older themes of Latin American cultural superiority. The United States was following the tradition of the Romans, Napoleon's France, and other peoples "overflowing with vigor" to seek empires. By not opposing this threat more energetically, his fellow Latin Americans were giving "proofs of an inferiority" that the Americans then used to justify their expansionism.[36]

Ugarte angrily claimed that Americans looked down on their neighbors to the south. Most Americans, he wrote, viewed Latin Americans as "savages, ridiculous phenomena, degenerates."[37] But, sounding like the French intellectuals who so influenced him, Ugarte made it clear that this was the way he felt toward North Americans. The United States was "great, powerful, prosperous, astonishingly progressive, supreme masters of energy and creative life, healthy and comfortable." But its people were also too practical, proud, and unprincipled, having the mentality of a "cowboy, violent and vain of his muscles, who civilizes the Far West by exterminating simultaneously the virgin forest and the aboriginal races in the same highhanded act of pride and domination."[38]

At the U.S.-Mexico border, Ugarte explained, one could clearly see the difference between the "Anglo-Saxon . . . hard, haughty and utilitarian, infatuated with his success and his muscular strength," who dominates nature and uses other races as servants in exchange for some "crumbs of the feast." In contrast, Mexico's people had "easy-going customs," were closer to nature, and had "contemplative, dreamy tendencies" that made them generous.[39]

One of Ugarte's ideas, which was a forerunner of contemporary anti-American thinking, was that the very fact that the United States did not act like other imperialistic states proved that it was even worse than they were. By not seeking full or permanent political control of Latin American states, the United States showed that it was more subtly dangerous. "Only the United States," he wrote, understood how to be expansionist by using alternative tactics: "At times imperious, at other times suave, in certain cases apparently disinterested, in others implacable in its greed. . . . North American imperialism is the most perfect instrument of domination."[40]

In fact, the U.S. refusal to incorporate Latin America into a political empire was said to show clearly how devious, racist, and aggressive it was. The Americans did not want to annex people it viewed as inferior to avoid "any impairing or enfeebling of the superiority which he claims."[41] In other words, Americans looked down on the peoples of the south so much that they would not even take them as subjects. In later decades, this need to explain the imperialism of a country that consciously rejected such methods would spawn all sorts of theories of neocolonialism, whose supposed tools included cultural exports as well as economic investment and political plots.

Even many of those noting that local problems, not foreign oppression, was the real reason for the region's difficulties still made clear their disdain for the overwhelming, overbearing neighbor to the north. One example was Gabriela Mistral, an esteemed Chilean educator, writer, and poet who won the Nobel Prize in literature in 1945. Her work focused on practical progress for her society. Even when she called for continental unity against the Yankee menace, she emphasized the need for higher standards and harder work as the key factor.

It was necessary, she wrote in "The Scream," to fight "the invasion of blond America that wants to sell us everything, to populate our lands and cities with her machinery, to use our resources that we don't know how to exploit." But she also claimed not to hate the Yankee:

> He is winning . . . because of our fault—for our torrid weakness and for Indian fatalism. He is crumbling us by virtue of some of his qualities and because of all of our racial vices. Why do we hate them? Let us hate what is in us that makes us vulnerable to his . . . will and to his opulence. . . . We talk tirelessly while . . . meanwhile he sees, he founds, he saws, works, multiplies, forges, creates . . . every minute, believes in his own faith and because of his faith, he is . . . invincible.[42]

Despite all this talk, however, there was surprisingly little anti-American action by Latin American states. Perhaps that was largely because in most countries, the local factors of factional conflict and civilian-military rivalries determined matters and the United States was of little importance. In a few places, mainly in Central America, U.S. influence was indeed powerful enough to ensure that no hostile political movements succeeded and could be held responsible for repressive regimes at various times in the past.

In this context, then, it is not surprising that the most significant anti-American revolution was waged in one such country, Nicaragua. Under the leadership of Augusto César Sandino, the flag of revolt was raised in 1927 against what he called the "drug dependent Yankees," "Yankee cowards and criminals," and "adventurous Yankees who are trampling Nicaragua's sovereignty under foot." These people were nothing more than "blond beasts," "blond pirates," and "piratical assassins." Sandino's country had suffered far more than most from American depredations, and he himself was killed by a U.S.-backed army that soon backed the corrupt Somoza dynasty.

But Sandino, later hailed as a progressive (so enshrined by the Marxist Sandinista movement), expressed a racialist anti-Americanism that was consistent with the most reactionary traditionalist forces in the region. His view of the United States as evil, innately aggressive, and inhumanly greedy made him identify all Americans as the enemy. "The North American people," he said in 1930, "support and will always support the expansionist policies of their unprincipled governments." On another occasion, Sandino explained, "The North American people are as imperialistic as their own leaders."[43]

When later developed by radical intellectuals in Latin America and elsewhere, this kind of thinking would blame America for the failure of their own utopian revolutions. This view would also justify anti-American terrorism there or elsewhere in the world, since all citizens of that country were complicit in its profiteering and thus legitimate targets. In addition, the idea that everyone was suffering because of America made a good ideology for mobilizing an entire national or religious community. Everyone from the "victim" country could unite in their hatred for everyone in the "imperialist" state. Thus, Marxism, a supposedly class doctrine, became adapted for effective use by nationalist (or even radical Islamist) movements or demagogic dictators.

Two new developments helped put anti-Americanism at the center of revolutionary ideology in Latin America during the middle years of the twentieth century. One was the growth of what had hitherto been a small intellectual class there. As universities expanded in the 1930s and thereafter, students were attracted to new versions of Marxism, often indoctrinated in radical views by their professors. Anti-Americanism, which had previously been spread largely by random literary works, now was systematically taught by institutions to large elements of the elite in every country.

The other new development was the Cold War. In earlier decades, the United States had been little concerned with Latin America except where some collapse or short-term crisis forced involvement in a specific country. President Franklin Roosevelt had even ended interventions in the 1930s with his Good Neighbor Policy. But with the worldwide U.S.-Soviet conflict beginning in the late 1940s, and especially after the Cuban revolution opened a new Cold War front in 1959, the United States became concerned with a potential Marxist revolution in every country. Consequently, it also became more likely to back local military and right-wing forces who promised that they would forestall this danger if only given American help.

The first victim of this new situation was Guatemala, where the CIA helped overthrow a left-wing populist, but non-Communist, government in 1954 and replaced it with a military junta. That regime's previous president had been Juan José Arévalo,[44] who expressed his bitterness in a 1961 book, *The Shark and the Sardines*. In contrast to Sandino, Arévalo took a different approach. "The great North American people" were unaware "of how many crimes have been committed in their name." They were also "victims of an imperialist policy" steered by big business. Originally, the United States had been "inspired by ideals of individual freedom, collective well-being and national sovereignty," but in the twentieth century this "grandeur of spirit was replaced by greed" and the government became the "protector of illicit commercial profits."[45]

Yet even he did not forego all the long-standard clichés of Latin American anti-Americanism. In his fable, America, represented by a shark, is a great beast "that dismembers all, destroys all, and swallows all, in sporting slaughter." It is amused when it passes a sardine that trembles in fear. A serpent sees the scene and proposes they work together as brothers, a parody on the spirit of Pan-American or Cold War cooperation. The shark would use its money, power, and ferocity to help the sardine, which would be a good servant, applaud his speeches, and spy on others to make sure they are the shark's friends. The shark agrees, but then whispers to the sardine, "Just wait till I catch you alone!"[46]

But the man who was caught alone, in the most celebrated anti-American incident of the time, was Vice President Richard Nixon when he visited Latin America in 1958. At the University of San Marcos in Lima, Peru, he was confronted by an angry crowd that threw stones at him. Returning to his hotel, Nixon was spat at by another mob. In Caracas, Venezuela, his motorcade from the airport was attacked by an angry crowd that used both rocks and spit. The latter flew so freely that his driver had to turn on the windshield wipers, and the chanting crowd almost overturned his car. In Venezuela, aside from all the long-term causes of antagonism, and perhaps deliberate Communist efforts, there were two grievances against the United States: the unpopular military junta enjoyed U.S. support, and the United States had just imposed restrictions on oil imports from that country.

This was only the beginning. Latin America was about to become the location of the world's second major state sponsor of anti-Americanism.[47] The U.S. relationship with Cuba had long been one of the most complex in the region. While the United States had freed Cuba from Spain and then given it independence, there had been many U.S. interventions in that unstable country that were motivated by a high degree of investment in the sugar industry, tourism, and other areas. Still, there were also strong currents in American policy that believed that democracy and reform were the best ways to fight Communism. Thus, even after Fidel Castro overthrew the incumbent, U.S.-backed dictatorship on January 1, 1959, the United States tried to build a good relationship with him.

But revolutionary Cuba, soon transformed into a Communist state, was a new phenomenon in Latin America: a country dedicated to a continent-wide revolution against America. The Cuban regime called its land the first territory of the Americas liberated from the United States. The price for this step, though, included an economic and political dependency on Moscow, a typical (except for its rhetoric) Latin American dictatorship, and a degree of conflict with the United States far higher than if Castro had been an independent nationalist.

The main statement of Cuban foreign policy, the February 1962 Second Declaration of Havana, constituted a declaration of war on the United States and the enshrinement of a new theory of anti-Americanism. Latin American states had failed to develop and were even becoming poorer, it charged, because they were in thrall to American imperialism. "Like the first Spanish conquerors, who exchanged mirrors and trinkets with the Indians for silver and gold, so the United States trades with Latin America."[48] According to the declaration, only the United States was holding back the solutions for such Latin American problems as unemployment, inadequate housing, shaky economies, and a sagging infrastructure.

The whole purpose of American diplomacy and military policy was said to be maintaining this system, which, according to the declaration, could only be overturned by revolution. This struggle would provoke U.S. countermeasures, but by the same token it would ensure a spreading anti-Americanism that would fuel its triumph: "Even though the Yankee imperialists are preparing a bloodbath for America they will not succeed in drowning the people's struggle. They will evoke universal hatred against themselves. This will be the last act of their rapacious and caveman system."[49]

This basic approach to anti-Americanism would continue to dominate the Latin American left for many decades, and for good reason. It proposed that all local problems and rivalries were to be subsumed into a unity of the people against the United States. By this means, the limited appeal of Communism would be greatly extended by dressing it up as nationalism. Expelling U.S. influence was presented as a magic elixir that would quickly and decisively solve the region's long-standing problems. Anti-Americanism was no longer one feature of regional ideology; it was to be the centerpiece.

Moreover, unlike earlier intellectuals who only wrote books or poems, the Cubans tried to put their theory into practice. Che Guevara, Castro's lieutenant who was assigned the leadership role for the hemisphere-wide revolution, explained in 1961 that though the United States imposed its "domination over every one of the twenty republics," American imperialism was on its way into the dustbin of history.[50]

But Guevara was wrong. Choosing Bolivia as the first place to test his revolutionary theory, he launched guerrilla war there in 1967. But he underestimated his adversary while misunderstanding that country's people and society. Thanks to a U.S. counterinsurgency effort, it was not long before his bullet-riddled body was being displayed. The war first unleashed in Bolivia by Cuba and its followers did intensify anti-American hatred in Latin America, yet this strategy also blew up in their faces. There were no Communist revolutions but plenty of hard-line military regimes that seized power and repressed opposition in order to prevent such an outcome.

A score of radical groups with the words "People's," "Revolutionary," and "Army," in their names fought local regimes throughout the late 1960s and into the 1970s in almost every Latin American country. Even in Chile, where the elected government of President Salvador Allende was overthrown in a brutal coup, the army did not need much more encouragement than the knowledge that the United States would not oppose them. The battles were fought out mainly among local forces. The resulting costly violence in so many countries simply became one more factor holding back the continent's development.

Other than kidnapping a few Americans and attacking some embassies, the revolutionaries did little damage to U.S. interests. Anti-Americanism, though, depended less on weapons than on words, a tool more easily wielded by Latin American intellectuals. Dozens of writers emerged to bash the United States with varying degrees of literary skill, to repeat the charge that it was to blame for everything. Their ideas had far more impact on fellow intellectuals—including those in Europe and the United States—than on local workers and peasants. But, ironically, while they decried American culture, it was the ideas of such intellectuals that dominated American thinking about Latin America on campuses, in publishing houses, in Hollywood, and in much of the media.

Such anti-American intellectuals, the Peruvian writer Mario Vargas Llosa wrote sarcastically, took grants from American institutions while endlessly proclaiming "that American imperialism—the Pentagon, the monopolies, Washington's cultural influence—is a source of our under-development." They detected CIA plots in everything from "tours of the Boston Symphony [to] Walt Disney cartoons." This also gave them the ideal tool for delegitimizing critics: branding them as American agents.[51] Such was the charge, for example, against even the Colombian novelist Gabriel García Márquez when he resigned from the Communist Party.[52] No accusation was considered too extreme or undocumented, as was the case with claims that the United States advocated population control in Latin America to get rid of competing peoples, an imperialist measure just one step short of genocide.[53]

The radical intellectuals and revolutionary activists thought that they had permanently changed how Latin Americans view reality, but in fact their ideological hegemony lasted only about a quarter-century. On the political level, the revolutionaries could not win and—whatever their intentions—only generated more misery and instability. On the economic plane, their proposed solutions did not work. Only in the realm of words, where theories don't have to meet the test of reality, did they continue to ride high.

At the same time, leftist anti-Americans often simply refurbished the old conservative anti-American arguments, based on civilizational complaints rather than Marxist analysis. They spoke of the masses, imperialism, and liberation but, like their European counterparts, their arguments rested on a perspective that was elitist, traditionalist, and culturally conservative. Thus, the Mexican writer Octavio Paz, one of the most articulate of the critics, explained in 1978 that the innate nature of U.S. mass society ensured that its behavior would be a "mix of arrogance and opportunism, blindness and machiavellianism."[54]

There was, however, an important element highlighted in the anti-Americanism of this period that would have a tremendous impact on that doctrine down to the present day: America as the cause of underdevelopment. The United States was said to dominate the terms of trade, since it could price manufactured goods higher while devaluing the Third World's raw materials. Latin American countries could only develop by breaking this system. This standpoint was promoted by the UN Economic Commission on Latin America (ECLA) and most notably by the Argentinean economist Raul Prebisch, who headed that institution from 1948 until 1962. A more radical edge was provided in 1966 by a book, *The Development of Underdevelopment*, by the Marxist economist Andre Gunder Frank, a U.S.-trained refugee from Nazi Germany who taught in many Latin American countries.

Frank's title was a perfect expression of his thesis. Underdevelopment, he claimed, was not the result of archaic social structures, lack of education, low agricultural productivity, reluctance to embrace innovation, political instability, and a score of other such causes. Rather, it was an artificial creation of malevolent imperialists. Just as traditional Marxism argued that overthrowing capitalism would allow rapid progress and the creation of a utopia, the new anti-Americanism made the same claim for getting rid of the United States.

The solution was to be statist economies, high import barriers, and deemphasizing the market by the government setting of prices. This strategy was basically a collection of all the mistakes being made else-where in the Third World as well as in the Soviet bloc. Moreover, the money borrowed to finance industrialization and import substitution would be lost in failed schemes and corruption, producing mountainous debts.[55]

Nevertheless, this belief swept through Latin American universities as unquestionable truth and continues to this day to be accepted by many in academia and the left, though not by Latin American policy makers or the general public. As one critical Venezuelan observer put it in the late 1970s, "There is an almost general belief in Latin America today that the United States has siphoned off the wealth which could have led to the Southern Hemisphere's development [by saying] 'They are rich be-cause we are poor; we are poor because they are rich.'"[56]

The only reason why Latin America was not as developed as the United States, the theory claimed, was because that country has stolen all of its resources. And these same resources were said to be the basis for the success of the United States. As Eduardo Galeano, whose book, *The Open Veins of Latin America*, was a huge best seller, puts it, "Our wealth has produced our poverty. In the colonial alchemy, gold turns to lead and food to poison. . . . The North American economy needs Latin American minerals like the lungs need air."[57]

Promoting anti-Americanism, then, was an act of self-defense and a necessity. It was an absolutely central and essential doctrine. And this ideology was based not on any specific U.S. policy or intervention but on the supposed essence of the United States itself in both its domestic and international aspects.

At the same time, though, many Latin Americans could not ignore the local causes of their problems and the unworkability of the radicals' proposed solutions. Using another old Latin American theme that often accompanied hostility toward the United States, they understood the need to imitate that country in order to achieve their own success.

By 1977, the reaction against radical anti-Americanism had taken hold. Domestic reform and moderation were a more likely path to democracy, stability, and economic development than a revolution against foreigners based on radical doctrine. The Venezuelan writer Carlos Rangel argued that the left's more useful complaint toward the United States would be to demand that it did more to help Latin American progress rather than blaming America for everything and trying to drive it out of the region.[58]

What was the true function of anti-Americanism? According to Rangel, it was both an excuse and a useful political tool in the hands of dictators and demagogues. Such scapegoating, Rangel warned, was paralyzing, a way of perpetuating stagnation. If the fault lay completely with the Yankees, there was no need to change one's own society, especially when these arguments were cynically used by repressive governments to conceal their own incompetence and misrule.[59]

It was a costly mistake, Rangel warned, to refuse to "admit that the reasons for North American success and Latin American failure are to be found in the qualities of North Americans and in the defects of Latin Americans." There was much to be learned from the U.S. example. True, America was an overpowering, often harmful neighbor. Yet it also had saved the continent from European colonialism, shown the way toward modernization and development, and offered a democratic model. Why, when the main damage to Latin America for most of its history had been European influence from Spain, Britain, and France, was there no antagonism toward those countries?

The answer, Rangel suggested, was that Latin America views itself as an extension of European culture. Since America was considered to be so inferior, its success must be attributed to exploitation and evil actions.[60] But, by the same token, Latin Americans were frustrated "since we cannot explain satisfactorily why we have been unable to capitalize on the advantages we have over the Third World." Everyone thus resents their "failure to reach the level of the United States."[61]

No country was more tempted by this attractive yet poisonous view than Mexico, which always viewed itself as victim number one of U.S. perfidy. And yet, aside from the war of 1848, how much harm had the United States actually done to Mexico? Certainly far less than the accusers would have it and than virtually every Mexican seemed to believe.

While U.S. and Mexican interests differed on various issues, the United States had no deliberate intention of harming or dominating Mexico. In the twentieth century, there were few American interventions in Mexico's internal affairs. One would never guess this from the tone of Mexican politics. In March 1975, President Luis Echeverría Álvarez visited the Autonomous University of Mexico. In revenge for past government attacks on students, several hundred demonstrated and threw stones at him. Police opened fire, killing several of them. Mexico's president justified this response by saying that they were naïve youngsters manipulated by the CIA.[62] In the mid-1980s, Mexican officials and newspapers even accused the United States of stealing rain by diverting hurricanes from Mexican shores and thus contributing to the country's worst drought in twenty years.[63]

The crown jewel of Mexican anti-Americanism is the National Museum of Interventions, opened in 1981. But though Spanish colonialism had lasted 300 years, the focus is mainly on the depredations, real or imagined, of the United States. American hostility is portrayed as a constant. After all, in the exhibit on the Monroe Doctrine, Mexico's first ambassador to the United States, José Manuel Zozaya, is quoted as saying, "The arrogance of those republicans does not allow them to see us as equals but as inferiors. With time they will become our sworn enemies."[64] The relationship is portrayed as an immutable enmity, one for which the ups and downs of policy were merely punctuation marks.

Thus, too, in 1987 the Mexican historian Gastón García Cantú claimed, "From the end of the eighteenth century through 1918, there were 285 invasions, incidents of intimidation, challenges, bombardments of ports and [theft] of territory.... No people in the world have had their territory, wealth, and security as plundered by anybody as Mexico has by the United States."[65]

Young Mexicans, wrote Jorge Castañeda, "learn almost as soon as they can read [that] the United States has always had designs on our country, either through direct territorial ambition or by seeking to influence our affairs to make Mexico more amenable to American interests and wishes."[66]

Consequently, in a 1986 poll, Mexicans considered American business, government, and media as all allied to promote U.S. control over Mexico.[67] "Even the modern Mexican middle classes continue to harbor deep feelings of resentment and anger against the United States," explained Castañeda. "Their penchant for American lifestyles and products should not be mistaken for an ebbing of traditional suspicion and hostility toward the United States."[68]

Yet while such attitudes would be more understandable if coming from, say, El Salvador or Guatemala, they had little to do with the reality of U.S.-Mexico relations, which had involved few confrontations for many decades. Rather, such feelings stemmed more from a hurt pride at being so behind a more advanced, powerful neighbor, and a resulting ultrasensitivity to imagined slights.

The Mexican media was aware that its job was to find more items for this list, no matter how twisted or sensational. Journalists know that a report with an anti-American angle has a better chance of making the front page. Obscure Americans are quoted if their remarks can be portrayed as anti-Mexican or threatening future problems in the relationship, while Mexican officials or academics are pressed to criticize U.S. deeds or statements.[69]

Partly through the clever use of the anti-American card, Mexico's ruling—and appropriately named, Party of the Institutionalized Revolution—stayed in power for more than eight decades, a world record. The country suffered under a statist and corrupt system justified by the need to keep American control at bay. In the 1970s and 1980s, four straight Mexican presidents failed to improve relations with the United States due to their personal resentment as they, in Castañeda's words, picked fights with the Yankees "over innumerable major and minor issues, resorting to traditional, nationalistic postures and maneuvers, and listening to veteran intellectual, diplomatic or political establishment 'gringo bashing.' "

Believing that relations were inevitably going to be bad because Washington was determined to weaken and dominate Mexico became a self-fulfilling, self-victimizing policy. By purveying this fear, Mexican intellectuals and leaders were themselves making their country more feeble by putting the emphasis on foreign guilt rather than on the kinds of reforms that Mexico needed in order to modernize itself. Equally, any proposed changes could be denounced as imitations of the hated United States or the kinds of policies that Washington wanted Mexico to follow.

While this explained why the leaders fanned anti-American sentiments, Castañeda suggested that the people embraced these feelings because the two countries were so unequal in power, had such a complex history of relations, and had such different interests that "if one problem is solved, another will surface."[70] And yet anti-Americanism was also a shield behind which Mexicans believed they had to stand because otherwise they felt defenseless and feared that their national identity might be overwhelmed and their sovereignty lost.[71] Unable to compete, they had to wage combat; but unable to win such a competition, the struggle had to be limited to angry words.

Often, too, as in Europe, anti-Americanism was more the sport of intellectuals and opportunistic politicians than the sentiment of the masses. Polls conducted during the 1990s showed that 87 percent of Hondurans, 84 percent of Guatemalans, 83 percent of Salvadorans, 73 percent of Bolivians, 70 percent of Peruvians, 65 percent of Mexicans (though 55 percent said the U.S. government had too much influence there),[72] 57 percent of Colombians, and 55 percent of Venezuelans held favorable views of the United States. This was despite the fact that in a 1995 poll, majorities—for example, 80 percent in Panama and 71 percent in Colombia—thought the United States would demand that it get its way in any dispute.[73]

In general, the late 1980s and afterward saw a major decline of anti-Americanism in Latin America. The radical solutions had not worked and, however one portrays them, the American model with its culture and material wealth seemed closer and more attractive. The Cold War's decline also reduced U.S. intervention in the region and even transformed it into support for democracy as perceptions of a Communist threat receded. The number of Latin American dictatorships fell until, ironically, only Cuba remained firmly in that category.

Free-market economic ideas challenged the radical dependency theories. In addition, a declining status for intellectuals and the discrediting of the panaceas offered by the left—in Latin America as in Europe, the main purveyors of anti-Americanism—also undercut that argument's popularity. With the growth of mass media, consumerism, and the hope of better living standards, Latin America became more like the United States or at least openly aspired to that goal.

One of the countries that prospered most of all was Chile, which had been a victim of American intervention in the 1970s. While *Le Monde* in September 2003 featured a cartoon that showed a plane crashing into a World Trade Center labeled Chile—implying that it had been U.S. support for a coup there in 1973, almost thirty years earlier, that was responsible for the September 11 attack—there was very little anti-Americanism in Chile itself. As shown by the polls cited above, even in countries like Panama and Nicaragua—which had also suffered direct U.S. interventions—anti-Americanism was low.

Aside from political shifts and rethinking, cultural changes also contributed to a decline in anti-Americanism. Historically, the United States was viewed as an alien, non-Spanish-speaking culture. Now, material from the United States was increasingly offered in the Spanish language, produced by recent Latin American immigrants with the flavor of that region, from such stations as Telemundo and Univision (based in Miami), as well as CNN in Spanish.

The growing population of Latin American immigrants in America from every country in the hemisphere is another factor. Many people now knew others living in the United States and find it easier to get firsthand, more accurate information on that country. Members of the elite may own homes in the United States or at least visit there frequently. They also know that the United States is the most likely place to find investment, technology, and educational opportunities or aid. Poorer people may hope to go there themselves.

Anti-Americanism had a lasting place in Latin American political culture for a variety of "local" structural and ideological reasons that transcended any current U.S. policy toward the region. As happened elsewhere, its causes had as much or more to do with the problems and nature of those societies than it did with the United States itself. Even when these attitudes were related to U.S. policies, attitudes toward the United States were reflected through the lens of a particular self-image and worldview with a long tradition. As the Mexican writer Octavio Paz admitted, the United States was simultaneously "the enemy of our identity and the secret model of what we wanted to be" but were unable to become.[74]

COLD WAR AND COCA-COLA

6

When the twentieth century began, the United States was not a very important country. Even as late as 1940, that situation had not changed too much. Anti-Americans had raged for decades about the American threat and the possibility that its model might take over the world, but such ideas remained largely speculative.

Equally, despite all the hatred generated against the United States, it had arguably done little to injure any other state in the world, at least outside of Latin America. European anti-Americanism at this point, until at least 1945, was clearly based not on policy but on a view of the United States as having an inferior civilization, society, and culture.

But gradually the old anti-American nightmare of a powerful United States that was playing a strong international role began to appear as more than a fantasy. A major U.S. role in World War I seemed, ironically, only to increase anti-Americanism in France, the country that American forces had fought and died to free. The new Soviet Union claimed that the United States was the ultimate capitalist power and its inevitable enemy. The same could be said for German attitudes, which had far more to do with Nazism's self-conception and goals than with any anger over the conflict with the United States during World War I.

By the late 1940s, though, the U.S. role in the world was finally developing along the lines that both pro- and anti-Americans had begun predicting as early as the 1790s. By 1945, the United States was now either the world's most important country or, at least, one of two superpowers. That transformation had an enormous impact on anti-Americanism. While the traditional criticisms remained consistent, their importance increased alongside that of the target country. Now that the United States was so active in the world, its specific deeds or policies abroad could be cited as proofs of its bad nature, intentions, and actions.

For the first time in history, too, anti-Americanism really mattered in the world. Being so big was an incorrigible offense to many, especially since the United States was usurping Europe's role. As the British historian Arnold Toynbee put it regarding America, "The giant's sheer size is always getting the giant into trouble with people of normal stature."[1]

A growing American cultural and economic power made the alleged danger all the more immediate and threatening. Now it was possible to think that the United States might be a model for the rest of the world. For others, when U.S. positions conflicted with those of their own country or faction, the ready-made anti-American thesis could be pulled off the shelf as explanation or weapon.

The entire world had to view the United States in this context. As the Soviet Union's main adversary, the United States was now central to the antagonisms of Moscow, Communist states or parties, and radical movements. It was now the United States, not England or France, that was the world's chief "imperialist" power that must be discredited and defeated. Promoting anti-Americanism was a way to weaken the U.S. side in the global Cold War battle and to undermine its local friends. Those hating America would not side with her, and those hating the United States intensely enough might either join the Soviet camp or become neutral.

For its part, Western Europe and its peoples had to decide whether to support the United States, support the USSR, or try to become a "third force." Suddenly, the country so long decried as inferior became Europe's leader; nations so long used to primacy had to take a back seat to the American upstart. While most states, except France, made this adjustment relatively easily, the power shift left lasting scars that would encourage more anti-Americanism in the future. It was understandably hard for Europeans to put their very survival in the hands of a country they often differed with about policy, style, and ideas.

The Third World underwent a parallel experience. Outside of Latin America, few peoples or countries previously had important interactions with the United States.[2] Now U.S. decisions and actions would affect their fate. As their dealings with the United States increased, it was also hard for these countries, too, to understand an unfamiliar American society and strange U.S. system with a history, institutions, and world-view so different from their own.

Moreover, whatever the United States stood for or advocated would inevitably offend some and threaten others. And the more that some people in any given country wanted to copy America or cooperate with it, the more that others would be antagonized. As the United States sought allies among governments, oppositions might see America as their enemy as well. Whether the United States did or didn't act, spoke or didn't speak, gave help or did nothing could provoke resentment.

In 1957, the Paris-based American humorist Art Buchwald placed an ad in the London *Times* personal column that said that he would like to hear from people who disliked Americans and their reasons why. He received over a hundred replies and concluded:

> If Americans would stop spending money, talking loudly in pub-
> lic places, telling the British who won the war, adopt a pro-colonial
> policy, back future British expeditions to Suez [a reference to the
> 1956 attack on Egypt], stop taking oil out of the Middle East, stop
> chewing gun, . . . move their air bases out of England, settle the
> desegregation problem in the South . . . put the American woman
> in her proper place, and not export Rock n'Roll [music], and speak
> correct English, the tension between the two countries might ease.[3]

Of course, there were far more than frivolous issues that led to controversy and friction. Many aspects of U.S. policy during the Cold War both abroad (notably, support for Latin American or other dictators and the Vietnam War) and at home (especially the McCarthy era and civil rights) would draw foreign criticism.

Again, though, it is important to emphasize that mere criticism of a U.S. policy or aspect of American society did not in itself constitute anti-Americanism. Rather, anti-Americanism required a view in which particular objections became systemic. In the eyes of such people, the United States could do—or at least would do—nothing right. They portrayed it as bad or inevitably misbehaving, misrepresenting its policies, slandering its institutions, and distorting its motives. Or, to put it most simply: the good make mistakes; the evil act deliberately or according to their nature.

It was in this spirit of questioning American motives and the country's nature that anti-Americanism could be found. A good example of such thinking is provided by the British playwright Harold Pinter who complained that from 1945 onward the United States "has exercised a sustained, systematic, remorseless, and quite clinical manipulation of power worldwide, while masquerading as a force for universal good. . . . [The United States has been] the most dangerous power the world has ever known."[4]

The origins of such a systematic response to the United States lay less in the details of U.S. behavior than in the accusers' motives and misunderstandings. Moreover, their beliefs and claims rested firmly on two centuries of well-established anti-American traditions. As always, anti-Americanism—as distinct from criticism—arose from such factors as other nations' ignorance, jealousy, class or partisan interest, ideology, and conflicting goals.

Of course, the second half of the twentieth century was also an era of great popularity for the United States in the world, and at times anti-Americanism fell to relatively low levels. Following the end of World War II, there was a great deal of gratitude toward the United States among non-Communist Western Europeans. They appreciated the U.S. role in first helping to save them from fascism, then giving so generously to rebuild their countries, and also preserving them from Communist takeovers or Soviet aggression.

Clearly, too, it was harder to deny that the long-derided U.S. democratic and economic system had worked pretty well. In contrast to Europeans of earlier times, the Italian writer Luigi Barzini meant it as a compliment when he explained in his big-selling 1953 book on America, "The United States has created the greatest organization for the production and distribution of goods in history."[5]

Finally, one could argue that at least part of the old predictions about the spread of the American model, or at least aspects of it, were becoming true. Western Europe was far more similar to the United States than it had been a half-century or century earlier. Since Europeans generally tended to adopt the things they preferred, most were comfortable with these changes. The left and intellectuals might worry that this was merely the beginning of a slide toward full-scale Americanization, but most people were less horrified or unsympathetic to the United States as the gap between their and American society narrowed.

For a time, anti-Americanism in Europe, outside of Communist circles and France at least, was in eclipse. While some resentment and grumbling resurfaced, these would remain minority viewpoints. In Germany and Italy, where the people were liberated from fascism and treated well by the United States, anti-Americanism was unacceptable among non-Communists. An exception was the novelist Hermann Hesse, who told his colleague Thomas Mann, "In Germany the dangerous criminals and racketeers, the sadists and gangsters are no longer Nazis, nor do they speak German, they are Americans."[6]

But most of the defeated West Germans did not want or could not afford to slander America. Their own great power pretensions were shattered, and they had made too many mistakes of their own to retain the old snobbish dismissal of American institutions. Not only was self-confidence in their own civilization's superiority eroded, but they also knew that only U.S. willpower and forces had saved them from Communist occupation.

In Britain, too, anti-Americanism was largely defused or driven underground by the close alliance between the two countries. Since 1945, the British debate has been over whether to look toward America or Europe, a division of loyalties not fully shared by any other Europeans.

Even while England could be jealous of American success and sorrowful about the loss of empire, it was able to cope with this relative decline. Given its common language and "Anglo-Saxon" (as the French and Latin Americans put it) heritage, Britain was already close to America. Now it institutionalized a "special relationship" and "Atlantic alliance." Britain could soften the blow of being junior partner by seeing itself as America's tutor (playing Greece to America's Rome, as some put it). In short, Britain's attitude to the United States could be patronizing without being antagonistic or hostile.

Tired of a long postwar austerity, the British masses saw no disgrace in wanting the gadgets and luxuries they knew were enjoyed by their American counterparts. For the left this posed a problem, though the difficulty was smaller since the left was largely non-Communist and even non-Marxist. On the political side, the British left knew that pro-Soviet or neutralist sentiments on the Cold War were political suicide. But the United States could still be derided as a land of lynching and McCarthyism.

On the cultural front, it could criticize the Americans in traditional terms as a people whose material goods only made their lives emptier. When the working-class literary rebel Kenneth Tynan wrote a sarcastic letter in 1957 on how to be successful in British cultural life, one of his recommendations was "adopt a patronizing attitude to anything popular or American."[7]

The main British expert on America was Harold Laski, a London School of Economics professor and leading Labour Party intellectual. Laski reflected the ambiguity of British attitudes that were more critical than anti-American. He had taught at Harvard in the 1920s and had many American friends, including Franklin Roosevelt. This love-hate relationship was shown by his 1949 book, *American Democracy*, which mixed a doctrinaire Marxist condemnation of the United States with affection as well. Some of his distortions were extreme. For example, he portrayed the North as treating the South like a colony and promoting racism among poor whites in order to keep the working class divided.[8]

A few on the left diluted their vitriol more sparingly. The novelist J. B. Priestly was so antagonistic to U.S. mass culture that he was dubbed by journalists "the man who hates America."[9] His fellow writer Graham Greene held similar views. He wrote in 1967, "If I had to choose between life in the Soviet Union and life in the United States I would certainly choose the Soviet Union." He viewed America as a mindless consumer society based on an "eternal adolescence . . . to which morality means keeping Mother's Day and looking after the kid sister's purity." It was useless to pretend "that with these allies it was ever possible to fight for civilization."[10]

These old cultural critiques were displaced to more exotic climes as American behavior in the Third World came under scrutiny. Greene was perhaps the first European writer to focus on this issue, which would assume tremendous importance in later years. In Greene's novel, *The Quiet American*, set in South Vietnam, the American figure is an idealistic but greatly naïve young man determined to promote democracy but actually causing widespread bloodshed to innocent people. The book's hero, a worldly wise but cynical British journalist, says of the Americans: "I was tired of the whole pack of them with their private stores of Coca-Cola and their portable hospitals and their too-wide cars, and their not quite latest guns. . . . My conversation was full of the poverty of American literature, the scandals of American politics, and the beastliness of American children. . . . Nothing that America could do was right."[11]

Others maintained the old aristocratic conservative strain of ridicule about America. "Of course, the Americans are cowards," Evelyn Waugh cheerfully told Graham Greene. "They are almost all the descendants of wretches who deserted their legitimate monarchs for fear of military service."[12] But this kind of talk was mainly restricted to private social conversation and jokes.

As so often happened, anti-Americanism became more significant when it became caught up in local disputes, for example the Labour Party's factional battles of the 1950s. The party's left wing, led by Aneurin Bevan, criticized the United States because it did not want to follow so closely America's Cold War leadership and saw that society as an unwelcome alternative to the socialist future that the Labour Party wanted for Britain.

In the context of the British internal debate, to imitate America's success meant to put more priority on making capitalism work than on promoting state ownership of industry. Thus, if the United States was highly regarded and became a model, traditional Labour Party goals would be watered down into merely managing the existing society better rather than transforming it. This is precisely what the rival party faction, led by Hugh Gaitskell, wanted to do by moving Labour toward the political center. It would be better, he argued, to make Britain more like America, which he saw as a place with greater social equality, no aristocracy, and, in the words of Gaitskell's chief intellectual ally Anthony Crosland, a "natural and unrestrained" atmosphere.

Gaitskell's faction also favored a close alliance with the United States in the Cold War, a stance that Bevan's group saw as undermining Britain's independence and the party's leftist orientation. Of course, the more pro-American were the party's moderates, the more incentive radicals had to bash the United States in order to discredit their foes and gain support for themselves. In response, Crosland complained in 1956 that anti-Americanism was a "left-wing neurosis, springing from a natural resentment at the transfer of world power from London to Washington, combined with the need to find some new and powerful scapegoat to replace the capitalists at home," whose power Labour had already diminished by promoting the "welfare state."[13]

George Orwell, the great British intellectual who never felt intimidated into conformity, agreed with this assessment and thought anti-Americanism was a marginal phenomenon. Those who advocated it were a minor, though vocal, mob. "I do not believe the mass of the people in this country are anti-American politically, and certainly not culturally." In attacking the United States, the intellectuals were merely uttering their own group's "parrot cry." Indeed, as would so often happen regarding anti-Americanism, such people were "indifferent to mass opinion" but trembled at the orthodoxy of their peers.[14]

Orwell was right about both the causes and limits of anti-Americanism in his country. Generally in Britain, anti-Americanism was usually voiced by a minority that knew it to be an unpopular idea. Even in the Labour Party, the moderate left maintained control. By 1961, the Bevan faction had been defeated and even revised its own views. Future Labour prime ministers, like Harold Wilson in the 1960s and Tony Blair in the 1990s and early 2000s, were strongly pro-American in the Gaitskell tradition.

It was, of course, the Communist bloc, a state sponsor of anti-Americanism, and the many in the West it influenced directly or indirectly who carried the banner of anti-Americanism in the postwar world. But there was one other country—France—where that attitude continued to be powerful despite the central role the United States played in its liberation and postwar reconstruction.

Ironically, France—unlike Britain and Germany—had never been at war with the United States. On the contrary, American troops had fought on French soil to protect that country in two world wars. Few issues had ever actually created friction between these two countries. Many anti-American attacks in France came from the Communists or others repeating Soviet propaganda. But this alone is not a sufficient explanation, since the Communists were even more powerful in Italy without having an equivalent impact.

Yet France's primacy as the world center of non-Communist anti-Americanism is easy to understand. The idea had a long, continuous history in that country, where it had always been mainly cultural and civilizational rather than policy-driven in origin. Only France, among Western industrialized states, still believed it should have global primacy. It was the sole such country that saw itself as a political and cultural rival to the United States.

France also had a powerful class whose practical interests were well served by anti-Americanism. The country's intellectual circles, dominated by the left, were skeptical about the justness of the U.S. cause in the Cold War. In material terms, French cultural and intellectual producers were economic competitors of American products. They were especially horrified by a country whose system devalued the importance of intellectuals. If France became Americanized, the intellectual and culture-producing sectors would suffer the greatest loss of status and influence. One way to put it was that the United States was often seen by intellectuals in general, and especially French intellectuals, the way capitalists perceived the USSR: as a direct danger to their power, prestige, and way of life.

There were many other factors, too. France—unlike Britain—had a different language from America and a cuisine more worthy of a spirited defense against fast food than did England or Germany. It was dedicated to a policy of propping up a disproportionately large peasantry in order to preserve the country's traditional character, making it vulnerable to the import of American food or technology that could displace these people. In short, France simultaneously felt culturally superior and better qualified to be a superpower yet threatened by an inferior American hegemony on both political and cultural grounds. As General Pierre Billotte, Charles de Gaulle's wartime chief of staff, explained, "France has an inferiority complex." But it also had a superiority complex toward America and the combination made for a great deal of antagonism.[15]

Rather than diluting French anti-Americanism, as one might expect, the U.S. role in liberating France during World War II actually intensified it—as had happened with World War I. The need to be saved by the United States offended the country's sense of greatness. As it declined from world power to supplicant for U.S. help, the bitterness intensified.

At the same time, the French had rather ungrateful complaints about the way the United States had rescued it. De Gaulle and his colleagues felt the Americans had mistreated them during the war by making their Free French movement only minor partners and carving up Europe with the Soviets without consulting France. A decade later, explaining France's withdrawal from NATO, de Gaulle added the criticism that it had taken too long for U.S. help to arrive in both world wars.[16]

Even when the United States paid for France's reconstruction with the Marshall Plan, Communists said—and many were convinced—that this was merely an American plot to dominate the country. Other left-wing parties were hostile, and center-right parties were suspicious.

As one study of French perceptions put it, this resentment at feeling overshadowed, undervalued, and ignored was made all the worse by their actual need for U.S. help and protection. "If only the Americans hated the French and were open enemies, as the Germans once were, something could be done about it," as one observer wrote.[17] The U.S. government was aware of this problem. Between 1948 and 1952, it launched a massive cultural and informational campaign to improve its image there, with radio programs, films, libraries, cultural exchanges, and organizations to encourage mutual understanding.[18] None of this solved the issue. Indeed, the McCarthy era in America convinced many Frenchmen that the mob mentality and low intellectual level they expected to find really was dominant. The United States was unfit, they believed, to lead the Free World, especially since France could do so much better.

There were few practical consequences of French anti-Americanism during this era, but the anti-American barrage was nevertheless deafening. It was an article of faith to many French intellectuals, for example, that South Korea had been encouraged by the United States to attack North Korea in 1950 rather than the other way around. No less an artist than Pablo Picasso did a painting entitled *Massacres in Korea*, which showed a squad of American soldiers murdering women and children.[19]

Hubert Beuve-Méry, founder and director of *Le Monde*, the favorite newspaper of French intellectuals, wrote in 1944, one month before American soldiers laid down their lives for French freedom on Normandy's beaches:

> The Americans represent a real danger to France. A very different danger than the threat of Germany or than a Russian threat could be. . . . The Americans can prevent us from making the necessary revolution and their materialism doesn't even have the tragic greatness of the totalitarian materialism. If they retain a real cult for the

idea of freedom, they do not feel the need to liberate themselves from the bondage their capitalism leads to.[20]

What came directly from Communist or fellow traveler writers, then, was often echoed by many or most other intellectuals—a situation that did not really happen anywhere else in Europe. Thus, when American schools were accused of ignoring European culture and fearing science because it challenged religion, these ideas gained broad acceptance in France. After Irène Joliot-Curie, a physicist and leading Communist supporter, was detained overnight at Ellis Island when trying to enter the United States, she said that Americans preferred fascism to Communism because "fascism has more respect for money." The leading Communist novelist Louis Aragon restated an old French anti-American theme: "The Yankee, more arrogant than the Nazi iconoclast substitutes the machine for the poet."[21] In Britain, Germany, or Italy, such statements would have been considered outrageous fringe opinions, while in France they were not atypical.

Still, American machines were also ridiculed. The Communist daily, L'Humanité, ran articles in 1948 to prove to the French that Americans were not better off than they were despite having a collection of household technological gadgets. Headlines included, "One could starve with a telephone" and "Not everyone has a bathroom." American refrigerators, the newspaper explained, were good only to make ice cubes for whiskey cocktails and not for storing food.[22]

Similarly, a 1948 article in a Communist literary journal complained, "We here are sick to death of having Yankee superiority shoved down our throats. A state the size of Europe that isn't capable of putting out even half the book-titles we publish in our [small] country. . . . Is that the ideal, the model, the leader they want us to look up to?"[23] Perhaps the most absurd irony of all was that one of the greatest postwar promoters of anti-Americanism in France was the fellow-traveling magazine Esprit, whose staff included former collaborators with the Nazis who were now "clearing" their credentials by moving close to the Communists. Incredibly, one of their accusations was that the United States had backed the collaborationist Vichy regime, which they had supported and the United States had opposed.

Not only was American society repugnant, but it also was said to threaten France directly. As an article in Esprit put it in 1948, "The Russians are a long way away. What we see are tons of American [volumes] and American ideas and American propaganda in our bookstores."[24] According to *Esprit* in 1951, daily life in the United States was a constant attack on personal liberty because of advertising, the banality of conversation, and the sameness of lifestyles. People feared not buying the latest refrigerator or television because that was to be different, and difference was "un-American." As a result, the Americans suffered from "a sort of dictatorship without a dictator."[25]

Even as Soviet tanks were rolling into Budapest to crush the 1956 Hungarian rebellion, *Esprit* found the United States to be worse than the USSR. Asked the magazine, "What can one expect from this civilization that mocks and caricatures Western spiritual traditions and is propelling mankind into a horizontal existence, shorn of transcendence and depth?"[26] According to a 1959 article, "American society is totalitarian; it is possibly the most totalitarian society in the world."[27]

Le Monde published a series of attacks on America by Pierre Emmanuel, a contributor also to *Esprit*, who explained that both the United States and USSR were totalitarian, "the one in power, the other in deed." Europeans formed a third camp that would eventually triumph over America because they retained an "idea." No matter how much Washington became the world's power center, the "heart and brains will remain in Europe." Every European who had been to the United States was appalled by its social conformity and the sight of its people being reduced to mere producers and consumers.[28]

These kinds of statements, equating the United States with the USSR while hinting that the latter was less objectionable, continued to be common on the French left in later years. For example, Jean-Marie Benoist, a former French cultural attaché to England and a professor at the prestigious College de France, writing in 1976, drew parallels between "the twin monolithic tyrannies of uniformity. . . . Woodstock and the jean uniform on the one side; the Gulags on the other."[29]

Possibly, Soviet concentration camps were worse, he suggested, but they were also the counterpart of how the propaganda of America ("Atlantic imperialism") tried to control Europe. Viewing an American movie was thus portrayed as some type of rough equivalent for laboring in a Siberian mine at subzero temperatures.[30]

While these two forms of totalitarianism were different in some ways, they were "equally fearsome," said Alain de Benoist, a leader of the

French intellectual right. "The Eastern variety imprisons, persecutes and mortifies the body but at least does not destroy hope. Its Western counterpart ends up creating happy robots. It is an air-conditioned hell. It kills the soul."[31] And European intellectuals professed to consider the soul far more important to protect than the mere body, which was the supposed priority of American materialism.

Generally, the USSR might at most be criticized for specific policies, but only the United States was subject to a systematic ridicule for its history and culture, inadequacy as a system, and mass culture. Ironically, this was left-wing criticism tinged with a reactionary aristocratic snobbishness, since it was condemning any departure from high culture in order to cater to popular tastes. Yet this apparent paradox made sense, since those claiming to speak in the French masses' name were actually defending their own prerogatives as a self-perpetuating elite that looked down on the people and sought to ensure its continued control over the intellectual means of production.

Criticizing America also had a special role as one of the few issues on which French conservatives—both right-wing extremists and staunch nationalists—agreed with the left. During World War II, French collaborators with the Nazis spent more time denouncing U.S. society than did their German counterparts. They charged it was a country dominated by Jews. "The American abomination is the Jewish abomination," as one of them put it. Precisely because it was a democracy, it was "a rotten nation, horribly powerless, unable to anticipate, to get organized, to vanquish."[32] Even American capitalism displeased them. The United States was merely "the country of [monopolies] and gangsterism and the American is a vile profiteer who only respects money."[33]

When it came to the United States, de Gaulle, the scourge of traitorous collaborators, also held the traditional hostile beliefs of the French right. In 1934, as a young officer, he wrote of the American "social system, in which material profit is the motive of all activity and the basis of all hierarchy."[34] It is certain," concluded the historian Philippe Roger, "that he feared Europe's submission to the culture, the economy and the linguistic power of the United-States."[35]

On forming his own political party in 1947, de Gaulle, fearful of Communism, at first favored a strong alliance with the United States. But as early as 1952, he gave a speech charging that the United States collaborated with Germany against French interests.[36] By 1954, his party was criticizing American society in terms like those of the left while also echoing the right-wing French accusations from the post–World War I era, which de Gaulle had grown up hearing.

A decade later, in 1964, de Gaulle was still emphasizing the civilizational confrontation between the United States and France. He appealed to a visiting Arab journalist for an alliance of those living around the Mediterranean to create "an industrial civilization that does not follow the American model and in which man is not merely means but purpose and aim."[37] René Pleven, one of his closest comrades, said de Gaulle "was a man for whom history counted more than anything else.... But where the United States were concerned he was at a loss; he found no historical keys." He did not think "it could be compared to that of 'real' nations."[38]

Similarly, U.S. Ambassador to France Charles Bohlen, who met de Gaulle many times, said that the French leader thought the United States "lacked most of the attributes [he] felt were essential for a stable country." It lacked a military tradition or unifying religious heritage, while its people were merely "immigrants from dozens of countries—in his eyes a somewhat messy collection of tribes that had come together to exploit a continent. He felt we were materialistic without a solid, civilizing tradition of, say, France. We were too powerful for our own good."[39]

Nevertheless, despite such factors, the overall levels of anti-Americanism in France or in Europe among the people as a whole during this era should not be overstated. Polls in the 1950s and 1960s showed overwhelmingly positive attitudes toward the United States in Britain, Germany, and Italy, while those friendly and hostile to the United States in France were near to being evenly divided. A 1953 poll in France showed that 61 percent were "sympathetic" to the United States, while only 8 percent expressed antipathy, 5 percent distrust, and 1 percent hatred.[40] A 1955 poll found those positive about America in France to be 4 percent more; a 1957 one showed the negatives as 3 percent greater.[41] Yet even among the French elite, a 1964 poll found that 87 percent saw the United States as a country that had common interests with France, almost the same as in other Western European states. In contrast, only 5 percent of those in the USSR dared make such a statement.[42]

Publicly, though, it often seemed that the French intellectual and cultural elite did hate America. One of the most revealing accounts was written by Simone de Beauvoir, one of France's more respected intellectuals and a leading figure in the emerging philosophy of existentialism. After a four-month-long trip to the United States in the late 1940s, she published her diary of the visit as a book. A key moment was her description of a meeting with a *New York Times* editor: "From the height of his own power and American power in general he throws me an ironic look: So France amuses itself with existentialism? Of course, he knows nothing about existentialism; his contempt is aimed at philosophy in general and more generally still at the presumptuousness of an economically impoverished country that claims to think."[43] But was perceiving such smug arrogance something out of the baggage de Beauvoir brought with her on the trip?

At any rate, she claims to prefer the "intimidating indifference" of those powerful in France to American flippancy. She detects hints that Americans know they are really inferior to Europe in their "restlessness, gum-chewing, and bold self-assurance." Perhaps some of this attitude derives from her certainty that the American system is not good for her caste. "America," she wrote, "is hard on intellectuals." She feels that publishers and editors size up a person's mind in a critical and distasteful way, "like an impresario asking a dancer to show her legs. They have contempt from the start for the produce they're going to buy, as well as the public on whom they'll foist their goods."[44]

Rather than fight to seize spiritual power in America, de Beauvoir complains, college students are paralyzed with "intellectual defeatism" because they believe the United States is "too huge a machine with too intricate gears" for them to conquer.[45] America is simply too caught up in "the banality of daily life" in which "people amuse themselves with gadgets and, lacking real projects, they cultivate hobbies. . . . Sports, movies, and comics all offer distractions. But in the end, people are always faced with what they wanted to escape: the arid basis of American life— boredom."[46]

One aspect of this misrepresentation is especially significant in such European assessments, a false comparison that has persisted for a century. The average French citizen does not sit around all day and discuss existentialism, literature, and the meaning of life. They are no less interested in sports, movies, and personal life than Americans. The pursuit of an elevated life of the spirit, sprinkled with "real projects," is the lifestyle of a relatively small elite. In that respect, there is not so much

difference between France and the United States except when one mis-
leadingly compares intellectual elite in the former country with average
people in the latter.

What is different between the two countries, though, is something of
the greatest importance for French intellectuals. In their own country,
they have a virtual monopoly on discourse. Intellectuals are featured on
television, on radio, and in the elite press as central figures, comparable
perhaps to sports or musical stars in America. In the United States, there
has also been a degree of intellectual life and high culture that is proportionately probably about the same as in France. But it is far less
central to the overall life of the nation.

The reason is that in America, this high-level cultural and intellectual
"product line" must compete with a more powerful popular culture represented by Hollywood, professional sports, pulp literature, and pop music. Intellectuals get far less respect or attention. Indeed, they are sometimes regarded with scorn, as indicated by such negative epithets ranging
from "egghead" in the 1950s to "nerd" in later decades. The problem is
that in a free market, the intellectuals have a great deal of difficulty
competing with cheaper items aimed at the least-common-denominator
audience. Of course, these stereotypes on both sides of the Atlantic are
easily exaggerated, but they certainly do have some validity.

No doubt, the majority of the French people might welcome—and
indeed have done so over time—such an alternative for themselves rather
than being the intellectual elite's captive audience. That is precisely what
that group in France and elsewhere in Europe has feared: once Europeans
caught on to the option of a legitimized mass culture, they would be
swept away by an American-style mass, populist, lowest-common-
denominator culture.

To this must be added one more small, but significant, point. French
and European intellectuals or artists have always underestimated the impact of their own works and culture on American society. Not all the
cultural transmission has been one way. A few years after de Beauvoir's
visit, existentialism was all the rage among the American intelligentsia,
just as French-produced postmodernism would be a few decades later.
If the willingness of Americans to borrow from others was appreciated,
their society would not be so derided by clichés about its narrow, provincial, and arrogant nature.

Other important aspects of French anti-American thinking were reflected in André Siegfried's 1955 book, *America at Mid-Century*. Many of the points made there can be found in similar volumes written by French visitors to America a century earlier.

One key concept, so prevalent in European anti-American thinking yet so strange to the American discourse, was the view of the United States as a separate civilization from their own. Americans, however, have almost never viewed themselves as a distinctive civilization but rather as a Western one closely linked to Europe. The acceptance of this kinship limits the development of any sense of superiority or antagonism toward Europe that is so often attributed to Americans by Europeans.

Siegfried was more balanced than many of his contemporaries in his view of the United States. On the positive side, he is effusive about Americans' energy. He finds it to be "an astonishing country where everything is focused on the future! . . . Its psychology remains characteristic of a youth that we Europeans have lost. America [is] the embryo of a [distinct] civilization, which has faith in the possibility of changing the very rhythm of nature. One might also call it the great American adventure, the end of which is not in sight. . . ."[47]

Yet he worries that this new society represents the triumph of technical progress over Western civilization. It is antihuman because it tries to "dissociate" man "from nature." Americans, he writes, are more interested in methods than in things for their own value.[48] Universities care more for buildings than the humanities. The country "requires dosing with a large portion of classicism," because it "produces competent people but it does not guarantee that they should be cultured." He seems surprised to discover that American companies actually preferred to hire people who had scientific and technical skills rather than a background in literature or philosophy.

Siegfried also suggested that the American emphasis on "high output" diminished "the critical spirit, which is by its very nature individualistic." Culture is eclipsed by technical progress and equipment. As a result, "The individual acting alone and thinking alone is reduced to powerlessness. Mass man has triumphed over the anarchic individuals, for the necessities of modern production have so willed it. . . . The man who really counts is the expert, before whom everyone must bow."[49]

Among other things, this analysis shows a failure to see how technological advances permit a higher degree of culture. Someone with a video recorder can watch any film in the world any time they want, while one who must go to a movie theater is more dependent on mass tastes and limited selection. Improved printing technology and distribution lowered the cost of publishing; mass education raised literacy standards. Fine literature, including the classics, was now available to everyone. Of course, it could be argued that American society conditioned its citizens to prefer junk, but those reading that junk would probably have been reading nothing else otherwise, and while impossible to prove it seems accurate to say that a higher percentage of the overall American population actually read as good, if not better, quality fiction or nonfiction as do the general population of Britain, France, or Germany.

Of course, there are many in America—especially in the 1950s—who would have agreed with the kind of critique offered by Siegfried and other French intellectuals. But there is a tiny but very significant difference. Americans condemned the "conformism" and "materialism" of the 1950s, as well as such phenomena as the power of Senator Joseph McCarthy, as the results of an era. Anti-Americans outside the country portrayed them as core aspects of America's essence, as typical and inevitable products of its society. These stereotypes were taken to extremes. When Jean-Paul Sartre visited the United States in 1945 and 1946, he concluded that it is when an American is "showing the most conformism that he feels the freest."[50] According to Sartre, just as Americans worship conformity ("The American uses his mechanical bottle-opener, fridge or car at the same time as all other Americans and the same way they do"), they feel that everyone in the world should behave and think exactly as they do.[51]

Never quite out of sight in all these evaluations was a fear that the United States wanted to impose its system on France and would succeed in doing so, at least if not fought fiercely. This belief had been the mainstay of French anti-Americanism going back to the nineteenth century. While declaiming their own system's superiority—and finding the United States inferior because it was different—they attributed the same arrogance to the Americans, who did not in fact go through life believing themselves better than the French. Equally, French anti-Americans often argued that the U.S. system was going to collapse yet were obsessed with a pessimistic expectation that their own system was doomed to be overwhelmed by Americanization. But why would this happen unless their own people—even if only because they were hypnotized by advertising—

"betrayed" them and preferred American or American-style culture and customs?

The French vision was one of a competition between their own "civilizing mission" against the "anti-civilization" drive of the United States. The Americans were seen as the new savages, and not noble ones either. In this scheme of thinking, America took the place of those classical inferiors, the peoples of the Third World, whose cultures—in terms now held to be racist and imperialistic—were previously seen by Europeans as the epitome of what was backward and primitive. There was no country in the world that had imposed its culture, language, and worldview on its colonies more than did France. And this is what French intellectuals expected America to do to its new "colonies," which might consist of the entire world.

But the trade goods of American culture were considered worthless and meaningless, plastic beads and trinkets intended to replace the priceless works of great artists. The perception, as two French scholars critical of anti-Americanism explained, was that the United States had nothing to export except "its lack of culture. [Americans] are condemned to cause all the cultures they touch to perish and to uproot all traditions. By exporting their way of life they end up killing the national soul everywhere since they themselves are the progeny of such murder."[52]

This was a powerful belief in France and among many European intellectuals, which they helped spread to the rest of the world. Once that concept was accepted, it was a simple matter to embrace Communist-style anti-American propaganda as accurately portraying the political aspects of this vandalism and brutality. If one thought so badly about the United States, it was easy to assume that all the charges against it were inevitably true.

For example, during the trial of Julius and Ethel Rosenberg for spying on the American nuclear program for the USSR—a charge that history has shown to be accurate—Sartre wrote, "Don't be surprised if from one end of Europe to the other we are shouting, 'America is a mad dog!' Let's cut every tie that binds us to her lest she bite us and we go mad too."[53] When the United States defended South Korea (under UN auspices, no less) from the aggression of its northern Communist neighbor, de Beauvoir thought after seeing two American soldiers, "They were defenders of a country which was supporting dictatorship and corruption from one end of the globe to the other."[54]

Such political outrage was often based on cultural distaste, while cultural distaste in turn was often grounded in fear of conquest. When de Beauvoir in 1952 was so stirred to hatred by seeing those two American soldiers enter a hotel in France, she reflected that they looked as if they were members of an arrogant occupation force. True dictatorship and corruption were seen as being more closely related to the forces of American cultural invasion than to the USSR's repressive tyranny.

As she mused in a 1960 book, in trying to understand her own attitude toward the United States:

> We regarded America as the country where capitalist oppression had triumphed in the most vile fashion. We detested the exploitation, unemployment, racism and lynch-law there. . . . Nonetheless, leaving aside its good or evil aspects, there was something gigantic and unfettered about life there that we found fascinating. . . . Ironically, we were attracted by America whose government we condemned, whilst the USSR, the scene of an experiment we found admirable, left us cold.[55]

Yet this frank assessment about the mixed nature of attitudes toward the United States only seemed to show how dangerous was America's attractiveness. Its ability to seduce people with freedom, success, hot music, trashy films, or fast food—despite its horrible features—was one of the most frightening aspects of America, a subversive threat to hostile Europeans as it would later be to radical Islamists. To catch oneself falling under America's spell was the moment in which it was imperative to rebel and reject the lure of Satan.

The spawn of Hollywood was deemed particularly dangerous in this respect. The number of American films imported into France during six months in 1946 was 36. A year later, the number had risen to 338 for that same amount of time. In 1947, a Committee of Defense for the French Cinema was created to warn that spending money to see "the rubbishy American movies" would destroy France's economy as well as its mind.[56]

Nevertheless, by the 1950s, American films were over 50 percent of all those distributed in France. Inevitably, most were of poor quality, but they were certainly popular.[57] One French cinema expert made this success sound like a foreign military invasion aided by local traitors: "With the complicity of some politicians and even newspapers . . . relying on the support of a bombproof distribution system, the Americans force their movies on us."[58]

Yet hidden away here is the obvious implication of such views: the real traitors were the average people ready to consume American products. They must be shamed into changing their behavior. Yet, after all, they were not being captured and marched, with guns at their backs, to the cinemas. They were simply exercising their own preferences. For French intellectuals who saw themselves as the generals in the army of culture, these people were deserters. But if French tastes were so elevated already, why would the masses want to see American films in the first place? Perhaps it was because the French and American masses were really not so different after all.

Another good example of this phenomenon was the battle over Coca-Cola. Coca-Cola is a sweet soft drink that people around the world seem to like. As Arthur Koestler, a Hungarian-born intellectual who after embracing many different ideologies was at the moment pro-American and resident in London, pointed out in 1951, there was no coercion involved: "The United States do not rule Europe as the British ruled India; they waged no Opium War to force their revolting 'Coke' down our throats. Europe bought the whole package because Europe wanted it."[59]

But precisely because Coca-Cola had become a symbol of Americanization, there was strong opposition to its introduction. The company expanded operations into Holland and Belgium in 1947, and then to Switzerland, Italy, and France two years later. Local competitors tried to stop the drink from being sold. There were lawsuits and campaigns by Communist parties to portray the beverage as containing dangerous amounts of caffeine, poison, or addictive substances. The popular Italian Communist Party newspaper warned that it would turn children's hair white, while, more imaginatively, the small Austrian party said the local bottling plant could be transformed into a factory making atomic bombs.[60]

In France, the Communists found an argument to appeal to every sector of French society. During a 1950 debate on the Coca-Cola menace in parliament, a Communist deputy laid it on the line: "We've seen successively the French cinema and French literature attacked. We've watched the struggle over our tractor industry. We've seen a whole series of our productive sectors, industrial, agricultural, and artistic, successively attacked without the public authorities defending them."[61] Perhaps he feared France being reduced to the same status as East Germany, Poland, and Czechoslovakia by Moscow.

Warning that France might be "coca-colonized," the Communist daily *L'Humanité* said the new drink would damage wine sales and worsen the trade deficit, while the distribution system would double as an American espionage network. Not even the most sacrosanct French symbols were said to be safe. A rumor claimed that the company wanted to put a Coca-Cola ad on the front of Paris's Notre Dame Cathedral.[62] Not to be outdone in patriotic rhetoric by the left, the right-wing Poujadist movement proclaimed that the rooster, symbol of France, would only sing "Cocorico" (the French equivalent of cock-a-doodle-do) "And not Coca-Cola!"[63] A Catholic newspaper was equally defiant: "We must call a spade a spade and label Coca-Cola for what it is—the avant-garde of an offensive aimed at economic colonization against which we feel it's our duty to struggle."[64] *Le Monde*, the icon of the French intellectuals, joined in and made it clear that the issue was far broader than what people drank at lunch. One writer explained: "Conquerors who have tried to assimilate other peoples have generally attacked their languages, their schools, and their religions. They were mistaken. The most vulnerable point is the national beverage. Wine is the most ancient feature of France. It precedes religion and language; it has survived all kinds of regimes. It has unified the nation."[65]

Le Monde put the issue clearly in terms of anti-Americanism: "What the French criticize is less Coca-Cola than its orchestration, less the drink itself, than the civilization—or, as they like to say, the style of life—of which it is the symbol."[66]

In 1950, parliament passed an anti–Coca-Cola bill that authorized the government, acting on scientific advice, to draw up new regulations for beverage companies. While Coca-Cola was never outlawed, fewer people drank it in France than in any other country in Western Europe.

By way of contrast, it is interesting to note how Americans treated the French national beverage differently by importing its wine while developing a massive industry of their own. Something few native-born Americans would have drunk in 1950 became extremely popular without either damaging America's distinctiveness or persuading French intellectuals that the United States was a friendly and equally advanced civilization.

Another symbol of the Americanization threat became the chronic

French hysteria about the Anglo-Saxonization of their language. René Étiemble, professor of comparative literature at the Sorbonne, wrote the 1964 book, *Parlez-vous Franglais?*, that assesses the French language's supposed corruption. With the adaptation of such words as the "twist" dance, "segregation," and, of course "Coca-Cola," he warns, the American way of life is "going to contaminate and botch what we have left of cuisine, wine, love, and original thoughts."[67] Another writer described "the scheme to homogenize [French] by means of Angloid pidgin."[68] And a third, in 1980, claimed that the contamination of French was part of an emerging universal pidgin English that was to communication what "fast food is to gastronomy."[69] Yet despite all this fear of an assault on the French language, less than 3 percent of new words in French come from English.[70]

In France, it often seemed as if every event was analyzed regarding its relationship to the alleged American threat. After another writer exalted the upsurge of revolutionary fervor in France during 1968 as a European revolt against Americanization, Régis Debray—a political philosopher whose main claim to fame had been his wrong prediction that Cuban-style revolution would sweep Latin America and expel U.S. influence—explained that the radical upsurge was merely one final gasp before France surrendered to America, abandoning its great dreams of a just society, national community, and solidarity with the world's exploited and oppressed.[71]

When Disneyland opened a European theme park near Paris in 1992, intellectuals denounced it as the equivalent of a "cultural Chernobyl," a reference to the defective Soviet nuclear reactor that spewed out large amounts of radioactive poison across the Ukrainian countryside.[72] Yet the theme park proved very popular even with the French, a fact that only proved for intellectuals the dangers such things posed to their way of life.

This feeling of being beleaguered and on the defensive reached the highest levels of French government. The idea that the United States was a threat, as presented in the best-selling 1967 book by Jean-Jacques Servan-Schreiber, *The American Challenge*, became a major issue in policy debates. Hubert Védrine, a French foreign minister under the socialist President François Mitterrand, coined the term "hyperpower" in the 1980s to describe U.S. domination over a "unipolar world."[73]

In 1982, Michel Jobert, who held that same post under the conservative

Gaullist President François Pompidou, saw Cobol, a computer language invented in the United States, as worse than the Soviet invasion of Kabul, the capital of Afghanistan. Cobol, he explained, was "more insidious and more part of our daily life than the threat from the East." Whereas the Soviets had been discredited by their attack on Afghanistan, the "Cobol coup" is taking place so quietly that those being taken over by the Americans were not even aware of it.[74]

The next year, cabinet minister Jean-Pierre Chevénement, a Socialist who seven years later would resign from office to protest French participation in the first war against Saddam Hussein, raised a hysterical alarm: "Never since the Hundred Years' War [which ended 500 years earlier] have our people known such an identity crisis. Our language is threatened with extinction for the first time in history. America has become the last horizon of our young because we have not offered them a great democratic design."[75]

That last point was a critical one for understanding the growing anti-Americanism expressed in France beginning in the final years of the twentieth century. There was a strong belief among many that the young generation was becoming too Americanized. Customs, music, film and clothes, the Internet, and many other things were cited as proof. One college professor explained that she feared her daughter was becoming Americanized because she had begun to make herself snacks rather than engaging only in formal meals.[76] This sense of being in the midst of a losing battle was shared with movements in many parts of the Third World as well.

But despite these fears of subversion, there were not many signs of retreat among the anti-American forces. Indeed, they generally succeeded even in barring the use of the term "anti-Americanism" in the French media and universities. To talk of such a phenomenon was to suggest that there was some systematic bias against America that should be corrected. There was no such prejudice, ran the response, but merely an accurate recounting of that country's genuine faults. Those criticizing anti-Americanism were often branded as American agents.[77]

During the 1950s and 1960s, the leading French critic of anti-Americanism was Raymond Aron, who suggested that his compatriots respected the USSR more for oppressing its intellectuals than the United States for ignoring them.[78] In the 1970s, the most popular dissenting interpretation was that of Jean-François Revel, who claimed that anti-

Americanism was part of the European left's larger effort to discredit liberalism by attacking its main model and champion. Misrepresenting the United States as a repressive, unfair, racist, nearly fascist society was a way to say, he later wrote, "See what it looks like when liberalism is implemented!"[79] Yet the fact that Revel's books also sold well in France proved that many people were open to alternative points of view.

Despite all the bluster about French—or, in other cases, European—superiority, the paranoid attitude so often evinced toward America represented a tremendous breakdown of confidence and a closing off of possibilities, the fearful rejection of change or of considering alternatives that is the very essence of the reactionary worldview. As the Frenchman Claude Roy wrote in his 1949 book on America, "Nothing is more ridiculous than the snails of the Old World who withdraw into their shells at the sight of the New World."[80]

Yet France, a society priding itself on its great history and even greater culture, trembled at any infusion of American culture because it assumed that there was no possibility of competing fairly. Instead of viewing such input as an inspiration for new forms of creativity, the wagons were circled to blot out images deemed too horrifying for French people to endure. By shutting itself off, France risked the danger of shutting itself down.

As a result, while France could easily have won any sneering contest, it lost the battles that truly counted. For example, France was the world's first country to have a public Internet, yet a reluctance to use such a demeaning medium and a demand that it set all the international standards for the new system resulted in the country lagging far behind in high technology. Equally, while it was eager to assert the superiority of its language, France watched as English increasingly became the world's common language. When a Japanese auto company merged with Renault, the company's French executives had to learn English in order to communicate with the Japanese.

Typical of the ostrich defense of putting one's head firmly into the sand, an approach too often adopted by the French intelligentsia, was the proposal of Claude Hagège, a respected professor of linguistic theory at the Collège de France, that French primary schools should teach two foreign languages, but neither of them would be English.[81]

All that this left for the French intellectuals was the hope that America might somehow decline, that its own people and the whole world might catch on to its sheer awfulness, that the contradictions detected in Paris would bring the edifice crashing down. One of the most famous of such exercises in wishful thinking was a 1968 book, *L'Empire Américain* by Claude Julien, who, as Washington correspondent for *Le Monde*, was the French intellectual establishment's expert on this issue.

America was vulnerable on two fronts, he explained. At home, presented as a paradise, consumer society actually was a hell of poverty, racism, injustice, unbearable tensions, hypocrisies, neuroses, and explosions of violence. Like European writers of the early nineteenth century, he suggested that this unworkable system might soon implode, ridding the world of its unwelcome presence.

Then there was the international situation. Surely the world would rebel against America, perhaps with France as its leader? After all, Americans accounted for only 6 percent of the world's population but consumed a large portion of its resources. As the gap between rich and poor grew and the United States relied on dictators to protect its raw materials, the end might be near in a revolutionary maelstrom.

Such events did not happen, however, during Julien's generation. Later, the American victory in the Cold War was a grave setback for these expectations. Later still, however, it seemed to some that the events of September 11, 2001, were a sign of some new heroic resistance, another round in the struggle that might succeed in overthrowing the beast from outside if not from within.

The idea of France reclaiming its glory and great power status as the champion of an anti-American coalition was not merely the fantasy of a few writers and intellectuals. It was also at times embraced by the country's highest officials. At a UNESCO conference in Mexico in 1982, Minister of Culture Jack Lang declared cultural war on the United States. The dominance of American songs, films, and television, he claimed, represented an "immense empire of profit," an empire against which must be waged "real cultural resistance, a real crusade against ... this financial and intellectual imperialism which no longer grabs territory or, rarely, but grabs consciousness, ways of thinking, ways of living. ... We must act if tomorrow we don't want to be nothing but the sandwich-board of the multinationals."[82]

For a group that portrayed itself as the world's most brilliant and superior set of thinkers, however, it was amazing how consistently wrong the French intellectuals were about the United States. As a result of these misconceptions and contorted claims, they remained mystified about why that country was so successful.

In 1986, Jean Baudrillard, author of a widely read travelogue about America, pondered this paradox as he considered its largest city: "It is a world completely rotten with wealth, power, senility, indifference, Puritanism, and mental hygiene, poverty, and waste, technological futility and aimless violence, and yet I cannot help but feel it has about it something of the dawning of the universe. Perhaps because the entire world continues to dream of New York, even as New York dominates and exploits it."[83]

There was, of course, anti-Americanism elsewhere in Europe, though compared to what went on in France, it was a rather anemic affair during the Cold War. After all, there were few points of friction between the United States and Britain, Germany, or Italy. America was defending Europe from a Soviet threat that could not easily be dismissed. Communist parties dissented but were increasingly discredited. The far left in Western Europe railed against America periodically but was a marginal force. Negative sentiment existed, especially among intellectuals, but rarely had any major role.

"Culturally, the British masses are much more friendly to America than what passes for our literary and academic intelligentsia. It is there, from Harold Pinter on the squawking left to Le Carré on the surly right that the more frenzied expressions of hatred tend to come," as one British observer described it.[84]

But the views of these opinion-forming sectors, dispensed to the general public through books, newspapers, radio, television, educational institutions, and other routes, did have an effect on the thinking of far larger groups. And these long-term influences would erupt when changes or events triggered already-existing attitudes.

For example, an in-depth 1988 study of the British public showed the continued existence of many traditional negative stereotypes among conservatives as well as leftists. "The Americans I meet tend to put me off ... because they appear to be brash and shallow and loud," said one affluent conservative. Added a left-of-center counterpart, Americans are "showmen ... braggers," people who always believed they were the best. "Gunboat diplomacy—it all ties in with their brash showmanship." And American culture was junk. As one Manchester citizen summed up the United States, "It's more of a racket than a society."

Such cultural clichés shaped the interpretation of political actions. While accepting their country's close alliance with the United States, the British tended to judge the United States more harshly than they did the USSR. In international affairs, it was seen as a "cowboy shooting from the hip."[85] As one well-heeled conservative put it, "I would trust the Russians to think things through and perhaps win a point because they've stayed calm and steady and thought it through like a chess game," while the Americans tended to lose their temper and act less rationally.[86]

Yet the specific cases used by interviewees to prove these views were in themselves revealing of an anti-American bias. Among these were the 1980 rescue attempt of American diplomats held hostage in Iran and a 1986 U.S. bombing raid on Libya following that country's involvement in a terror attack on American soldiers in Germany. These were, though, defensive actions, and certainly nothing so different—and far less motivated by imperial self-interest—from the kinds of things Britain had done when it was the world's leading power.

The most serious discrepancy was a tendency to see the United States and Soviet Union as morally equivalent, mirror images in following a selfish and ruthless policy. Expecting far less of the USSR, it was easy to take that country's misdeeds for granted: since they were expected, they didn't count. One might be quick to seek some positive attribute to balance matters somewhat, as well as to give hope that the Cold War might be kept peaceful and resolved quickly.

In contrast, the fact that the United States was an ally might make for harsher judgment of it. As leader of the West, the United States might drag these once-powerful countries in its wake, risking their futures by its adventurism. Those interviewed in the British study resented America as insensitive to their country's suggestions and dismissive of its positions. Lingering resentments at old issues intensified this feeling. Respondents cited the United States' "late" entry into World War II (forgetting its tremendous aid for Britain while ostensibly still neutral) or failure to support Britain during the 1956 Suez crisis (ironically, criticizing an anti-imperialist U.S. stance that ran counter to a common anti-American stereotype).

This last example is especially revealing and ironic. After all, however justified in strategic terms, the 1956 British and French invasion of Egypt was a prime example of the kinds of things over which they criticized the United States. On that occasion, rightly or wrongly, the American government had backed the leftist Egyptian regime as the victim of imperial machinations. France, where such criticisms of the United States were even more common, had engaged in far more international adventures, including many unilateral interventions to overthrow or preserve dictatorships in its former African colonies.

This issue of evaluating what American culture or society proved about its foreign policy or how, in turn, such international behavior revealed an underlying pattern of U.S. methods and goals, was a critical element making anti-Americanism so distinctive. After all, despite decades of aggression, imperialism, and exploitation by Britain, France, Spain, Germany, Italy, and Russia, no systematic doctrine of antagonism to those societies ever came into existence. Whatever they did—and did wrong—was not attributed mainly to the essence of their culture or character of their people.

There was also a new element in late-twentieth-century anti-Americanism that only became really salient after the Cold War's end and Communism's collapse. It still seemed far out in 1983, when the British travel writer Jan Morris proclaimed "the reluctant and terrible conviction that the greatest threat to the peace of humanity is the United States. I can no longer stomach America's insidious meddling across the face of the world. Wherever I go I find myself more and more repelled by the apparently insatiable American urge to interfere in other people's business."[87]

Yet Morris was prefiguring a new worldview that would be fully launched against America in the 1990s, albeit one under construction since the time the United States was a little country huddled along the Atlantic seacoast. In the words of the British philosopher Bertrand Russell, "Whenever there is hunger, wherever there is exploitative tyranny, whenever people are tortured and the masses left to rot under the weight of disease and starvation, the forces which hold the people stem from Washington."[88]

In short, the fifth and highest phase of anti-Americanism would be that the United States was responsible for virtually all the world's problems and evils. For two centuries, both pro- and anti-Americans had been predicting that America would become the future of the human race, the model of civilization, and the greatest cultural and strategic power. Anti-Americans warned that one day, the United States would threaten the world in its lust for conquest, exporting its malformed society and destructive culture. Now, at last by the 1990s, that moment would be at hand.

Whatever the injustices of the Vietnam War, it was not widely credible, even in France, to portray the United States as responsible for all the world's ills as long as the USSR existed to take some of the blame and provide a rationale for much of what happened. Only when that rival bloc collapsed could America be believed to be the planet's greatest villain, because now it really was the globe's greatest power.

THE GREAT SATAN

If at least one good thing might come out of September 11, 2001, the most terrible terrorist attack in modern history, surely it could have been expected to be heightened world sympathy for the United States in the Middle East. In fact, however, the opposite happened. Usama bin Ladin and his al-Qa'ida group organized the operation in the first place because they wanted to identify America as an evil country that was the source of the world's problems.

To some extent, they succeeded far more than just hijacking four planes and crashing three of them into the World Trade Center and Pentagon. It was also the greatest graphic demonstration of anti-Americanism and advertisement for that doctrine that had ever happened.

There were two types of anti-American responses. The first and more extreme was the idea, mainly in the Middle East and among Muslims, that bin Ladin was right, the attacks were justified, and there had to be more armed struggle against the United States and its influence. The other approach—more popular in the Middle East, Europe, and elsewhere—was to say that there was much truth in bin Ladin's claims and large legitimate grievances against the United States, though the attack itself was excessive and American influence should be fought with non-violent means. While the first school of thought wanted to fight America, the second was content merely to blame America.

For almost a half-century before September 11, anti-Americanism had been a major force in the Middle East. But before that date, it had usually been part of a larger worldview, an accessory (albeit an important one). Now, anti-Americanism was placed at the very center of these ideologies.

The Middle East version of anti-Americanism possessed its own distinctive roots, course of development, and list of complaints. At the same time, though, it had, like counterparts elsewhere, the same dual concept of America, two mutually reinforcing ideas in building an anti-American vision.

On one hand, the United States was portrayed as a bad society, especially dangerous since its model might displace the Arab/Muslim culture and way of life. On the other hand, the United States had an evil foreign policy, antagonistic to Arab/Muslim interests because it sought to injure, conquer, and dominate the Middle East. The root of anti-Americanism in the Middle East, then, is not so much the substance of American words or deeds but the deliberate reinterpretation of American words or deeds to make them seem hostile and evil.

What were some of the causes that made Middle Eastern anti-Americanism so intense? First, and ironically, was the fact that anti-Americanism developed later in the Middle East than in Europe or Latin America, largely because that region's significant contacts with the United States only took place in relatively recent times. It came onto the stage at the time of that phenomenon's highest, most intense, phase. Middle Eastern views of America were formed at the time in which that country was a global power and seen mainly in that light.

Second, and perhaps even more significant, was that cultural distance made it far easier to distort the nature and motives of the United States. Europe and Latin America knew they shared a great deal in common with America. Ultimately, the United States was only a variation—even if some considered it a perverted one—of their own civilization. For the Arab and Muslim world, however, the United States was not only far more alien but also often seen as the embodiment of the entire Western world.

A third key element was the entwining of anti-Americanism with the

Arab world's, and later Iran's, political system. At the root of this version of anti-Americanism was less a factually based set of grievances than a campaign far more systematic and keyed to political advantage than elsewhere in the world. Most of the ruling and opinion-making elite—even those whose countries maintained good relations with the United States, as in Saudi Arabia or Egypt—had strong political motives for endorsing anti-American views and making them a key part of their strategy for retaining power.

As in the Soviet Union and Nazi Germany, anti-Americanism was a state-supported doctrine. The reason was that in the Arab world and Iran, ruling ideologies—Arab nationalism and Islamism, respectively—saw themselves as alternative models of how society should be organized. For them, America was a rival for the loyalties of their own people and the preservation of the way of life they wanted. Consequently, it had to be discredited and defeated in order for their vision to triumph.

Unlike in Europe or Latin America, these dictatorial and ideological regimes controlled all social institutions, including the media, mosque, and schools, using them to spread systematically their version of the United States. Also in comparison to other places, the liberal forces that had always been the main foes of anti-Americanism in Europe and Latin America were far weaker there.

Fourth, the Middle Eastern regimes' visible failures made them need to wield anti-Americanism all the more. How else could they explain their own inability to unite the Arab world, destroy Israel, bring rapid economic development, or give their people more freedom than by citing U.S. sabotage? To survive, they needed to persuade their people that the main threat came from a powerful and evil external enemy, which required them to unite around their government to fight.

Even governments considered relatively moderate that maintained good formal relations with the United States, such as Egypt or Saudi Arabia, still vigorously promoted anti-Americanism to deflect attention and blame from their domestic and foreign policy failures, to mobilize internal support against a make-believe enemy, to forge militant credentials, and to appease radical neighbors. They were happy to receive U.S. help and protection while denouncing the country that gave it.

Finally, anti-Americanism also became an important tool for revolutionary movements, which tried to portray their rulers as American stooges and themselves as patriots that fought against imperialism. This was not such an unusual posture, as it had been adopted elsewhere by Communists and nationalists in many countries. What made it different, however, was the fact that in the Middle East, these forces were increasingly Islamist, meaning that America was also seen as a threat in the passionate and sensitive area of attacking one's religion.

Such men as Ayatollah Ruhollah Khomeini, who seized power in Iran in 1979, and Usama bin Ladin, who tried to foment revolution in Saudi Arabia in the 1990s, viewed America as an alternative model of society that was subverting Muslim culture and religion. For them, too, like the Arab nationalists, the United States seemed to block their ambition to rule the region: it was a demon against whom they could mobilize the masses, and anti-Americanism was a rationale for their inability to overthrow Arab governments. Millions of their followers were persuaded by their slogans that Islam was the answer and that America was the problem.

Moreover, while the Islamist revolutionaries were trying to overthrow their Arab nationalist rulers, the latter actually agreed with them on the point of promoting anti-Americanism. The mutual accusations against the United States by Arab nationalist regimes and Islamist oppositions reinforced each other. Rulers even increased the volume of their anti-American rhetoric to co-opt potential supporters of the opposition and to shore up their Islamic, as well as patriotic, legitimacy. The result was a spiraling upward of anti-American propaganda.

As a result of government policy, anti-Americanism became official doctrine throughout the Middle East, even in those countries where relations seemed best and regardless of U.S. actions favoring Arab or Muslim interests. Since anti-Americanism became state policy in the Arab world in the late 1950s—and in Iran since 1979—schools, religious authorities, intellectuals, political figures, and the media have repeated these themes with little or no alternative point of view being available to their audiences.

But it was not merely a matter of regimes twisting the arms of an intellectual class, which has been the main carrier of anti-Americanism throughout the world. The overwhelming majority of Arab teachers, writers, and journalists were true believers in Arab nationalist (and sometimes Islamist) ideology, and they promoted anti-Americanism to serve these causes. Whatever their own degree of personal Westernization, doing so validated their militant credentials and cultural authenticity while also bringing them rewards from the regimes that generally paid their salaries and gave them access to the means of communication.

The message presented from all these sources was of a hostile, imperialistic, and repressive America. Since there were supposedly no real conflicts among Arabs or Muslims, the quarrels and disagreements between countries, parties, and communities were said to be largely due to U.S. machinations. Israel, whose elimination was also high on the Arab and Islamist agenda, supposedly only existed because of U.S. backing. Thus, America—and not the rulers' misgovernment or the ideologies' bankruptcy—was mainly responsible for the fact that the Arab (or Muslim) world is not united, strong, happy, pious, filled with social justice, freed of Israel's existence, and wealthy.

Indeed, the high degree of distrust and rejection that results is characterized by a Syrian journalist's claim that the United States follows a Nazi model: "Lie, lie, until the lie becomes truth. But U.S. lies have not become truth."[1] In most of the Arab world and in large parts of the Muslim world, though, it was anti-Americanism that became accepted as truth despite the absence or distortion of evidence for such assertions.

In the words of Salman Rushdie, the Indian-born British writer, the reason for the power and prevalence of anti-Americanism is its value as

a smokescreen for Muslim nations' many defects—their corruption, their incompetence, their oppression of their own citizens, their economic, scientific and cultural stagnation. America-hating has become a badge of identity, making possible a chest-beating, flag-burning rhetoric... that makes men feel good. It contains a strong streak of hypocrisy, hating... America because it has made of itself what [they] cannot.... What America is accused of—closed-mindedness, stereotyping, ignorance—is also what its accusers would see if they looked into a mirror.[2]

Thus, the main U.S. utility for the region's oppressive dictatorships was not as a protector but as an excuse for their failings. For the Arab world's ills, as the Lebanese-American scholar Fouad Ajami wrote, anti-Americanism was the "placebo."[3] Given anti-Americanism's intensity and pervasiveness in deliberately misexplaining the meaning of U.S. policy and values, ordinary people accepted its claims as truth. Surrounded daily by anti-American messages taught by teachers, journalists, religious authorities, and government and opposition leaders alike, it was hardly surprising that the masses accepted and echoed such sentiments. They were fed on a steady diet of distortions about the nature of American society and foreign policy, with little or no different views to be heard.

Living with so much corruption, repression, economic stagnation, social restrictions, and lack of hope, people had an urgent need to find someone to blame. Since they were powerless to criticize publicly or replace their own dictators, it is hardly surprising that the United States became their principal scapegoat or that anti-Americanism was a popular way to blow off steam.

As Ajami put it:

> The populations shut out of power fell back on their imaginations and their bitterness. They resented the rulers but could not overthrow them. It was easier to lash out at American power and question American purposes. And they have been permitted the political space to do so. They can burn American flags at will, so long as they remember that the rulers and their prerogatives are beyond scrutiny. The rulers ... know when to indulge the periodic outbursts at American power.[4]

Given this relentless effort by regimes, radical oppositions, and intellectuals belonging to both camps, the Middle East became one of the few places where anti-Americanism has truly become a populist doctrine actually accepted by a large majority of people. "For many Arabs, regardless of their politics," writes the Arab-American academic Fawaz Gerges, the United States was portrayed as "the embodiment of evil, [responsible for all the world's] ills and misfortunes."[5]

The masses were programmed in this direction not only by direct criticism of the United States but also by the systematic distortion of its deeds and policies. "There can be no written praise of America, no acknowledgment of its tolerance or hospitality," wrote Ajami. No serious Arab work "has spoken of the American political experience or the American cultural landscape with any appreciation."[6]

Those defending the United States or pointing to the dictatorial regimes as the real problem were few in number. Since they were labeled as traitors to Islam or the Arab nation, such people required a great deal of personal courage but were silenced or denied media access, and faced considerable career and even personal risks. At any rate, advocates of such Western ideas as pluralist democracy, free enterprise, human rights, civil liberties, or friendship with the West saw these arguments dismissed and discredited as the misleading and ruinous notions promulgated by American imperialism.

But the goals of regimes and ideologies were not all that was at stake. Anti-Americanism also reflected the degree to which modernization, Westernization, and globalization has been highly problematic in the Arab world. Nowhere else is resistance to such influences so uncompromising and thoroughgoing as in the Arab and Muslim world along both religious and nationalistic lines. Equally, nowhere else were these new ideas and institutions so identified specifically with the United States.

After all, for Europe and even Latin America, the United States and its influence or way of life represented only one aspect of modern society, pluralist democracy, or a free-enterprise economy. Many features of American life and thought had originated in Europe and also existed there, perhaps with relatively minor variations.

But for the Arab world, coming to full self-consciousness in the aftermath of European colonialism and during the era of American supremacy, these were alien ideas and ones highly identified uniquely with the United States. There was often talk about "the West," but the focus was overwhelmingly on America. As a result, anti-Americanism existed in a much purer form in the Middle East, as a doctrine for disparaging a whole set of ideas that included matters ranging from equality for women to equality for ethnic and religious groups, from new styles of music to greater personal freedom. Westernization, modernization, and globalization became mere synonyms for Americanization.

The man who could most credibly claim to be the intellectual author of anti-Americanism in the Arab world was Sayyid Qutb, who was also the most important founding theorist of revolutionary Islamism. Qutb's critique of America was an exclusively civilizational one, with virtually no reference to American policies. In 1948, the forty-two-year-old Qutb was sent by Egypt's education ministry to the United States to study its schooling methods. In articles written for Egyptian periodicals and later in a 1951 book, *The America I Have Seen*, Qutb expressed his horror about life in Greeley, Colorado, where he studied curriculum at the Colorado State Teachers College.

Like his European and Latin American predecessors in anti-Americanism, Qutb saw his own people as spiritual superiors threatened by an inferior and dangerous culture. Yet, in Qutb's case, because of his miscomprehension, knee-jerk hatred of the "other," and perception of any society different from his own as inferior, he and his anti-American successors embodied in far more extreme ways the very characteristics they condemned as distorting America's alleged vision of Arabs and Muslims.

To show that Americans had bad taste, he described a young American man with large, brightly colored tattoos of animals.[7] The attention paid by residents of Greeley to their lawns proved that Americans were selfish people interested only in material things. The competition among the town's Christian ministers showed how everything in America was invested with the spirit of business, while a church dance scandalized him by its "seductive atmosphere" and the visibility of women's legs.[8]

In terms close to historic French anti-Americanism, Qutb explained that all high culture was imported from Europe and that the only art form Americans did well were films, since this media combined "craftsmanship and primitive emotions." American material civilization might be successful, he concluded, but its people were not, and their abilities were only materialistic ones that subverted spirituality and mocked the proper way of life and relationship between people and God.[9]

According to Qutb, then—in terms not so far from classical European anti-Americanism—the United States was technologically advanced yet spiritually primitive. Perhaps it could be respected for its technological ingenuity, productivity, and living standards, but the conclusion, in Qutb's words, was that "man cannot maintain his balance before the machine and risks becoming a machine himself. He is unable to shoulder the burden of exhausting work and forge ahead on the path of inhumanity, he unleashes the animal within."[10]

Its society "reminds one of the days when man lived in jungles and caves" because it appreciates only "muscular strength rather than values in family or social life." Violence is another characteristic in the Arab anti-American lexicon. For Qutb, this was demonstrated by a preference for such sports as boxing and football. Thus, "the American is by his very nature a warrior who loves combat."[11] This explains why the United States is brutal and aggressive abroad.

In contrast to secular Europeans who disdain America as fanatically religious, however, Muslim anti-Americans see it as distressingly atheist and thus a godless threat to any pious society. Qutb wrote that despite its profusion of church buildings, no one is less able to appreciate religion than Americans."[12]

Similar themes recur in the relatively sparse—compared to Europe's—Arab travel literature about the United States. Yusuf al-Hasan, a Palestinian, in a 1986 travel book about the country, said it lashes out to punish others without reflection or reasoning, "Just like the cowboy who lives in a world in which only the fastest to pull his gun survives."[13] As a result, explains Egyptian satirist Mahmud al-Sadani, "America is the greatest, largest, and most obnoxious empire in history." It helps the strong against the weak, Israel against the Arabs. It invades Panama on the "pretext" that its dictator is involved in drug-dealing but really only to control the Panama Canal, or opposes Cuba as a dictatorship while supporting other Latin American dictators.[14]

Middle Eastern anti-Americanism is thus based on a comprehensive critique of America based on such issues as America's history, its society, and analogies with its behavior elsewhere in the world. In some cases, these ideas are drawn by European sources, either read or absorbed during studies there, though increasingly they may come from the direct experience of those who attended universities in the United States.

Many of these sentiments arise from cultural clashes, a pattern similar to nineteenth-century European anti-Americanism. Indeed, even on issues where Arab-Muslim differences to the West in general are the greatest, there is still a striking similarity between the anti-American reactions of Arabs and Muslims and the expressions of horror at America by those from conservative European perspectives.

Such is the case with the view of women's role in America. Qutb's discussion of this issue positively drips with a sense of sensual danger, a frightening power that might overwhelm the pious and subvert Arab-Muslim society as the social equivalent of a nuclear weapon. He describes the American female as a temptress, acting her part in a system Qutb described as "biological": "The American girl is well acquainted with her body's seductive capacity. She knows it lies in the face, and in expressive eyes, and thirsty lips. She knows seductiveness lies in the round breasts, the full buttocks, and in the shapely thighs, sleek legs—and she shows all this and does not hide it."[15]

Like their European counterparts, Middle Eastern critics also viewed

America as a country where women suffered from the loss of their proper role and an excess of social power. Islamist Iran's spiritual guide Ali al-Husseini al-Khamene'i explained that this was why women were better off in his country than in America.[16] A secular Egyptian journalist used an argument identical to Islamists and nineteenth-century European anti-Americans: since the United States was controlled by "money and sex... the materialistic ambition of some American women ends with ... broken hearts and homes, and sick, exhausted souls, and with them drowning their wretchedness in drugs and alcohol."[17]

If American women had subverted their own men to destruction, they could also be portrayed as playing that same role of seducing Arab men into cultural surrender. The secular leftist Egyptian Sherif Hetata wrote a novel entitled *The Net* in 1982 with a plot like a Soviet Cold War story. The Egyptian hero is tempted by a glamorous, mysterious American woman spy to leave a state-run pharmaceutical company to work for an American multinational. He also abandons his wife, who represents traditional Egyptian virtues. But the evil American's real purpose is to destroy the Egyptian left. The love affair ends in disaster, the woman is murdered, and her Egyptian victim is executed as a traitor. The moral is that Egypt will face disaster if it heeds the siren call of a falsely glittering but treacherous America.[18]

This idea of a disgusting society inevitably producing a repellent foreign policy often appears in Middle Eastern anti-Americanism. And so while the political side of anti-Americanism is more commonly expressed than the cultural-civilizational side, this is in no small part due to the fact that the latter is taken for granted. In a remarkable passage, Saddam Hussein brought the two aspects together when he told his subjects, "The United States exports evil, in terms of corruption and criminality, not only to any place to which its armies travel, but also to any place where its movies go."[19]

Ironically, the main architect of Arab nationalist anti-Americanism, the secularist Egyptian President Gamal Abdel Nasser, was the man who executed Qutb on charges of fomenting an Islamist revolution against himself. As the Arab world's leader and would-be unifier, Nasser knew that the United States would not back his plans to seize control of the region and overturn all the other regimes. Therefore, he had to declare America as the enemy of the Arabs in general and stir up hostility to it.

But the United States did not quite live up to the role that Nasser assigned it, another sign of the broad gap between reality and the image of the United States held or disseminated by Arab regimes. Not only was anti-Americanism in the Arab world formulated at a time when the United States played a relatively minor role in the region—and had little to do with Israel—but America had even supported Nasser's 1952 coup and saved him from being overthrown by a British-French-Israeli attack in 1956.

It was, in fact, Nasser's alliance with the USSR in his bid to subvert moderate Arab countries like Jordan, Saudi Arabia, and Lebanon and to become the region's leader that made U.S. policy makers oppose his ambitions.[20] Even then, despite the aggressive and imperialist reputation imputed to it, the United States did not do much against him. Moreover, far from being anti-Islam in this era, U.S. policy became literally its political patron, seeing traditionalist Muslims like those in Saudi Arabia as a bulwark against Communism and radical Arab nationalism.

Meanwhile, Arab nationalists came to run the most aggressive, repressive regimes in the region, intimidate moderate traditionalists, and win over almost the entire intellectual class. They claimed that their own doctrine represented the people's will and that anyone who disagreed was a U.S. stooge. As Arab nationalist regimes seized control of Iraq in 1958, Syria in 1963, and Libya in 1970, this system spread, as did the systematic anti-American indoctrination it used.

There were no limits to what could be claimed and believed about the United States. After the 1967 Arab-Israeli war, for example, Nasser explained away his humiliating defeat at Israel's hands by falsely claiming that his forces had been destroyed by the U.S. Air Force. Egyptian schoolchildren were taught ever afterward the lie that the United States attacked Egypt and fought alongside Israel in the 1967 war. Israel was portrayed as either America's stooge or master.[21]

In reality, though, the United States had no significant relationship with Israel until the 1970s. And the sole actual U.S.-backed coup was in 1953 in Iran, where American leaders feared that Prime Minister Muhammad Mossadegh's government was being taken over by Communist forces. Helping to overthrow Mossadegh, though the coup enjoyed considerable support even among Iran's Muslim clerics, was the one American deed that could be portrayed as a grievance equivalent to those prevalent in Latin America. Unlike in Latin America or Asia, however, where the United States openly confronted, fought, or overthrew governments it deemed hostile, in the Middle East America courted even Arab radical forces, worrying that those it antagonized would side with the USSR. This strategy eventually worked with Egypt in the late 1970s, and that country became the recipient of large-scale U.S. aid and assistance without having any effect on the regime's massive production of anti-American propaganda.

The Arab nationalist regimes were virtually the world's only non-Communist forces aligned with Moscow during the Cold War. When it came to the United States, they borrowed extensively from that bloc's arguments and propaganda. Like the Communists, they had no use for the democratic, free-enterprise, human rights–oriented system of the United States. They created dictatorial mobilization states that were in every respect antithetical to American ideas, values, and institutions.

Such views were also expressed by PLO leader Yasir Arafat, who saw himself as part of a global Third World revolution against the United States. At a 1969 student convention in Amman, long before there was any U.S. alliance with Israel, he led the crowd in singing a song entitled, "America, the Head of the Snake."[22] Arafat repeatedly denounced U.S. policy as "an imperialist plot to liquidate the Palestinian cause"[23] and claimed that America had caused all the region's problems.[24] This was despite the fact that the United States never attacked the PLO, even though it killed Americans on several occasions and sided with America's enemies.[25]

The idea that the United States wanted to conquer the region for itself was echoed almost universally by Arab ideologues and leaders. Syrian President Hafiz al-Asad explained in a 1981 speech, "The United States wants us to be puppets so it can manipulate us the way it wants. It wants us to be slaves so it can exploit us the way it wants. It wants to occupy our territory and exploit our masses. It wants us to be parrots repeating what is said to us."[26] Yet, in fact, the United States did not attack Syria and even accepted that country's occupation of Lebanon.

President Saddam Hussein spoke the same way, arguing for example in 1990 shortly before invading Kuwait that the United States would seize control of the region unless the Arabs united behind him to fight against it.[27] But not only had the United States never fought against Saddam before the 1990s, it even helped him win his war against Iran in the 1980s.

As radical Islamists rose to prominence beginning with the 1979 Iranian revolution, they made similar arguments. Khomeini, leader of Iran's revolution, insisted that the United States was a demonic force that made the world a terrible place and prevented the emergence of an Islamist utopia.[28] Yet Khomeini's labeling of the United States as the "Great Satan" was an intriguing clue to the real issue. In Islam as in Christianity, Satan is not an imperialist bully but a smooth persuader, a tempter who makes his wares seem so attractive that people want to sell him their souls. Precisely because America was so attractive for Iranians, Khomeini had to convince them it was so ugly.

Many Arabs and Iranians find America alluring. This makes the task for ideologues, intellectuals, politicians, and revolutionaries to discredit America all the more urgent. What better symbol for this reality than the fact that at their last meeting with U.S. diplomats before taking them hostage in November 1979, Iranian officials spent half the time denouncing America and the other half requesting visas for their relatives.

Thus, anti-Americanism may be based on accusations that American society is ugly but is actually motivated by fear of its lure. Many extremist Islamists, including most of the September 11 terrorists and the militant Iranian students who seized the U.S. embassy there in 1979, had much personal contact with the West. Having come close to embracing "temptation," they barricaded themselves inside a radical Islamist identity to shield them from their own desires.

Similarly, anti-Americanism simultaneously portrayed the United States as an arrogant bully and cowardly weakling. Calling America an imperialist giant is a good way to provoke outrage against it, but insisting that the United States is weak is more likely to mobilize people to fight it. A real superpower, after all, makes a frightening enemy and a useful ally. Indeed, most often anti-American rhetoric is a substitute, not a prelude, for confrontation. Almost everyone in the Arab world and Iran wants the benefits of U.S. aid, products, and protection. Despite much talk about boycotts, Arab businessmen seek American trade and investment, while young Arabs are eager for its mass culture, and many would jump at a chance to immigrate to the United States.

Thus, despite constant claims that victory over America was certain, knowing the political-military power and cultural-technological appeal of the United States often gave a decidedly defeatist tone to Middle Eastern anti-Americanism, which heightened its passion and stridency.[29] As in Europe and Latin America, much anti-Americanism was inspired by the conclusion that the cultural Americanization of society and the U.S. triumph strategically were inevitable.

At any rate, the idea that the United States was embarked on a program of world conquest—a mainstay of historic European anti-Americanism—was taken for granted in the Arab world and Islamist Iran. For instance, in a long analysis of American history, the mainstream secular Egyptian intellectual Samir Amin explains in his country's most important newspaper that America is different from Europe because its "extremist Protestant sects" saw themselves as a Nazi-like master race with a "God-given mission" to conquer the globe, making it the most brutal threat the world ever faced. It is no democracy but rather a capitalist dictatorship, where politics is merely a form of entertainment to fool the masses into believing they really have some say. The people are doused with disinformation, while critics are isolated and forced to sell out or are murdered. "The establishment can easily manipulate 'public opinion' by cultivating its stupidity." Somehow, the American people just don't see this obvious truth.[30]

Given this internally repressive system based on illusions, the United States must create a foreign enemy during times of internal stress in order to keep itself going. Once this was Communism; now it is terrorism. But the real American goal is world domination: "to prevent the emergence of any other power which might be capable of putting up resistance" and to ensure that other countries are merely "satellites." All American presidents agree, Amin explains, that "only one country has the right to be 'big' and that is the United States."[31]

And thus, what American policy in the Middle East and elsewhere is really about is to "impose the new imperialist order" on everyone. They must "either accept U.S. hegemony, along with the super-strength 'liberalism' it promotes, and which means little more than an exclusive obsession with making money—or reject both." The world will be remade "in the image of Texas" unless it defeats America's "neo-Nazi challenge."[32]

Of course, not everyone accepts such a comprehensive system of explaining America's true nature. But many did accept the basic assumption that the United States is hostile to the Arabs, the Muslims, and the various countries where they live. Consequently, American actions are portrayed in the worst possible light, no American deed is shown as being positive, and U.S. policies are not described accurately enough to be understood even by those who might be skeptical about the line they are being taught.

Should Egypt show any appreciation for the $2 billion in aid it receives every year from the United States? No, explains the state-owned newspaper *al-Akhbar*. Egypt did not ask for the money; it was an American initiative. And besides, America is not seeking "friends but agents, which is unacceptable" to Egypt.[33] But why, then, does Egypt accept the aid, and why does U.S. aid to Israel constitute support while assistance given Egypt is a form of subversion?

Does the desire of many Arabs to migrate to America prove that it is an attractive society? No, explains a panelist on al-Jazira television, because "America's plunder of Arab resources and its colonialism . . . imposed the regimes that repress the peoples and oppress them—that is what has forced hundreds of thousands and millions of Arabs to emigrate to Europe and America."[34]

Can the United States help promote democracy in the Middle East? No, explains an Egyptian newspaper columnist in 2003, because "[the American] culture of death and murder cannot lead to the creation of [the] opposite culture [of democracy]." Americans need war "to feed their aggressive military economic machine." In this context, terrorism is seen as simple self-defense by "the weak who possess no means of resisting destruction, plunder, and death . . . to confront the American culture of murder and destruction."[35]

The key issue, then, was that specific U.S. actions were only used, and distorted, to fit a preexisting conception in which nothing America did could vindicate itself. The core principle was of America as an imperialistic state that operated on three levels: as a bad model, cultural-intellectual seducer, and military aggressor. It controlled what went on in the Middle East and was responsible for all the bad governments and for the failure of revolutions. Israel was either a tool of this imperialist drive or the master of it by controlling America itself. As a result of this pervasive anti-American case, many were ready to agree when bin Ladin's lieutenant Ayman al-Zawahiri presented the view that the United States "will not permit any Muslim power to govern in any of the Islamic countries," and were equally ready to make the same conclusion if the word "Arab" were to be substituted for Muslim and Islamic.[36]

These arguments, long on passion and short on evidence, escaped critical scrutiny because they had a monopoly in terms of government sponsorship and acceptance by the intellectual establishment. "You come to us to exhaust our oil and steal more of our land," explains a leader of the Palestinian Islamist group, Hamas. "We see on your hands nothing but the blood of our peoples . . . downtrodden and miserable." The real U.S. goal is to divide the Arabs and destroy our identity, "so that we forget our names and our memory in order to instill the evil you spread all over our land" in fighting among ourselves.[37]

Amin, in *al-Ahram*, explained all this in terms not at all atypical of mainstream writing about America, "The United States practices international terrorism against the whole world." Its rulers are a "junta of war criminals," whose police force has "powers similar to those of the Gestapo."[38] An Iranian newspaper made a similar comparison, since America terrorizes and bombs other countries and breaks all international rules. "The Americans are infected today with satanic pride and arrogant egotism" and have been "throughout the 20th century." It had trampled on the rights of "Afghanistan, Iraq, Japan, Korea, and the Philippines, and other places in the world that are on the brink of conflagration."[39] A Saudi writer agrees, accusing the United States of committing terrorist acts "all over the world" as it seeks global hegemony.[40]

America must be fought and punished because otherwise, as an Iranian newspaper warns, "No country . . . anywhere in the world will be immune to the cruel nature of [American] arrogance."[41] This kind of talk came not only out of radical Iran and Iraq. Even Egypt's leading newspaper also proclaimed that there was still time to fight America: "The world has not yet become a single sphere of influence entirely subject to a single superpower. . . . There is still ability to resist."[42]

When actually stated in some detail, however, the case against the United States was remarkably thin, certainly compared to what a Latin American, African, or Asian could muster. There were three basic components in the charge sheet: alleged U.S. aggression against Muslim states, supposed U.S. backing for dictatorial regimes, and support for Israel.

Before the 2003 Iraq war, the first category consisted mainly of references to Libya and Sudan, which the United States hit with one bombing raid each in response to terrorist attacks, as well as the 1991 UN- and Arab League–sanctioned war on Iraq and the postwar UN-mandated sanctions when Iraq clearly did not implement its own agreements. Despite the attempt to portray post–September 11 counterterrorist activities as objectionable, such acts of aggression, then, were virtually nonexistent.

Equally, there was nothing that could reasonably be called economic exploitation. Arab oil-producing countries had been the main beneficiaries of petroleum pricing and production since the early 1970s, and there was little U.S. investment elsewhere. It was hard to argue that Arabs are poor because Americans are rich—though this did not stop some from doing so—and it could not be claimed that Arab raw materials are sold at low prices in exchange for high-priced Western industrial goods, a situation quite different from that of those countries that export only cacao or other agricultural products.

The false claims of injury at American hands take on remarkable forms. In 1999, an Egypt Air passenger plane that took off from New York crashed in a way suggesting sabotage by a copilot due to Islamist political motives or a psychological breakdown. Egyptian official statements and the state-controlled media presented this tragedy as the result of a U.S.-orchestrated conspiracy or at least cover-up designed to slander Egypt. Yet rather than confront this slander, the U.S. government acted typically in trying to avoid offending Egyptian sensibilities in its report by leaving open the crash's cause, though it would never gain credit for an approach so at odds with the false image being purveyed to Egypt's people.[43]

The second variety of complaint contained a paradox. If the United States was criticized when it went against Arab states, it was also condemned for cooperating with them. As one writer put it, Arabs said that their governments were so "corrupt and authoritarian" because the United States gave them billions of dollars each year, so they must be U.S. puppets.[44] But the only country to which the United States gave large-scale aid was Egypt, which in turn promoted anti-Americanism because, it complained, America was not helping the Arabs enough.

The United States was constantly said to dominate everything and, through conspiracies, to be behind every government or event. It was blamed for supporting "unpopular" or "repressive" regimes even by those who themselves represented the worst examples of this genre. Khamene'i, Khomeini's successor as Iran's spiritual guide, complained in 1997, "The American government speaks of . . . democracy and support[s] some of the most despotic regimes."[45] Even high-ranking Saudi officials complained that the United States backed "autocrats" and "oppressive" regimes.[46]

But what "despotic" and "oppressive" Arab regimes did they have in mind as being backed by the United States? The most brutal Arab rulers were also the most energetic advocates of anti-Americanism, yet many Arabs believed that the United States was so powerful that it controlled even those most outwardly hostile to it. Thus, Saddam, Arafat, Khomeini, Asad, and others were said to be American agents. After all, it was explained, the United States could easily remove those it really opposed.

Thus, the United States was not only blamed by the dictatorships but blamed for them as well. Yet, whenever it pressed regimes for reform or moderate policies, they accused it of a bullying imperialism; when it dealt with them as legitimate rulers, they accused it of blocking democracy and keeping tyrants in power.

In fact, during the twentieth century's second half, no Arab government existed because of U.S. backing. Incumbent rulers retained power without its help. At most, U.S. policy gave occasional protection to more moderate Arab regimes against foreign attack, a tradition culminating with an American-led coalition freeing Kuwait from Iraqi aggression in 1991. If anything, the story of U.S. policy in the Middle East has proven how little it was able to affect the policy of Arab regimes, or Islamist Iran, for that matter.

Equally, on no occasion did Arab governments get direct U.S. help against internal threats. In contrast to Latin America, counterinsurgency against radicals—at least until after September 11—was never done with U.S. assistance or at American behest. For example, it was Britain that aided Oman to battle a Marxist insurgency in the 1970s and France that helped Algeria fight Islamist revolutionaries in the 1990s. Aside from fighting Iraq in 1991 as part of a UN-mandated, Arab league–endorsed coalition, there had been only two short-lived U.S. military interventions into Lebanon—in 1958 and 1982—that had little effect on that country's internal politics.

Claiming that the United States controlled governments over which it had little influence was merely another way of expressing the idea that America was both malevolent and omnipotent. It was fancifully implied that these countries would become democracies if America did not subvert this process. Regimes that systematically defied the United States—

like Saddam Hussein's Iraq and like Syria, which were outright hostile, or Egypt and Saudi Arabia, which ignored U.S. requests they didn't want to fulfill—were said by anti-American ideologues to be really doing its bidding. As Abdel-Bari Atwan, the editor of an influential Arab newspaper, put it:

> [Arab regimes] sell oil at prices said to be determined mainly by America, open their countries for U.S. military bases, facilitate American control and domination over the Arab world's economic resources including oil, and convert the Arab world into a huge consuming market for U.S. products. In addition they are purported to make unnecessary huge arms deals worth billions of dollars which allegedly give them a capacity to suppress the people rather than using the money for socio-economic development.[47]

Finally, there was an attempt to reduce all of American policy to a single issue defined as "U.S. support for Israel," while also distorting the nature and policies of Israel itself. A typical example of this approach was made by Khalid Amayreh in an article published in 2001: "America is the tormentor of my people. It is to me, as a Palestinian, what Nazi Germany was to the Jews. America is the all-powerful devil that spreads oppression and death in my neighborhood. . . . America is the author of 53 years of suffering, death, bereavement, occupation, oppression, homelessness and victimization . . . the usurper of my people's right to human rights, democracy, civil liberties, development and a dignified life."[48]

As the phrase "53 years" showed, the real accusation was that America's sin was not permitting the violent destruction of Israel. But the United States backed the creation of a Palestinian state in 1948 and had little to do with this conflict until the 1970s, when it began energetically pursuing a long process of trying to negotiate a compromise solution to the dispute. It never conspired to help Israel dominate the Middle East, oppress or exterminate Arabs or Muslims, or carry out any of the similar notions daily put forward as unquestionable truth in the Arab world. Its policy toward Israel revolved around two basic principles: to help it survive real threats to eliminate that state and to broker a negotiated peace agreement acceptable to both sides in order to end the conflict.

For decades, the Arab states and the Palestinian movement were unwilling to make peace with Israel. Yet whenever opportunities seemed to arise for diplomatic progress, the United States seized them, believing a peace agreement to be in its interest precisely because it wanted good relations with the Arab world. By resolving this issue, the United States would be better able to promote regional stability, reduce the possibility of war, and ensure its own regional position.

By the same token, U.S. peacemaking efforts were dangerous to those whose plans required continued strife and declining American influence in the region. This is precisely why those who wished to destroy Israel and to block any negotiated settlement objected to U.S. policy: because it would deprive them of this issue as an excuse for retaining or fomenting revolution. Thus, their real anti-American complaint was not that the United States wasn't doing enough to resolve the conflict but that it might succeed.

During the 1993–2000 peace process, the United States tried hard to achieve a solution, putting the issue at the top of its agenda, moving considerably closer to the Arab/Palestinian standpoint, accepting a Palestinian state, negotiating directly with Arafat and giving him financial aid, and urging Israel to make concessions. The biggest wave of anti-American sentiment in history would thus take place immediately after the greatest U.S. effort to resolve the Palestinian issue to the satisfaction of Arabs and Muslims in 2000 at the Camp David meeting and in the Clinton Plan.[49]

In this context, then, anti-Americanism was more of a weapon than a grievance, with different forces in the Arab world and Islamist Iran using it in various ways. For Saddam's Iraq, anti-Americanism became a tool in its battle to escape sanctions and rebuild its military might. America, not Iraq, it told neighbors, was the real threat to their well-being. For Iran, anti-Americanism was used to discredit domestic demands for reform by claiming that moderates were U.S. agents and that fighting the American threat took precedence over internal changes. For Syria, anti-Americanism was a substitute for economic or democratic reform, a rationale for the country's dreadful state.

For Palestinian leaders, anti-Americanism concealed their own rejection of peace offers and resort to violence. By sponsoring anti-Americanism, Egypt showed it was no U.S. stooge and asserted its leadership as protecting the Arab world from American control. And the Saudis joined bin Ladin, their sworn enemy, in decrying America so as to prove their own radical Islamic credentials, while trying to attribute all U.S. criticisms of Saudi support for terrorism to malevolent anti-Muslim motives.

Finally, there is a truly remarkable factor, unique in the Middle East, of trying to use the promotion of anti-Americanism as a means of blackmail to gain rewards from the United States. Arab governments frequently tell the United States that a popular anti-Americanism over which they have no control threatens both their ability to cooperate with America and U.S. interests themselves. Consequently, they—and those who believe them in the West—insist that the United States must change its policies to be more to their liking or face disaster.

All these tactics were major parts of the Middle Eastern response to the September 11, 2001, attack. While individual Arabs and Iranians saw the tragedy as a cause for reevaluating their own countries' policies and societies, this was a distinctly minority standpoint. Much of the post–September 11 anti-Americanism concealed or justified the attackers' openly stated motives—to spark an Islamist war against an alleged American attempt to destroy Islam and take over the Middle East.

Instead, the attackers and their supporters or apologists declared it to be a defensive act in response to the fact that a corrupt and evil United States was attacking Arabs and Muslims. This argument fit with what the Arab masses had long been told. Seeing bin Ladin act on this idea brought it to life and won adherents for a more systematic, high-profile anti-Americanism. The U.S. measures taken in response—attacks on Afghanistan and Iraq, efforts to battle terrorists elsewhere, and even the American public information campaign and changes in domestic laws— were then portrayed as proof of the very imperialist expansionism, anti-Arab intentions, and anti-Muslim motives against which the attacks were a supposed reaction.

A good example of this indictment came from Ali Uqleh Ursan, head of the Syrian writers' association and himself the faithful servant of a repressive dictatorship that had sponsored terrorism, occupied its neighbor, Lebanon, and killed thousands of its own citizens:

> The fall of the symbol of American power reminded me of the many innocents whose funerals we attended and whose wounds we treated. . . . I remembered the funerals that have been held every day in occupied Palestine since 1987. . . . I remembered Tripoli [Libya] on the day of the American-British aggression, and the

attempt to destroy its leader's house as he slept; then, his daughter was killed under the ruins. . . . I remembered the oppression of the peoples in Korea and Vietnam. . . .

[I felt] tremendous bitterness, revulsion, and disgust towards the country that, in the past half-century, has racked up only a black history of oppression and support for aggression and racism.[50]

The Americans, he argues, should get back the kind of treatment they have given all of the world's people, especially the Arabs. Feeling as if he was soaring above the corpse of the World Trade Center, the "symbol of arrogant American imperialist power," is what he describes as the greatest moment of his life.[51]

This false, if passionately held, sense of victimization by America was why so many exulted at the September 11 attack. Few took up arms, but many articulated the basic tenets of anti-Americanism. They had been driven to it, they claimed, by U.S. behavior. America, explained one Palestinian militant, "offers me one of two choices: Either I submissively accept perpetual enslavement and oppression . . . or become an Usama bin Ladin."[52]

By showing that the United States could be hit and wounded, the attack seemed to promise revenge and even ultimate victory. An Iraqi newspaper declared, "The myth of America was destroyed with the World Trade Center in New York. . . . It is the prestige, arrogance and institutions of America that burn. . . . It has dragged the dignity of the U.S. government into the mud and unveiled its vain arrogance."[53]

Bin Ladin's great "accomplishment" of September 11, then, was a defining moment in making anti-Americanism the central issue on the regional agenda. This was the front that bin Ladin identified as the top priority for his global Jihadist strategy. For a quarter-century since Iran's revolution, Islamists had put the emphasis on efforts to overthrow Arab governments but had failed in such places as Lebanon, Egypt, and Algeria. Now, bin Ladin proposed a new strategy. Instead of attacking fellow Muslims, an unpopular tactic, Islamists would try to appeal to the masses by killing foreign and infidel Americans. After all, since they were rejecting an "American" paradigm for modernization and change, why not go after the United States, directly to the source of that despised program?

Contrasting with the official statements of regret by governments after

September 11 were scores of responses like that of Saudi cleric Safar bin Abd al-Rahman al-Hawali: "A tremendous wave of joy . . . was felt by Muslims in the street, and whoever tells you otherwise is avoiding the truth."[54] Many of his countrymen passed out candies, slaughtered animals for feasts, or sent congratulatory text messages to each other on mobile telephones.[55] In Bahrain, a journalist wrote, "The United States now is eating a little piece from the bread which she baked and fed to the world for many decades."[56] A Lebanese man in the street exulted, "We're ecstatic. Let America have a taste of what we've tasted."[57]

A University of Lebanon lecturer explained that people were rejoicing because the attack had been carried out against the headquarters of American colonialism:

> No one thought for a moment about the people who were inside the tallest of the world's towers as they burned; everyone thought of the American administration and rejoiced at its misfortune, while its leaders scrambled to find a place to hide. . . . Can anyone really believe that a people of whom the United States has killed hundreds and thousands times the number of people killed in New York . . . is sorry, and is not happy, when he witnesses this smack to the face of its most bitter enemy?[58]

But what had the United States actually done to any of these people or nations, compared certainly to what they had been told it had done to them? The Americans had not really killed 300,000 or 3 million Arabs, the statistical claim that this college teacher was making. What was this gigantic grudge based on if not the falsely implanted belief that American imperialism had been responsible for their problems and was trying to seize control of their destinies?

In Saudi Arabia, the country from which bin Ladin originated, the United States was seen as the key promoter and model of modernization, a process opposed by the powerfully conservative opinion there. Since the government had gone along with some U.S. policies in the Persian Gulf, bought American arms, and permitted a U.S. military presence on its soil after the 1991 liberation of Kuwait, it was a target for traditionalist Muslims and revolutionary Islamists alike. In August 1996, when bin Ladin published a "declaration of war" against America and the Saudi royal family, his main grievance was the claim that the army of the

"American crusaders" had occupied the most sacred of all Muslim countries.[59]

Perhaps the specific issue most mentioned within the Middle East as promoting anti-Americanism—though it had been rarely mentioned by bin Ladin himself—was the Arab-Israeli conflict. One Lebanese observed after the September 11 attack, "People are happy. America has always supported terrorism. They see how the innocent Palestinian children are killed and they back the Zionist army that does it. America has never been on the side of justice."[60] A Palestinian insisted, "This is the language that the United States understands and this is the way to stop America from helping the Zionist terrorists who are killing our children, men and women everyday."[61]

Yet September 11 occurred only shortly after the United States had spent eight years trying to broker a peace agreement that would have ended any occupation and created a Palestinian state, only to have its proposals rejected by the Palestinian leader and given almost no backing by Arab states. Arab governments and media had not informed their citizens of these facts, and instead systematically distorted the U.S. role and efforts in order to provoke the maximum anger against it.

One good example of the type of knee-jerk hostility that prevails regardless of what the United States does or says was the response to an *al-Ahram* op-ed piece written by U.S. Ambassador to Egypt David Welch on the September 11 attacks' second anniversary. Welch's article praised Egypt but asked in the politest of terms for one small favor: that the (state-controlled) media stop claiming American or Israeli forces carried out the attacks, pointing out that bin Ladin had even claimed responsibility.[62]

The response was an outpouring of anti-American hatred, including a petition by dozens of Egyptian intellectuals, authors, and journalists—who regularly are told by their own government "how to think and write"—demanding the ambassador be removed because he allegedly

> spoke as if he were addressing slaves or the citizens of some banana republic, not those representing the voice and conscience of the Arab nation whose roots lie deep in history and whose culture is ... the cradle of the conscience of the entire world. ... It is odd that the ambassador of any foreign country, whether it be America or Micronesia, should dictate to free Egyptian intellectuals and

journalists how to think and write, and [tell them that they] must believe everything America and its media think, even if it is lies. ... Even if America thinks that it has conquered the globe, it will not succeed in conquering and subduing the free wielders of the pen.... We advise the U.S. ambassador to try to salvage his country's reputation, shamed by its silence on Israel's crimes, which are in no way less than Hitler's crimes. If he has time to advise and interfere in Egypt's domestic matters, we say to him ... that it would be better for him to return to his country.[63]

There are many ironies in this situation. Governments declare themselves friends of the United States on a diplomatic level at the same time as they encourage hate campaigns against it. Behavior gives the lie to rhetoric. If, in fact, the United States was really the swaggering, imperialist bully these governments portrayed, they would not be so quick to defy and denounce it.

Nevertheless, Saddam, bin Ladin, Iran's leaders, and thousands of journalists, professors, and intellectuals in the region argued that America could be defeated by the proper methods. Khomeini had once said America "cannot do a damn thing" to stop Islamist revolution.[64] Saddam urged Arabs to battle the United States. Bin Ladin insisted that a small group of terrorists willing to sacrifice their lives would prove America's vulnerability. The perception of American weakness inspired as much or more anti-Americanism than did that of its great power.

But in its broad outlines and despite the many differences in details or emphasis, the modern form of anti-Americanism in the Middle East was quite parallel to that elsewhere in the world, including Europe, a doctrine predicated on the belief that the United States wanted to conquer the world politically, militarily, economically, and culturally. As in Europe, the Cold War's end and the Soviet Union's collapse was seen as paving the way for America's global primacy as the sole superpower.

Such factors as the indispensable U.S. role in preserving Gulf security or achieving Arab-Israeli peace, its military might, the pervasiveness of its cultural products, and the lack of any other power able to match its strength were taken as meaning that the United States could create a world empire. But very few would ask—or be allowed to contest— whether this was an accurate depiction of American motives, deeds, and intentions. While at least in Europe there was a real debate over these issues and a long history of contrary standpoints, in the Middle East those who had the loudest voices and a virtual monopoly on communications presented only evidence of America's guilt.

Thus, in Lebanon, long beset by intercommunal violence, locally produced terrorism, and a Syrian occupation that had nothing to do with the United States, it was America that was accused of waging a "barbaric onslaught on the nations and countries of the world" because it "is a society of absolute violence and, free from any moral restrictions, scruples, or religious and humanitarian values."[65]

In Egypt, America's closest ally in the Arab world, newspapers claimed in the aftermath of September 11 that the United States had used weapons in the 1991 war against Iraq to cause cancer among Iraqi children, a million of whom had supposedly been butchered by sanctions imposed by the UN but blamed only on America.[66] The editor of Egypt's most important newspaper, *al-Ahram*—who was both the country's leading journalist and a friend of President Husni Mubarak—wrote that the United States air-dropped poisoned food to murder Afghan civilians during its attack on the Taliban in 2001.[67] The editor of Egypt's second most important newspaper, Jalal Duweidar of *al-Akhbar*, explained that the world was now in the hands of a devil called the United States that orders everyone to surrender to its selfish and destructive purposes.[68]

The 2003 U.S.-led war on Iraq was met with an even more intensive campaign highlighting such themes. In August 2003, Fatma Abdallah Mahmoud wrote in *al-Akhbar* that the United States was a "primitive, barbaric, blood-letting" country that "destroys, annihilates, and plunders treasure and oil" from others while perpetrating "abhorrent crimes" in Iraq, Liberia, Afghanistan, Sudan, and Palestine. Everywhere, evil deeds are carried out by the "children and grandchildren of the gangs of pirates and blood-letters who run [U.S.] policy . . . the [descendants] of the original criminals, who plundered North America and murdered its original inhabitants, the Indians, to the last man." There is no basic difference between their "repulsive and loathsome present and their black past, stained with crime and murder." The author concludes by urging the world's people to fight America and kill Americans.[69]

Three weeks later, an *al-Ahram* editorial accused the United States of fomenting all the main acts of terrorism in Iraq, deliberately murdering hundreds of Muslims including a key religious leader, as well as bombing UN headquarters and the Jordanian embassy in Baghdad. The fact that those responsible for the incidents were really Saddam loyalists or Islamist terrorists was dismissed as American "propaganda aimed at causing world-wide damage to Muslims." The editorial then called on Iraqis to unite and fight the true enemy, the United States.[70]

These were not mere idle words but incitements to anti-American violence. To tell Muslims that the United States had deliberately murdered a high-ranking cleric and scores of other Muslims and that it was slandering and dividing Muslims so they would kill each other was to encourage future acts of terrorism and murder against Americans.

The bad will promulgated by these arguments and interpretations showed up in public opinion surveys. In a Gallup poll released in February 2002, 36 percent of Kuwaitis, who U.S. troops had liberated from Iraq in 1991 without trying to exploit the situation to gain any power over them, said the September 11 attacks were justifiable, the highest percentage of any country polled, and 41 percent viewed the United States unfavorably. Pakistan, a country the United States had repeatedly supported with aid against India and the Soviet invasion of Afghanistan, was highly antagonistic due to Islamist fervor, with 68 percent unfavorable. Jordan, which the United States had treated generously despite that country's support for Iraq in the 1991 crisis, showed 62 percent unfavorable.

In Saudi Arabia, 64 percent said they had an unfavorable impression of the United States. The figure was 41 percent in Morocco and 63 percent in Iran. Residents of Lebanon had the highest favorable opinion of the United States, at 41 percent, followed by NATO ally Turkey with 40 percent. The lowest numbers came from Pakistan, at 5 percent. Twenty-eight percent of Kuwaitis, 27 percent of Indonesians, 22 percent of Jordanians, 22 percent of Moroccans, 16 percent of Saudis, and 14 percent of Iranians surveyed had a favorable view of the United States.[71]

The Iraq war crisis was to raise these negative public opinion figures even higher, since the conflict was put into a context of a U.S. imperialist assault on an Arab and Muslim country. A May 2003 poll showed that anti-Americanism in Jordan peaked so that 99 percent of the people now had a somewhat or very unfavorable opinion of the United States. Hostility was also extremely high in the Palestinian Authority (99 percent). Just 15 percent of Turks, 13 percent of Pakistanis, 27 percent of Lebanese, and 27 percent of Moroccans had a positive feeling toward the United States.[72]

There was, however, one point on which anti-American propaganda was sometimes unsuccessful: most Arabs did not accept the derogation of American society itself. Polls showed favorable views regarding the level of education, freedom, and democracy in the United States.[73] This basic distinction between the views of the masses and intellectuals was similar to patterns in Europe and Latin America.

As one writer put it: "Ask anyone in Egypt what country they would like to visit, and they will probably say America. Ask them what movie they would like to see and it will probably be an American film. Ask them what school they would like to attend and they will name an American university. They may disagree violently with American policies, but they don't hate America."[74]

The highly politicized nature of these attitudes was revealed by the irony that anti-Americanism was declining in Iran. Despite the fact that Iranians had been fed such propaganda for a quarter-century and the United States had invoked economic sanctions against that country, open discontent with the Islamist regime, a more diverse press, the absence of Arab nationalism, and the existence of a strong pro-democracy movement mitigated the factors that pushed anti-Americanism higher in the Arab world.

A 2002 poll indicated that over 64.5 percent of Iranians wanted renewed relations with the United States, contrary to their own government's policy. On the hostile side, 70.4 percent felt they could not trust the U.S. government, and 62 percent were suspicious of the real purpose of the U.S. war against terrorism. Yet 46 percent said that U.S. policies on Iran were "to some extent correct," while 45 percent even endorsed U.S. intervention as a possible way to fix Iran's problems.[75] The government's response to these results was to close the National Institute for Research and Opinion Polls and to charge its director with criminal offenses.

Ironically, one articulate representative of this view was Hussein Khomeini, grandson of the ayatollah who had been one of the main architects of Middle Eastern anti-Americanism. The younger Khomeini told a Washington audience after the United States overthrew Saddam's regime, "I don't see any benefit [that America could have expected] from attacking Iraq. . . . It was just the hand of God that led America down to Iraq, to rid Iraqis of the tyrant." He hinted that the United States should do the same thing to the Tehran government. "America," he insisted, "should not be dispassionate about the misery and pain of Iranians. Rather, she should help Iranians gain democracy."[76]

Of course, this was the kind of pro-interventionist appeal that had often sparked U.S. involvement (and subsequent anti-Americanism) in the Middle East, including Iraq, and elsewhere in the world. The United States could use normal diplomatic behavior by dealing with existing regimes that might be unpopular and dictatorial, and open itself up to charges of backing repressive, unpopular governments. Or it could promote democracy and human rights, and open itself up to charges of being an imperialist power subverting legitimate governments.

The attempt, certainly well-intentioned whether or not it was misguided, to counter anti-Americanism by showing that the United States wanted to help the Arab people and Muslims by promoting democracy was one important factor in the decision to overthrow the Iraqi dictatorship in 2003. Before that war, Saddam himself had made a self-interested anti-American argument that nonetheless reflected majority Arab opinion:

> The United States wants to impose its hegemony on the Arab world, and as a prelude it wants to control Iraq and then strike the capitals that oppose it and revolt against its hegemony. From Baghdad, which will be under military control, it will strike Damascus and Tehran. It will fragment them and will cause major problems to Saudi Arabia. . . . This way the Arab oil will be under its control and the region, especially the oil sources—after the destruction of Afghanistan—will be under total control of the United States. All these things serve the Israeli interests, and based on this strategy the purpose is to make Israel into a large empire in the area.[77]

While some Arabs and more Iraqis welcomed the U.S. attack against Iraq, most in the first and many in the second group did not. Instead, the overthrow of Saddam was more often than not portrayed in the Arab world as an act of imperialist aggression, another reason for distrusting and disliking the United States. Coverage on al-Jazira and other Arab media of the U.S. role during and after the war was constantly hostile, placing Americans in the worst light as deliberately committing atrocities and having the worst of motives.[78]

Mahmoud Abd Al-Mun'im Murad, an Egyptian columnist, claimed that the U.S. plan was to turn "all human beings, into mute robots serving the American and the Israeli," and to destroy Iraq as part of its plan to control "the entire human race."[79] The ruling Palestinian Fatah movement indicted Bush as a war criminal who killed Afghan and Iraqi civilians, supported Israel, wanted to "kill many of the world's children," and was trying to seize control of the globe's natural resources.[80] Buthayna Sha'ban, official spokesperson for the Syrian Foreign Ministry, called the United States a terrorist that sought "to take control of the entire region."[81] The government's official newspaper claimed that "greedy warmongering monopolist U.S. companies" wanted "more destruction and more devastation" so as to profit from rebuilding Iraq at that country's expense.[82] The U.S. policy of paying for reconstruction itself without taking Iraqi funds was never mentioned.

The United States cannot find a solution for Middle Eastern anti-Americanism because the answer is not within its grasp. The problem is a product of the regional system itself, of the governing regimes and ideologies that find anti-Americanism to be so useful for their own needs. In this sense, it is like the state-sponsored anti-Americanism of Communism and fascism and different from the far more marginal varieties seen in Europe and Latin America.

Hatred of America is thus used to justify a great deal that is bad in the Arab world and helps keep it politically dominated by dictatorships, socially unfree, and economically less successful. Blaming national shortcomings on America means that the Arab debate avoids dealing with the internal problems and weaknesses that are the real cause of their problems. It justifies the view that the only barrier to complete success, prosperity, and justice for the Arab (and Islamic) world is the United States. Instead of dealing with privatization, women's equality, democracy, civil society, freedom of speech, due process of law, and twenty other issues the Arab world needs to address, attention can be diverted to conjuring American conspiracies and threats.

In discussing the 2003 war in Iraq, the relatively moderate Jordanian Fahd al-Fanik claimed, "The world has not witnessed such blatant aggression since the days of the Tartars. . . . While pretending to save the Iraqi people it will in fact murder them."[83] And a Gulf newspaper insisted that the United States should leave Iraq after murdering 1 million people there in "an unlawful embargo and a colonial war." That article ends by asking, "Are the Americans willing to admit their mistakes? This is the most important question of the 21st century, since much of the world's safety depends on it."[84]

Yet the United States has always been willing—even eager—to admit mistakes. It is part of that penchant for self-improvement and constant change that some of the world finds admirable and others find dangerous or sinful. One might better say that much of the world's safety and the course of the twenty-first century will depend on whether the world is willing to admit its mistakes about misjudging and hating the United States.

AMERICA AS SUPER-VILLAIN

In thriller novels and films so typical of the modern era (and, ironically, a frequently exported American cultural product), the hero battles a super-villain seeking world domination. At times, these evil forces have been Communist or fascist, individual megalomaniacs, or even extraterrestrial or supernatural invaders.

Yet today, it is the United States—in Europe, the Middle East, and elsewhere—which itself is assigned the role of Great Satan by the post–Cold War version of anti-Americanism. Hating America is no longer just an idiosyncrasy or historical footnote. It had become part of an ideology involving not only a view of the United States but also an all-encompassing ideology explaining how the world works. And this perception, in turn, is more widely and deeply spread across the world than at any previous time.

The basic points of historic anti-Americanism have fused into a new powerful ideology that combines the stereotypes of two centuries with critical developments from recent times. On one hand are the internal factors of bad culture and society used to condemn America; on the other hand are the international sins of evil foreign policy and pervasive cultural influence.

All these factors relating to values, institutions, and policies are mutually reinforcing. To some extent, the intensity of anti-Americanism may prove to be a transient phenomenon related to specific events, U.S. policies or actions, and the personalities of U.S. leaders. But there are also deeper, longer-term forces involved as well.

From 1999 to 2003, the U.S. image plummeted in Europe from a good rating of 83 to 48 percent in England, 62 to 31 percent in France, 78 to 25 percent in Germany, and 76 to 34 percent in Italy.[1] Fifty-three percent of respondents in the European Union in late 2003 saw the United States in the same league as Iran and North Korea as a threat to world peace.[2] By March 2004, anti-Americanism was hitting all-time highs in Europe with 34 percent of British having a very or somewhat unfavorable view of the United States, as well as 62 percent of French and 59 percent of Germans. But Europeans also drew a distinction between the American people and the United States as a nation, and when polled about the former, favorable ratings were 73 percent in England, 68 percent in Germany, and 53 percent in France.[3] President George W. Bush did not fare much better than Usama bin Ladin, with 85 percent in France and Germany having an unfavorable view of him, compared to 93 and 96 percent against bin Ladin.[4]

And yet there was more to the problem than just the mannerisms of George W. Bush and the controversial Iraq war. Much of the world was in search of a post–Cold War threat. Europeans had reached a critical point in their progress toward continental integration, with many seeking a common identity and a foe to set themselves off against. The Middle East, bogged down in domestic and regional paralysis—including a failed revolutionary Islamist movement that needed a scapegoat—was ripe for an even more extreme interpretation with the United States defined as its chief enemy. That was the whole purpose of the September 11 attacks in the first place.

It was no accident, then, that this highest stage of anti-Americanism spread after the Cold War ended with the Soviet Union and its bloc collapsed. America was the world's sole superpower, an outcome appearing to be the ultimate proof of the United State's cultural, political, social, economic, and military success. And that was precisely the problem, for this was equally the moment when the long-feared American takeover of the world appeared credible. Even the spread of modernity throughout the world or "globalization" was widely seen, as it had been by nineteenth-century Europeans, as Americanization.

Post–Cold War anti-Americanism was inspired by the fact that now the United States was the world's sole superpower, deprived even of the justification of protecting others from Soviet imperialism. The immense power of the United States in itself was a cause for mistrust and alarm, upsetting people whose nation's or region's fate seemed to be in American hands.

Many countries, movements, and individuals could not imagine that a state finding itself in possession of such wealth and power would not seek global hegemony. They claimed to find ample proof to show that the U.S. ambition was to rule the planet in general and themselves in particular. After all, wasn't that what they would do in America's situation? In fact, though, the United States had not used its post–Cold War position of potential domination in a fashion deserving such a response. On the contrary, its response had been to reduce international involvement and focus more on humanitarian ventures.

Nevertheless, some charged that the world takeover had already happened, like the demagogic Pakistani-British Marxist Tariq Ali, a purveyor of anti-Americanism since the 1960s, who now proclaimed that America's "military-imperial state" had already conquered all: "In the absence of a countervailing power since the collapse of the Soviet Union, the United States has been able to impose its model of economics, politics and culture on the world at large."[5]

Such ideas were mixed in with all the traditional complaints about American values and institutions, which some hated because they understood them correctly, while others hated because they interpreted them in wildly inaccurate ways. Objections to U.S. policy were systematized in a way that easily fit into historic anti-American critiques.

With the Cold War and the danger of Soviet domination past, that victory's costs now came under increasing criticism. Saving the world from Communist dictatorship had often required—or at least occasioned—compromises with unsavory regimes as well as immoral behavior. Real and imagined trespasses could now be judged harshly, especially when the lack of choice and dangers to be surmounted were ignored.

As one British writer charged in discussing this era, "The United States forfeited any claim to moral leadership long ago. It has a history of undermining international law, contempt for the human rights of others and promoting its own brand of international terrorism."[6] The usual list of real or alleged American sins in Vietnam, Chile, and Nicaragua was recited as if this proved the case for that country's clearly evil nature. Even correct criticisms of specific past U.S. policies were often distorted by being made into basic and intrinsic traits of a distinctly American civilization.

In a far more moderate tone, the British scholar Timothy Garton Ash suggested America "has too much power for anyone's good, including its own. . . . Contrary to what many Europeans think, the problem with American power is not that it is American. The problem is simply the power. It would be dangerous even for an archangel to wield so much power."[7]

But why was such a view "contrary to what many Europeans think"? Why did they view the problem as distinctly American in origin? Here, the view of the United States as different, inferior, and dangerous came into play. The United States must be behaving as it did because it was the land of irresponsible cowboys, ignorant religious fanatics, greed-obsessed capitalists, uncultured fools, intolerant buffoons, and so on.

At a minimum, America's ways were not those of one's own country, religion, or society. At worst, they were thought rotten in their own right. Whether someone was devoted to Spanish, French, or Arabic; Islam, atheism, or Latin American Catholicism; preserving tradition or utopian revolution, America could be said to block their dream of the future or replace it with a nightmare. A different style of anti-Americanism existed for every need or taste. America was too revolutionary and too counterrevolutionary, too elitist and too mass-oriented, too far left and too far right, the friend of one's enemies or the enemy of one's friends.

Along with the fear of American world dominance and the criticism of the United States for its nature or actions was a new poisonous element. According to the old views of anti-Americanism from the nineteenth century through the Cold War, the United States had been a failure despite its apparent success. Its people were miserable and its stability questionable. Yet what happened when these claims were no longer sustainable, when the competing systems collapsed or seemed to be left behind?

A different approach to anti-Americanism developed along the following lines: not only was America a threat to the world, but also its achievements were based not on the virtues of its system, ideas, and institutions but rather on the massive oppression and exploitation of the world. America's higher level of development was at everyone else's expense and, by the same token, the relative failure of others to duplicate it was due to America's sins. Rather than what it was in practice—a reluctant activist in the world—America was portrayed as a vampire whose life depended on sucking others' blood.

This response arose from various nonmainstream Marxist theories, mainly in Germany and France, as well as Third World doctrines pioneered in Latin America and independently developed in the Middle East. Yes, the new perspective agreed, America may have a successful system with relatively happy and well-off people, but its prosperity and joy comes at everyone else's expense. Its success was less the result of hard work and innovation than of theft and oppression. Moreover, by refusing to revolt against the system and actually benefiting from it, the American people, not just a small capitalist class, were the enemy. There was an intriguing hint about this notion from Lenin. American workers, he wrote in 1918, were merely acting as "hired thugs" for the "wealthy scoundrels" who really ran the country.[8]

A comprehensive theory explaining why America was imperialistically different from all other capitalist or Western countries was built by intellectuals, academics, and journalists, sounding like a satire of traditional Soviet doctrine. While the last French anti-American generation had predicted that the United States was an imperialistic menace that would collapse, the task was now to explain how it still survived and flourished. Thus, Emmanuel Todd explained in a 2003 book how the system works: the United States deliberately fosters conflict "wherever it can" because it must keep up an inflow of loot to fund its voracious consumption. "It cannot live without the goods produced by the rest of the planet." So it invents bogus threats to justify its military presence and keep foreign clients in line. The fact that the United States actually runs a constant trade deficit and that military costs, many of which go to protect Europe, are a drain on its economy had no place in this analysis.[9]

It was hard to foresee such trends and ideas developing at the beginning of this era. Despite the total victory in the half-century-long Cold War, the coalition success over Iraq in 1991, and the lack of serious disputes with Europe, a majority—but fewer than might be expected—liked the United States at the start of the 1990s. In 1992, approval stood at only 66 percent in Britain and 51 percent in France.[10] At the same time, when asked whether American culture was a threat to their own, 54 percent in France, 40 percent in Britain, and 38 percent in West Germany said "yes" in 1993. While a 74 percent popularity rating was recorded in Britain that year, the figure in France had fallen to 48 percent.[11]

By 1995, while 78 percent in Italy and 72 percent in Germany had a favorable view of the United States (lower West German figures being increased by the merger with the more pro-American ex-Communist East), popularity in England stood at 62 percent and France at only 55 percent. Sixty-one percent of French people and 50 percent of those in England thought America to be a cultural threat.[12] In 2000, the favorability rating toward the United States stood at 83 percent of Britons, 62 percent of French, 78 percent of Germans, and 76 percent of Italians.[13]

As always, the ridicule of American culture was tightly linked to a fear that these characteristics, ideas, and products were successfully assaulting one's own country. This was even felt in England, where interchanges of ideas and culture with America were most common. In the 1990s (as had happened in the 1950s), the left responded to a pro-American orientation by the Labour Party's centrist leadership with a wave of anti-Americanism.[14] At a debate held at a mid-1990s British literary festival, 40 percent of the crowd supported a motion that "it is the duty of every European to resist American culture."[15]

If other Britons disagreed and decided that they liked American culture or ideas, that choice seemed to others a betrayal that made them even angrier. For if Europeans wanted to adapt such things then the danger of America being the model for the continent's future was a very real one. In the words of one British writer, in an article entitled, "America Has Descended into Madness":

> Every week one [cabinet minister] tells us it is all done far better in the United States before announcing policies to further the Americanization of Britain. We must have their damned highway [system]. . . . What next? U.S.-style justice which leaves the poor and disenfranchised without half-decent lawyers, merciless boot camps and barbaric death chambers? Or a health service which can give you wondrous help if you are middle class but which fails

millions of others who cannot afford to have the right kind of insurance? And schools and neighborhoods grossly divided along race and class lines?[16]

America, once disdained in Britain as too egalitarian, was now savaged for allegedly being the opposite. Often, as in this case, anti-Americanism is put in the context of a losing battle accompanied by bitterness that the "obviousness" of that country's evil nature is not obvious to everyone. In the words of another left-wing British writer in the *Guardian*, the flagship daily of the intellectual class there:

> All around you, you can hear people choosing to ignore the fact that America is greatly responsible for turning the earth into an open sewer—culturally, morally and physically—and harping on instead about American "energy" and "can-do." Of course, nine times out of ten, that energy is the energy of the vandal, psychotic or manic depressive, fuelling acts of barbarism and destruction from My Lai [a massacre by U.S. troops in Vietnam] to Eminem [a rap music singer]; and it's a shame that that legendary can-do usually translates as can-do crime, can-do imperialism and can-do poisoning the seas.[17]

But this was not entirely new. Deploring American popular culture precisely because it was seductively popular had been a mainstay of anti-American complaint for well over a century. Thus, even partaking of Americanism simply reminded one of the danger. Salman Rushdie, the British novelist who himself stirred up a minor anti-American wave among fellow intellectuals when he announced his decision to move from London to New York, remarked, "In most people's heads, globalization has come to mean the worldwide triumph of Nike, the Gap and MTV. . . . We want these goods and services when we behave as consumers, but with our cultural hats on we have begun to deplore their omnipresence."[18]

Indeed, during an anti-American demonstration over the 2003 Iraq war in London, a British journalist recorded her ironic observations along these lines. One student wearing Nike shoes and standing in a long line outside a Starbucks coffee bar told him, "September 11 was the fault of the Americans. They want to rule the world, like, literally, but also with cultural imperialism." A yuppie wearing a hat emblazoned with the name of New York City explained, "I'm marching against hypocrisy: America is the greatest terrorist in the world, but they call their terrorism war." Meanwhile, a hippie type eating a McDonald's hamburger insisted, "Socially, we're not allied with the United States."[19]

Nevertheless, one major reason for American culture's popularity in Europe is that it was something Europeans, regardless of their national origin, could share on an equal basis. It is less divisive to adopt something from the United States than a characteristic cultural product from one European country alone, whose success could be seen as representing that state's domination over a united Europe. For example, using American food, music, or clothes is less politically problematic than, for instance, Germans and Italians adapting the French equivalents.[20] As one expert put it, "There is no pan-European identity among youth" except for American popular culture.[21] "The only true pan-European culture is the American culture," said French television commentator Christine Ockrent.[22] Even the English language—though also, of course, Great Britain's native tongue—is more acceptable for common European use because of its third-party credentials.

Equally, Europeans, especially young people, tend to view the meaning of American ideas or items in a way far different from the mass-produced banality that is all the critics see. As a European student of popular culture puts it, the attraction is one of a "youthful and dynamic life full of excitement, adventure and glamour," providing anti-establishment escapism, "a projection screen for people's fantasies." Thus, for instance, American pop music is a symbol of rebellion to both Third World immigrants and white natives in Europe, an alternative to the existing society.[23]

Those rebelling against the United States intellectually may be simultaneously using America to rebel against their own cultures. It is precisely America's individualism—the opposite of the conformity and standardization alleged by anti-Americans to dominate there—which "offers a way out of everyday boredom" and the "restrictions set by existing social structures."[24] Rather than imposing imperialist and reactionary ideas, the impact of America is to encourage a demand for change at home, which is exactly what is feared, as it has been for two centuries, by those who govern European culture and society.

Missing all these realities, ideologically oriented writers argue that those attracted by American products are victims of an insidious political assault. One such critique claimed that America was like a terrorist using biological weapons to infect progressively larger groups of people until it can seize cultural-intellectual power. Using McDonald's as an example, a sociologist from a British university explains how American products, unlike others, are dangerously addictive and politically subversive: "When the natives start behaving more like the burger [companies] and start infecting themselves with their attitudes and behavior (impatience, obesity, heart disease, etc.), they become even more susceptible to even more American interventions."[25] By this time, they will be too weak to resist the spread of U.S. imperialism.

The real purpose of the "homogenization evidenced by Coca-Cola and McDonald's," according to a sociology professor in Britain, is to universalize dreaded American values and lead to an "end of history" directed by "arrogant American superiority and self-centeredness." The outcome will be a form of global slavery: "The Disneyfication of the world, its transformation to Waltopia, the cocacolonization of the globe, the McDonaldization of society." So predestined is this kind of "analysis" that even the fact that Ford produced a car called Mondeo (world) is simply one more example of the horrifying American view that its products are master of the globe.[26]

"Watch out, the process of globalization, lacking logic and seeking modernity, will inevitable lead us all to McDonald's," warned François Guillaume, member of parliament, former minister, and leader of the agricultural lobby, whose economic interests were damaged by the import of competitive American foodstuffs.[27]

In many ways, the campaign against McDonald's was simply a replay of the post–World War II battle of Coca-Cola.[28] As early as 1986, several thousand Italians demonstrated against the opening of the first McDonald's in Rome as signaling that city's "degradation" and Americanization. In August 1999, this battle greatly escalated when José Bové, French farm activist, trashed a McDonald's under construction in Millau, France. He complained, "McDonald's represents anonymous globalization with little relevance to real food."[29] He was also protesting American sanctions on French farm products in retaliation against a government-imposed ban on the import of hormone-treated American beef and led other protests as well to wreck genetically modified corn and soybean fields managed by a U.S. company.

In France, the stomach was often presented as the main front in the war against American imperialism. France's very identity, though certainly seeming solid to any observer, was allegedly under siege by an objectively inferior but more powerful rival intent on stealing its people's souls, or at least taste buds. Thus, a 1999 anti-American book, *No Thanks, Uncle Sam* written by Noël Mamère and Olivier Warin, accused the United States of trying "to make us gobble up his hormone-fed beef— we, the country of [the world's greatest chefs]."[30]

The argument continues with this oral fixation of outraged patriotism: "We are certainly used to humiliations; our soil is the most regularly invaded of the Western world. But who bites into the Frenchman always ends up finding him too spicy, probably because we season the stuffing: cut into the Gaul, he is copiously filled [with] José Bové."[31] The implication is that the American cultural onslaught is somewhat equivalent to three German invasions.[32]

Compared to the bon vivant French, the Americans are food fools. They are obese people who think only of eating pizza and hamburgers washed down with Coca-Cola. This choice between two items is what passes in America, the authors add sarcastically, for "varying the gastronomy." In exchange for the great French delicacies of foie gras, truffles, shallots, and Roquefort cheese, the Americans offer only to force the French to eat McDonald's beef full of hormones.[33]

But food is just one aspect of the problem; underneath the sauce is the traditional complaint of anti-Americans going back to the earliest days of the United States: "The symbol is McDonald's but the real enemy is the world organization of commerce, the conversion of the whole planet to the American model," Mamère and Warin wrote.[34]

Of course, there is—despite all the talk about bad food—a delicious irony in much of this contemporary America-bashing. There are endless complaints that Americans—in the words of the same French authors— don't "know who we are or where we are, and [don't] give a damn about us." The authors sum up the problem of America's global power in these words: "Omnipotence, added to ignorance: a dreadful cocktail."[35]

Yet such people repeatedly show their own remarkable ignorance about the United States and indifference to its concerns. Ignorance is not an American monopoly.

The same point applies to the real causes and effect of spreading American culture. To hear the anti-Americans speak about it, the future world will be based on Europeans eating breakfast, lunch, and dinner at

McDonald's, as Americans already presumably do. In fact, in most cases, American products simply join the European mix of mildly exotic things one does sometimes. Going for an occasional hamburger is the equivalent change of pace for Europeans as visiting a Chinese restaurant, which also explains why McDonald's has not wiped out all the wide variety of alternative eating places in America.

Even fast-food globalization is not as simple as it has been portrayed. If American companies want to succeed, they must adapt to local tastes rather than force American customs down people's throats. In London, McDonald's sells the McChicken Korma Naan, intended to please local South Asian immigrants. In India, where Hindus eschew beef, there is the lamb Maharaja Mac. In Hong Kong, Starbucks sells green tea cheesecake, while in New Zealand one can get a kidney pie at its outlets.

It is also easy to exaggerate cultural differences between Americans and Europeans, especially since these influences flow in both directions. As an Italian journalist explained, "When I moved to New York as a young Fulbright fellow, there wasn't a single McDonald's in Italy and it was impossible to buy a decent bottle of olive oil or sip a warm cappuccino in Manhattan. Now the McDonald's in my hometown, Palermo, attracts hungry teenagers, but I dress my salad with the dark green olive oil produced in Palermo that's now available all over the United States. And I rate American cappuccinos the best outside the old country."[36]

It is amusing to recall that next to hamburgers, the food probably consumed most at McDonald's is "French fried potatoes," an extremely popular dish from France, where it is called "pommes frites." And, finally, the columnist Thomas Friedman pointed out that while Europeans were shunning U.S.-grown food containing genetic manipulations, "even though there is no scientific evidence that these are harmful," everywhere he looked during a high-level European meeting, they were smoking cigarettes.[37] Moreover, contemporary French anti-Americans are unaware of how their ancestors once ridiculed health consciousness about diet as a silly American affectation.[38]

But the root of the problem was not merely misunderstanding. There was also a large element of old-fashioned economic rivalry involved, in which anti-Americanism was simply a way to run down the competitor. For example, French Defense Minister Michèle Alliot-Marie complained that U.S. Secretary of Defense Donald Rumsfeld allegedly believed that "the United States is the only military, economic and financial power in the world. We do not share this vision." She urged European firms to unite and resist what she called an American "economic war" against them, under French leadership.[39]

Of course, America was criticized over far more than just food, with many issues manipulated to put on it the worst possible light. For example, the use of the death penalty was portrayed as a profoundly revealing factor about the American psyche. Charging that Americans were extraordinarily violent had been a common theme in nineteenth-century anti-Americanism. Now, according to Raymond Forni, chairman of the French National Assembly, the death penalty in the United States was pure "savagery. . . . There used to be slavery, then organized racial segregation. Today there is the death penalty. . . . The country of scientific innovation deploys innovation in the service of death."[40]

One French anthropologist suggested that Americans engaged in human sacrifice because they knew their society was doomed: "Facing the threat of destruction of their social order, modern Americans, like the Aztecs, are terrified by the prospect of an end to the current cosmic cycle. Only the deaths of countless human beings can generate enough energy to counter the danger."[41]

But no one pointed out that the death penalty was a matter of choice by the individual states, not even practiced by a majority of them, and hence told nothing about America in general. Typically, U.S. engagement in a practice was seen as sinful and symptomatic even if others doing it were forgiven and not so stigmatized. For example, a prominent Italian writer exclaimed, "I'll never visit the United States while the death penalty is in effect" but then proceeded to travel to other countries at a time when they used that punishment.[42]

There were, of course, many variations in the causes of anti-Americanism among different countries. For example, the Soviet Union had been the most systematically anti-American country in the world, with such attitudes officially inculcated by every institution over many decades. Thus, when Communism fell, anti-American doctrine was associated with a discredited regime. After a brief interval, however, many of the same historic anti-American themes and arguments were revived.

According to a March–April 1990 poll, as they were only beginning to be able to speak freely, 25 percent of Soviet citizens had a very favorable view and 47 percent a somewhat favorable view of the United States. Only 7 percent had a negative view.[43] In 1994, 70 percent in Moscow and

St. Petersburg were favorable compared to 21 percent negative.[44] Yet while these results were typical, there was also an undercurrent of hostility visible in these polls, with a majority of Russians consistently believing that the United States was seeking world domination while reducing their country to a second-rate power dependent on raw materials' export and Western aid.[45]

In a November 1999 poll, only 4 percent of Russians thought "the West was doing everything possible to help Russia become a civilized and developed state," while 41 percent thought the West wanted Russia to be a weak "Third World" state and 38 percent saw its goal as destroying Russia entirely.[46] Polls taken in 2002 showed that as many people viewed the United States negatively as those who viewed it positively.[47] America was seen as being an alien cultural influence, a rival, and a would-be master.

An article in *Komsomolskaya Pravda* in March 2003 explained that it was now proven to be a myth that the United States was a paragon of virtue that respected human rights. It could now be seen to be a selfish, money-grubbing, oil-stealing war criminal. The American army's performance in Iraq, during the highly successful initial war there, supposedly proved it to be inferior to Russia's forces. And the same issue showed there was no freedom of speech in America because the mass media were obviously censored, despite the unprecedented live coverage of the fighting and the numerous commentators who felt free to criticize U.S. policy on television.[48]

In April 2003, Russians polled said they liked Saddam Hussein by a 22 to 17 percent margin (most were indifferent), but that they disliked George W. Bush by a 76 to 11 percent margin.[49] A poll conducted the following month showed that 44 percent had a "strongly negative or mostly negative" view of the United States, while 46 percent had a positive attitude. Speaking on the anniversary of the 1941 Nazi invasion, former defense minister General Igor Rodionov told war veterans that their own country was now occupied by America. "Our geopolitical enemy has achieved what Hitler wanted to do," he said in an emotional speech. General Andrei Nikolayev, chairman of the parliament's defense committee, warned that the United States was seeking to establish its domination over the world and that no one "would be able to stop the U.S. military machine."[50]

A popular film, *Brat-2*, showed a Russian hitman killing large numbers of Americans, telling his victims, "You've got money and power, and where has it got you? . . . You don't have truth." One hit song was entitled "Kill the Yankee." And sophisticated intellectuals, like economist Mikhail Delyagin, argued that Russia could only survive if it fought the "aggression of the U.S. and its NATO allies against Yugoslavia," a country for which Russians have a special feeling as fellow Slavs.[51]

As in Western Europe, nationalistic self-definition was often being built by invoking the need to battle an American threat and alternative. Not only had this idea been an element of the Russian left, but it also was incipient in the main opposing philosophy of Slavophilism, which exalted the Russian spirit, religion, and culture against a decadent Western counterpart. Although usually focused on Western Europe in the nineteenth century, it had been applied against the United States as early as Dostoyevsky and was taken up by the new Russian political right after the fall of Communism.[52]

The remaining Communists, of course, never changed their view and now even sounded close to the Slavophiles on this issue. The Americans, warned Communist leader Genady Zyuganov in 1996, "are trying to impose on us a style of behavior that does not fit in our character and our uniqueness." But these basic ideas were held far more broadly. Much of the media and even the government began to churn out a systematically anti-American message, including constant accusations of U.S. subversion against Russia.[53]

Very specific local factors are also at work in Greece, which provides a good example of how a mixture of historically "good" and "bad" American actions created hostility toward the United States. In the 1940s, the United States helped Greece defeat a Soviet-backed leftist insurgency. The United States was generally popular thereafter, though not among leftists, for having saved Greek sovereignty. But U.S. support for the 1967–1974 right-wing junta made it unpopular in many quarters, especially—ironically—after the United States refused to back an ill-conceived nationalist plot to seize Cyprus. Once the junta was overthrown, the ruling leftist PASOK party—led by a politician who had lived in the United States for many years and was married to an American—promoted anti-Americanism. In the 1990s, a new issue arose as the United States opposed Yugoslavia, a traditional Greek ally, over its dictatorship's brutal campaign against the Kosovo Muslims.

In the long run, then, Greeks were angry at two American actions that supported the Greek right against the left along with two others that opposed Greek nationalism. In the first category was the U.S. effort to stop a Communist takeover and later to support a military dictatorship in Greece, while the latter included a policy of blocking covert Greek aggression against Cyprus and to prevent massacres of Muslims in Kosovo. Thus, anti-Americanism was promoted by both ends of the Greek political spectrum but merged in a generalized patriotic hostility.

By the post–Cold War 1990s, the main Greek anti-American antagonism was Kosovo, and the main target of Greek anger was President Bill Clinton. Among the epithets flung at Clinton in the mainstream Greek media were criminal, pervert, murderer, imposter, bloodthirsty, gangster, slayer, naïve, criminal, butcher, stupid, killer, foolish, unscrupulous, disgraceful, dishonest, and rascal. One writer claimed, "Clinton is a miserable little Hitler that Adolph himself would not have made him even deputy commander of an army camp, because [Clinton] is stupid."[54]

This barrage of hatred was directed at Clinton's imminent visit to Greece in November 1999. A broad coalition of leftists declared this "representative of American imperialist policy" unwelcome because he would "contaminate the sanctified . . . soil of our motherland." Clinton was "a murderer of people, ideals, values, beauty and life," who aspired to be "the lord of the planet." Despite Clinton's apology for past U.S. backing for the junta, violent demonstrations erupted against his visit.[55]

The upsurge of anti-Americanism in the 1990s was strong in the Middle East and well under way in Europe before President George W. Bush took office in January 2001, before the terror attacks of September 11, 2001, happened, and before his administration began to talk about attacking Iraq during 2002. Bush's policies certainly further fed foreign suspicions of America—his rejection of a strong international court and environmental agreements, for example—and his personality and how it was perceived played a big role in setting the negative attitude toward him and intensifying it against America.

Many Americans who didn't vote for Bush also regarded him with disdain, but it would be hard to invent a person more likely than Bush to further inflame already rising anti-Americanism in Europe. Aside from any of his actual policies, he fit many of the main historic negative stereotypes that Europeans and others held about the United States. For a start, he came from Texas, the purported land of the cowboy and death penalty, and had a drawl, which played into European prejudices about cowboys and violent, ignorant, impulsive frontiersmen.

Definitely not an intellectual and hardly erudite or articulate, Bush appeared in every way a European intellectual's worst nightmare. As a conservative, Bush grated on the left-leaning sensibilities of these same people. Yet, ironically, it was his rejection of a traditionally conservative, realpolitik foreign policy that convinced his European critics that he was a virulent nationalist embarked on a drive for world conquest.

Whatever its basis in reality, the European image of Bush was drawn and exaggerated from the historical litany of anti-American charges. He was said to be an "ignorant, self-righteous Christian warrior," "smirking executioner," and "Toxic Texan." In this context, European intellectuals thought Bush to be a dangerous fool and madman. His professed religiosity was still another negative that fit the European stereotype of Americans as religious fanatics. And Bush's "just folks" manner was a feature of anti-American derision toward U.S. politicians going back to the early nineteenth century. He also came into office at a time when some Europeans were ready to view the United States as a threat replacing the USSR, and thus some found that "today's Washington has a whiff of Soviet ways; suffocating internal discipline, resentment of even reasoned, moderate opposition, and a refusal to admit even the tiniest error."[56]

But even before Bush had a chance to do anything, he was already classified in a hostile manner. When Bush was elected, a *Le Monde* headline called him the "global village idiot."[57] The mass-circulation British newspaper the *Daily Mirror*, which played up Bush's role as governor in a state that frequently used the death penalty, asked, "Do we really want a man like him making snap decisions on whether to drop bombs or go to war? Do we really like the idea of his finger on the big trigger? No, we don't." Bush, it continued, "is a thoroughly dangerous, unpleasant piece of work who shouldn't be let anywhere near the White House."[58]

Yet, ironically, it was his rejection of a traditionally conservative, realpolitik foreign policy that most convinced his European critics that he was a virulent nationalist embarked on a drive for world conquest. Bush's policies, from his early stance on agreements concerning an international court and environmental agreements to the Iraq war seemed to be flaunting and using his nation's power in a way that disregarded European viewpoints. It could be made to appear that this was at last the U.S. drive to world rule so long predicted by anti-Americans and which could be made to seem both logical and possible now that the United States was the world's sole superpower. Of course, this did not mean U.S. policies were necessarily wrong, they were also defined both by events—especially September 11—and a lack of European cooperation on key issues as well.

There was, however, another man more accurately described as a wild-eyed extremist ready to use any form of violence to further his own plan for world conquest, Usama bin Ladin. The attacks of September 11, 2001, simultaneously unleashed a wave of pro-American sympathy and anti-Americanism in Europe and everywhere else around the world.

To put it bluntly, many people, and not just in the Middle East, liked the terrorist assault. Some delighted at the blow against America because it was so evil, and hoped that this was the start of some new form of global revolution. Others, in their voyeuristic revenge, were happy that America was suffering because it was so powerful. Indeed, one hallmark of the anti-American reaction to September 11 was that it almost always came from people reacting against alleged injuries to others, very few of those who most felt and expressed hatred had suffered directly due to the United States.

An international poll of opinion makers worldwide two months after September 11 found that more than half of those outside the United States agreed that American policies in the world were a major cause of the attacks, and two-thirds agreed with the idea that it was "good that Americans now know what it's like to be vulnerable."[59] And, of course, there were also voices within the United States that said the same thing.

The attitude of either rejoicing in or rationalizing the September 11 attack was an especially powerful one in France. In Paris, right-wingers in the National Front Party drank champagne and cheered while watching the World Trade Center crash down. Elsewhere in that city, some leftists in the audience heckled a call by Communist Party national secretary Robert Hue for three minutes of silence in memory of the victims.[60] Such attitudes were reflected, albeit with more elegance, at the highest levels of the French intellectual and cultural establishment. Prime Minister Lionel Jospin hinted that there was some merited punishment in the attacks.[61]

Any such criticism was quite hypocritical, since bin Ladin would have been arguably more "justified" in destroying the Eiffel Tower as revenge for France's energetic backing of Algeria's military regime, a far more active intervention against Islamist rebels than any American involvement in such internal Arab battles. On such matters, there was a European double standard in judging America. No Europeans suggested that their own past colonialism or current interventions proved their societies had an evil character.

Ironically, the most famous French pro-American statement about September 11 demonstrated the broad extent of anti-American hostility in the country. A *Le Monde* editorial of September 12, by publisher Jean-Marie Colombiani, was entitled, "Nous Sommes Tous Américains" (We Are All Americans). In the article he asked, "Indeed, just as in the gravest moments of our own history, how can we not feel profound solidarity with those people, that country, the United States, to whom we are so close and to whom we owe our freedom, and therefore our solidarity?"[62] It provoked criticism by many in France as being too sympathetic toward the United States.

But even in this article, Colombiani suggested that the United States itself created bin Ladin. A few months later, he wrote a book, *Tous Américains? Le monde après le 11 Septembre 2001* (Are We All Americans? The World After September 11, 2001), questioning his own earlier thesis and unleashing the usual range of caricatures and charges, many of which had aged far longer than the finest French wines. For him, the United States was a country that violates all the world's laws, glories in the death penalty, and treats its own minorities in a racist fashion. What especially galls him is his vision of America as a fundamentalist Christian state, which is no better than fundamentalist Muslim ones. For him, September 11 clearly changed nothing and taught him nothing.

The same could be said for Jean Baudrillard, who wrote on November 3, 2001, in *Le Monde* that the perpetrators of September 11 had acted out his and "all the world['s] without exception" dream of destroying "a power that has become hegemonic. . . . It is they who acted, but we who wanted the deed."[63] Others, like the respected philosopher Jacques Derrida, found September 11 to be a "symptom" of globalization, which itself was an American sin.[64]

Yet such ideas arose from a European view of the United States with no connection to the actual motives of those involved in the attacks. Bin Ladin and his men were not acting as they did to fight globalization but to promote a radical Islamist revolution as a way of forcing their own brand of globalization on the world by force.

If there was anything further needed to prove the mad eagerness of many to blame September 11 on the United States and to create a European ideology justifying an anti-American jihad, it was provided by one Thierry Meyssan, a member of the far-right French lunatic fringe. Meyssan wrote a book entitled *L'Effroyable Imposture* (The Horrifying Fraud), which claimed that September 11 was in fact a propaganda stunt by American intelligence agencies and the military-industrial complex to justify military intervention in Afghanistan and Iraq.

This book became a gigantic commercial success in France and other European countries, with Meyssan also being lionized in the Arab world. But even while few in the West—the Arab world was a different story— believed that the United States faked the attacks, Meyssan's idea that September 11 was a mere excuse for advancing the American goal of world domination was widely accepted by anti-Americans in Europe.

Still, what could be more shocking than the fact that German polls showed that 20 percent of the population—rising to 33 percent among those below the age of thirty—believed the U.S. government might have sponsored the attacks on itself?[65] In April 2002, only 48 percent of Germans considered the United States a guarantor of world peace compared with 62 percent who did so in 1993. Meanwhile, 47 percent considered the U.S. war on terrorism as aggressive, with only 34 percent seeing it as justified.[66]

The following year, *The CIA and September 11*, published by a reputable German company and written by former minister of research and technology Andreas von Bulow, suggested that U.S. and Israeli intelligence blew up the World Trade Center from the inside, with the planes being a mere distraction. The motive was an American conservative plot to take over the world. The book was also soon on the best-seller list, as were left-wing American writings that made similar accusations. In June 2003, a German government-run television station broadcast a documentary challenging the American version of September 11. In cover stories with titles like "Blood for Oil" and "Warriors of God," the German newsweekly *Der Spiegel* described U.S. policy as a conspiracy to control the world fomented and led by the oil industry or Christian right-wingers.[67] Not to be outdone, a *Stern* magazine cover showed an American missile piercing the heart of a dove of peace.[68]

While less widespread than in France, partly because leftist intellectuals have less influence there, or Germany, parallel themes were developed in Britain after September 11. Chelsea Clinton, daughter of the former president who was working on her master's degree there, wrote, "Every day at some point I encounter some sort of anti-American feeling."[69]

That she felt this way is not surprising when scholars of the caliber of Mary Beard—a Cambridge University academic specializing in the classics, not contemporary affairs—explained, "The United States had it coming. . . . World bullies, even if their heart is in the right place, will in the end pay the price."[70] Anatole Kaletsky, chief economic correspondent for the *Times,* claimed, "The greatest danger to America's dominant position today is not Islamic fundamentalism. It is the arrogance of American power."[71]

Mary Kaldor, a professor at London School of Economics, came close to Meyssan's position: "It could be argued that if September 11 had not happened, the American military-industrial complex might have had to invent it. Indeed, what happened on September 11 could have come out of what seemed to be the wild fantasies of 'asymmetric threats' that were developed by American strategic analysts as they sought a new military role for the United States after the end of the Cold War."[72]

Mainstream politicians were also driven to crackpot extremes. Member of parliament and former environmental minister Michael Meacher insisted that the September 11 attacks were definitely known about in advance by the U.S. government and possibly even planned by America. The U.S. goal was to use this as an excuse to seek to dominate space and cyberspace, overthrow China and Iran, and permanently occupy the Persian Gulf region to secure the globe's oil fields. It was nothing short of "a blueprint for U.S. world domination" using the "bogus cover" of a "so-called 'war on terrorism.' "[73]

The flavor of such thought can also be gleaned by an extended quotation from *Guardian* columnist Charlotte Raven, who explained:

> The United States might benefit from an insight into what it feels like to be knocked to your knees by a faceless power deaf to everything but the logic of its own crazed agenda. There's nothing shameful about this position. It is perfectly possible to condemn the terrorist action and dislike the US just as much as you did before. . . .

If anti-Americanism has been seized, temporarily, by forces that have done dreadful things in its name, there is no reason for its adherents to retreat from its basic precepts. America is the same country it was before September 11. If you didn't like it then, there's no reason why you should have to pretend to now. All those who see its suffering as a kind of absolution should remember how little we've seen that would support this reading. A bully with a bloody nose is still a bully and, weeping apart, everything the US body politic has done in the week since the attacks has confirmed its essential character.[74]

In other words, anti-Americanism was too important to leave in the hands of the terrorists. It should return to the control of those responsible people who recognized that the United States was evil but were not themselves seeking to seize the globe on behalf of radical Islamism.

Such people were clearly not going to allow the United States to prove itself not guilty of these charges. The supposed proof that the United States was an imperialist aggressor, well before any debate began about a war with Iraq, was that it retaliated against those directly responsible for the attack. Every action in self-defense was taken as proof of their assertions, despite the dignified and determinedly antihysterical American reaction to the September 11 attacks, which included a strong rejection of prejudice against any people or religion—as, of course, the critics were doing to the United States—which actually disproved them.

As for the record of bullying, the United States at this point had spent more than the previous dozen years encouraging democracy in Latin America and a longer period without coercive intervention there. The same point applied to Asia and Africa, where the main U.S. effort was involved in humanitarian missions as in Somalia. In the Middle East, the main evidence for supposed U.S. bullying would have been its leadership of an international coalition against Iraq's aggression in 1991. It had expended extraordinary energy to resolve the Arab-Israeli conflict through compromise. In Europe, its involvements had largely been those of leading a multinational effort to protect groups—and Muslim ones at that—in Bosnia and Kosovo.

Raven condemns the United States for offering its own view of the events as proof that it is allegedly guilty of an imperialist attempt to "control meaning," and she is angry because the United States wanted to go "into a war [against terrorism] that doesn't exist."[75] Yet it had been bin Ladin, and his ally the Afghan government, which had declared war on the United States. Before September 11, far from being a bullying state, the United States had done little to respond to that assault. And if no such war existed, what in fact had happened on September 11? Indeed, the true war that did not exist was that purportedly being waged by the United States against the rest of humanity, the phony war of an alleged American drive for world domination.

In Latin America, one rarely found such sentiments, but they were most evident in Brazil, where the eminent economist Celso Furtado termed the September 11 attack a provocation by right-wing Americans to justify seizing power, as had the Nazis in Germany in 1933. The prominent theologian Leonardo Boff said he was sorry more planes hadn't crashed into the Pentagon. Even the country's president, the socialist Fernando Henrique Cardoso, told a cheering French parliament, "Barbarism is not only the cowardliness of terrorism but also the intolerance or the imposition of unilateral policies on a global scale." His audience knew who he was bashing. Cardoso, a French-educated veteran advocate of the view that the United States was responsible for Latin American underdevelopment, had also been frequently feted in America and received honorary degrees from Notre Dame and Rutgers universities. In a September 2001 poll, 79 percent of Brazilians opposed any military attack by the United States against countries that hosted those responsible for the destruction of the World Trade Center, with higher levels of opposition among the wealthiest.[76]

Such ideas were heard even from Canada, America's northern neighbor, though Prime Minister Jean Chrétien, in sharp contrast to many European statements, blamed the whole West generally for responsibility regarding the attack: "You cannot exercise your powers to the point of humiliation for the others. That is what the Western world—not only the Americans, the Western world—has to realize. . . . I do think that the Western world is getting too rich in relation to the poor world and necessarily will be looked upon as being arrogant and self-satisfied, greedy and with no limits. The 11th of September is an occasion for me to realize it even more."[77]

The fact that the attackers were mostly from well-off families and came, as did their political movement as a whole, from Saudi Arabia, the Third World's richest country, did not seem to affect his judgment. Part of the problem was that the critics reinterpreted the attack as a symptom of whatever complaints they had about the United States and its policies. Blaming the United States for the attack and denying it the right to self-defense were unfriendly actions reflecting hostility rather than some deeper wisdom.

Since the September 11 attack clearly originated with Usama bin Ladin, the United States had every right to respond with military action against him and his cooperating host, the Taliban government in Afghanistan. To the anti-Americans, however, this was an act of aggression. The attribution of responsibility to bin Ladin was doubted, the domestic oppression caused by the Taliban was ignored, American motives were called into question, and the worst possible face was put on the conduct of the war.

When the Taliban did fall in December 2001, the French radio correspondents at the scene spent more time attacking the United States for behaving in an imperial way and accusing American journalists of collaborating in this effort. They explained that claims that Afghans did not support the Taliban regime were an example of American propaganda. One common motive for anti-Americanism, jealousy, was in full display as the French reporters bitterly complained that their American counterparts arrived "with pockets full of dollars," which enabled them to rent helicopters and hire the best interpreters.[78]

Matters were somewhat different regarding the U.S. decision to go to war with Iraq in 2003. Whether or not the attack was warranted, this was a policy that certainly did feed into anti-American preconceptions that had already become quite powerful. It could be said to show that the United States was too powerful, ignored others' wishes or interests, and appeared eager to attack foreign countries. But the infusion of a massive dose of anti-Americanism into the debate made the opposition more passionate and hostile, and interfered with efforts to find someway to avoid the crisis or increase international cooperation to deal with it.

Of course, even in the United States, the war was most controversial and condemned by many, sometimes in terms similar to those heard in Europe or the Middle East. Yet once any of the actual motives for the United States to confront Iraq were dismissed, it was easy for people in many countries to see themselves as the potential victim of America. In this sense, the invasion of Iraq, having nothing to do with any element of the misdeeds of Saddam Hussein's regime, came to be seen as a precedent for the future conquest of any other given country in the world.

The extreme response was to accuse the United States of engaging in an imperialist action to steal Iraqi oil as another step in its plan for world domination. Another theme was that this was an action against the Iraqi people, who were in fact suffering under perhaps the world's worst dictatorship. Ironically, one of the main accusations against the United States by anti-Americans had been that it was indifferent to the depredations of such regimes. Anti-American critics played down the Saddam Hussein regime's misdeeds, a tremendous irony for those portraying themselves as defenders of human rights and freedom. Throughout Europe, antiwar demonstrations turned into hate-America rallies. A study of the five main French newspapers' coverage of the Iraq War showed twenty-nine headlines condemning Saddam's dictatorship and 135 blaming Bush for the conflict.[79]

At times, whipping up hysteria—as opposed to disagreeing with U.S. policy in a constructive manner—was related to cynical partisan considerations. This approach was clearly true in the September 2002 German election. The victory of Chancellor Gerhard Schroeder, who had been suffering during the campaign because of the country's poor economy, was probably due to his demagogic anti-American appeals. Among other things, Schroeder made a nationalist appeal by stating that to go along with the American policy would make Germany a puppet of the United States. His justice minister, Herta Daeubler-Gmelin, went so far as to compare Bush to Adolf Hitler, which in Germany was no mere rhetorical flourish.[80]

Indeed, Schroeder's German Social Democratic Party became a consistent sponsor of anti-Americanism. Ludwig Stiegler, a member of parliament, likened Bush to an imperialist Roman emperor bent on subjugating Germany. Oskar Lafontaine, the party's deputy co-chairman, called the United States "an aggressor nation." Rudolf Hartnung, chairman of the youth organization, accused the United States of "ideologically inspired genocide" in Central America and other places. State legislator Jurgen Busack claimed, "The warmongers and international arsonists do not govern in the Kremlin. They govern in Washington. The United States must lie, cheat, and deceive in an effort to thwart resistance to its insane foreign policy adventures."[81]

Anti-Americanism had become a coherent ideology, which seemed to have replaced Marxism as the left's dominant idea. The U.S. government, Tariq Ali explained, had long previously planned world domination and then "utilized the national trauma of September 11 to pursue an audacious imperial agenda, of which the occupation of Iraq promises to be only the first step." Iraq was seized in order to profit from its oil assets and benefit Israel.[82]

More broadly, the goal was to intimidate the rest of the world so that it would be subservient to American orders. In Ali's summary, "Just as the use of nuclear weapons in Hiroshima and Nagasaki had once been a pointed demonstration of American might to the Soviet Union, so today a blitzkrieg rolling swiftly across Iraq would serve to show the world at large, and perhaps states in the Far East—China, North Korea, even Japan—in particular, that if the chips are down, the United States has, in the last resort, the means to enforce its will."[83]

The real goal, according to Ali, was a classically imperialist one: "The United States is now deciding it wants to run the world. The United States should come out openly and say to the world, 'We are the only imperial power, and we're going to rule you, and if you don't like it you can lump it.' American imperialism has always been the imperialism that has been frightened of speaking its name. Now it's beginning to do so. In a way, it's better. We know where we kneel."[84]

There was also a seemingly less extreme, but roughly similar, anti-American version of events that had wider credibility. It began by saying that the United States was not a crazed, world-conquering nation but merely one with a bad government at the present time. But while Bush at first appears to be the target, the argument soon moved into a blanket condemnation of U.S. policies over a very long period.

This approach was exemplified, for example, by the *Guardian* columnist George Monboit. The United States, he said, had no right to wage "war on another nation because that nation has defied international law." He charged the Bush administration with having "torn up more international treaties and disregarded more United Nations' conventions than the rest of the world has in 20 years." This list included the Bush administration's rejection of agreements on biological, chemical, and nuclear tests. But Monboit then went on to accuse the United States of illegal experimentation with biological weapons, assassinating foreign leaders, and torturing prisoners.[85]

While he was apparently just criticizing the Bush administration's specific policies, the article is entitled "The Logic of Empire," viewing this as the logical goal of American society. This is the classical anti-Americanism that views its imperialist drive as an inevitable outcome of its structure:

> The United States also possesses a vast military-industrial complex that is in constant need of conflict in order to justify its staggeringly expensive existence. Perhaps more importantly than any of these factors, the hawks who control the White House perceive that perpetual war results in the perpetual demand for their services. And there is scarcely a better formula for perpetual war, with both terrorists and other Arab nations, than the invasion of Iraq. The hawks know that they will win, whoever loses. In other words, if the United States was not preparing to attack Iraq, it would be preparing to attack another nation. The United States will go to war with that country because it needs a country with which to go to war.[86]

Thus, the ostensible reasons for the war have nothing to do with it. The cause is a thirst for killing and conquest that America's survival— and the employment needs of certain individuals—require. This is a classic statement of anti-Americanism because it argues that the United States is integrally and inevitably evil. As a result, the people of France did not just oppose the war; many of them also hoped for a U.S. defeat. According to an April 2003 poll, 34 percent supported the U.S.-led forces, 25 percent wanted Iraq to win, and 31 percent declared themselves neutral.[87]

The key element in all this discussion was not so much opposition to the Iraq War based on the immediate issues but a generalized antagonism toward the United States. In the popular BBC radio show, *Straw Poll*, on July 26, 2002, Professor Mary Kaldor debated *Washington Post* reporter T. R. Reid on whether "American power is the power of the good." She argued that the U.S. role as the sole superpower was a danger to the rest of the world. At the end of the program, 70 percent of the studio audience said it agreed with her.[88]

When it came to the purer expressions of hatred, however, this was best expressed by literary figures who do not require even the most basic forms of alleged proof for their inflammatory claims. Harold Pinter, one of Britain's leading playwrights, put his view of the perpetually evil American into verse in "God Bless America, Here They Go Again." The war in Iraq is just one more example of "The Yanks in their armored parade," singing with joy "as they gallop across the big world/Praising America's God." The streets are full of bodies from those they have murdered, mutilated, brutalized, and massacred.[89]

America is thus prodded into mass murder by its fanatical religious beliefs that take joy in killing and destruction. Viewing Americans as a nation of religious nuts is as common among European anti-Americans as seeing the United States as a country of atheists who hate the deity is for Middle Eastern critics.

Arguing that the United States was wrong on any given issue was certainly a fair response, but often the point being made—and requiring major distortions of the facts—was that something intrinsically wrong with America caused the real or alleged shortcomings. It was blind, ignorant, and aggressive, driven by religious fanaticism and greedy imperialism. Perhaps most of all, it was different, not subject to the kinds of motives and ideas that shaped civilized Europe.

America was retaliating to terrorist attacks in Iraq because, according to an Italian writer, it was driven by the "Christian God of the army of the righteous" and was about to invade Iran mainly because it had the capability to do so.[90] A colleague suggested that the U.S. goal in Iraq was "to show the UN and Europe that the control of the entire world is firmly in American hands."[91]

The British novelist John Le Carré engages in an only slightly more sophisticated frothing by seeing the United States both as a serial murderer as well as a society whose repression is on a plane with that of Saddam Hussein. It is an approach merging critiques of U.S. foreign policy and domestic society into one big imperialist package:

> America has entered one of its periods of historical madness, but this [one is] . . . worse than McCarthyism, worse than the Bay of Pigs and in the long term potentially more disastrous than the Vietnam War. As in McCarthy times, the freedoms that have made America the envy of the world are being systematically eroded. The combination of compliant U.S. media and vested corporate inter-

ests is once more ensuring that a debate that should be ringing out in every town square is confined to the loftier columns of the East Coast press. . . .

But the American public is not merely being misled. It is being browbeaten and kept in a state of ignorance and fear. The carefully orchestrated neurosis should carry Bush and his fellow conspirators nicely into the next election. The religious cant that will send American troops into battle is perhaps the most sickening aspect of this surreal war-to-be. What is at stake is not an Axis of Evil—but oil, money and people's lives. Saddam's misfortune is to sit on the second biggest oilfield in the world. Bush wants it, and who helps him get it will receive a piece of the cake. And who doesn't, won't.

What is at stake is not an imminent military or terrorist threat, but the economic imperative of U.S. growth. What is at stake is America's need to demonstrate its military power to all of us—to Europe and Russia and China, and poor mad little North Korea, as well as the Middle East; to show who rules America at home, and who is to be ruled by America abroad.[92]

America, then, is a society that lies as systematically abroad as it does at home. Being struck by the largest single terrorist attack in world history has no bearing on its motives. Its very nature forces it into an imperialist role, the type of idea that would previously have been expressed only by doctrinaire Communists. The American media, which featured a massive discussion over every aspect of the U.S. response to September 11, including a heated debate over the prospective Iraq War, is merely a captive organ on the level of the Soviet press. The overwhelming conformity and lack of real freedom that nineteenth-century anti-Americans claimed characterized the United States are still mainstays of the critique. In short, the ignorance of America, a constant feature of anti-Americanism for two centuries, has not diminished among major groups of European intellectuals.

Indeed, bizarre interpretations of the American domestic scene were very much a factor in the anti-Americanism around the Iraq War. In England, an American journalist was asked on one show whether he saw "any parallels between the security state that George Bush has created in

America since 9/11 and the Gulag." Another British interviewer asked whether people in America are often arrested for insulting the president on the Internet.[93]

Canada, located right next door to the United States, might be expected to have a better understanding of such things. Indeed, hostility there is lower and more reasoned. While 53 percent of Canadians held unfavorable attitudes toward the U.S. government in 2003, 70 percent thought favorably about Americans, while 62 percent had a very or somewhat favorable view of the United States.[94]

Yet, at the same time, Canada has a specific problem in regard to its ten-times-more-populated neighbor. Whatever the differences between the two countries, they are close enough in language, history, and customs that Canada must define itself as the "un-America" to have any identity at all. Canada's self-image is that of a kinder, gentler nation that is nice to people around the world, is environmentally conscious, and has a more sedate pace of life. In a book published in 2003, *Fire and Ice*, Michael Adams assures his fellow citizens that the two countries were moving in opposite directions. Americans were becoming more socially conservative, fat, and deferential to authority figures. Meanwhile, Canadians were becoming more tolerant, open to risk, and willing to question the institutions that governed them.

In intellectual and media circles, however, Canadian attitudes toward the United States do not always display such high levels of tolerance. These are the groups that are on the front lines of defining Canada's difference from the United States, since, otherwise, they had no marginal advantage over their more powerful American competitors. Like European counterparts, they evince a great deal of fear, jealousy, and resentment. The Canadian novelist Margaret Drabble is typical of a large element of this group's opinions; she wrote in February 2003:

My anti-Americanism has become almost uncontrollable. It has possessed me, like a disease. It rises up in my throat like acid reflux, that fashionable American sickness. I now loathe the United States and what it has done to Iraq and the rest of the helpless world. I have tried to control my anti-Americanism, remembering the many Americans that I know and respect, but I can't keep it down any longer. I detest Disneyfication, I detest Coca-Cola, I detest burgers,

I detest sentimental and violent Hollywood movies that tell lies about history. I detest American imperialism, American infantilism, and American triumphalism about victories it didn't even win.[95]

In Australia, too, where the government supported U.S. policy on Iraq, the parliamentary debate revealed hatred and resentment far beyond this specific issue, as demonstrated by the title of a book by Richard Neville, *Amerika Psycho: Behind Uncle Sam's Mask of Sanity*. Such attitudes were amply demonstrated in parliamentary debates. Australians "are sick and tired of this government's compliance with every demand the United States makes," said Australian Member of Parliament Martin Ferguson. Fellow MP Julia Irwin complained, "In the empire of the United States of America, are we to be merely citizens of a vassal state . . . not as a proud and independent nation but as a deputy sheriff to the United States; a mercenary force at the bidding of the president?" Leader of the Australian Labor Party and MP Mark Latham added, "Along with most Australians, I do not want a world in which one country has all the power." And Harry Quick remarked, "The dilemma facing the world is that America has a caricature of a Wild West gun-toting Texas bounty hunter masquerading as a U.S. president and desperate for a rerun of the Gulf War."[96]

Here were several of contemporary anti-Americanism's basic themes. Any support for the United States was subservience, a complaint that combined hurt national pride and a partisan opposition effort to score points against one's own government for doing so. Using the crudest stereotypes of the United States, critics claimed that America was an irrational state lusting for war and world dominance.

Clearly, the problem here is not just the Iraq War, regardless of how much that specific event inspired expressions of anti-Americanism or seemed to provide proof of its claims, or even the personality of George W. Bush. These attitudes were caught up in traditional views of America, the struggle to maintain one's own national identity, the left's search for some new political doctrine, the snobbishness of an elite that hated mass culture, fear of American power, and many other factors.

Of course, America had its defenders, in part inspired by the extremism of the critical barrage and not necessarily because of support for the Iraq war. The Italian writer Oriana Fallaci celebrated American impudence, courage, optimism, geniality, and integrity:

I compliment the respect [the American] has for common people and for the wretched, the ugly, the despised. I envy the infinite patience with which he bears the offenses and the slander. I praise the marvelous dignity and even humility with which he faces his incomparable success, I mean the fact that in only two centuries he has become the absolute winner. . . . And I never forget that [if the United States] hadn't . . . defeated Hitler today I would speak German. Had he not held back the Soviet Union, today I would speak Russian.[97]

The British journalist Gavin Esler added that the caricatures of America had exceeded all bounds. He questioned whether there were many Americans who matched the image of fat and lazy, gun-obsessed people who are loud and arrogant and who seek to dominate the world. Observing the daily fare of the British media, Esler pointed out, "Americans are the only people for whom it is acceptable to have negative stereotypes, modern-day Nazis with cowboy boots instead of jackboots." It was a no-win situation for the United States, since if Americans "do nothing about the world's problems . . . they are ignorant and isolationist, selfish and gutless," while if they do try to act, "they are arrogant and naive, greedy and bullying."[98]

Even in France, there were those who defended the United States. The leading French intellectual Bernard-Henri Lévy recorded that whatever one thinks of any specific mistaken policy,

America does not threaten peace in the world. Peace in the world is threatened by North Korea, Usama bin Ladin, by the Pakistani jihadist groups and maybe its secret services, by the terrorist organizations financed by Saudi Arabia. No, you can't say America threatens the peace of the world without a certain hatred that makes you completely blind and deaf to reality. . . .

Certainly, America has its faults and has committed its share of tragic errors. But that is not the issue. . . . Anti-American sentiment we see today, not only in Europe but in the world at large, hates not what is bad in America but what is good. . . . What they hate is democracy. They hate sexual freedom and the rights of women. They hate tolerance. They hate the separation of religion and state. They hate modernity.[99]

What contemporary anti-Americanism really represented, he concluded, was the structuring passion for "the worst perversities of our time," including the contemporary manifestations of fascism, communism, and Islamism.

Indeed, for two centuries anti-Americanism had always represented something more than merely a critique of the United States, a specific political position in opposition to what that country was seen as representing. At times, the focus might be on a specific policy or feature of American society that might well be worth criticizing.

Yet there were also long-term themes that were merely applied, often without serious examination, to some current situation. Such an approach might involve an assault on real or purported American values, exaggerated or inaccurate stereotypes about the United States itself, or distortions about the facts or motives regarding U.S. policies. There was also the factor of self-interest on the part of the anti-Americans themselves, who used the doctrine as a weapon to promote the interests of a group, party, or state.

Despite the effect of contemporary personalities and issues that heightened it still further, the upsurge of anti-Americanism following the end of the Cold War and enhanced by September 11 was a natural continuation—a fulfillment, as it were—of a trend that can be traced back two centuries.

AN EXPLICABLE UNPOPULARITY

Back to the days of Franklin and Jefferson, Americans have always cared deeply about their international image. "A nation whose citizens seek popularity more than any other kind of success [finds] it . . . galling (and inexplicable) [to be] so extensively unpopular."[1] Thus wrote the French writer Jacques Barzun in his popular 1965 book about America.

Even Alexander Solzhenitsyn, the Russian writer who had his own withering and angry criticisms of American society, noted in 1978 how hurtful and apparently inexplicable anti-Americanism could seem. "The United States has shown itself to be the most magnanimous, the most generous country in the world. . . . And what do we hear in reply? Reproaches, curses. American cultural centers are burned, and the representatives of the Third World [are eager] to vote against the United States."[2]

In general, there have been two distinct American responses to this supposedly paradoxical hatred of America. Most commonly, there is a sense of anger and annoyance coupled with curiosity. How could people be so antagonistic to a country of such decent intentions and frequent successes? How can the good side of America at home and the positive things it has done internationally be so ignored? This must arise from hostility to America's basic values such as democracy, free enterprise, and liberty.

The alternative view is that the hatred is deserved, a result of bad American policies. For this group, the criticisms are generally accurate, though perhaps exaggerated. Indeed, much of the ammunition for contemporary anti-Americanism—so clearly visible in European bookstores and publications—comes from the statements and writings of U.S. citizens who dislike many aspects of their own country.

Consequently, the debate over anti-Americanism's meaning and what to do about it has been structured between these two conceptions. In the former case, the response has been to fight (with words or other means) those who attack America while trying to explain the country's case better. The contrary position is that changing U.S. policies will inevitably dissipate antagonism. While both arguments have many valid things to say, this values-versus-policy debate is ultimately sterile, simultaneously marked by extreme partisanship and the omission of far too many factors that better explain anti-Americanism.

Neither school of thought pays serious attention to the structural and political uses of anti-Americanism or to its historical development. The United States has been hated neither solely because of its nature nor due to its deeds. To begin with, both American policy and values must be interpreted by others. Why do some put the most negative possible light on these things? In other words, anti-Americans may deride policies and values in ways that so distort them as to transform both into made-up stereotypes and monsters. The opposition, then, is not to the American values and policies that actually exist but to the stupid or evil things they appear as in these caricatures.

If the problem is American policies, then why has anti-Americanism been so continuous over time, repeating the same false claims in dramatically different circumstances? If the problem is American values, then why is it that those supporting relatively similar values, notably in Europe, are often the most hostile? The story of anti-Americanism recounted in this book raises many other points, showing that neither of these two largely ahistorical approaches accounts for the facts.

If there is any central factor explaining the power, durability, and multiple variations of anti-Americanism, it is one that has existed going back to the birth of the United States and even earlier: America has always been perceived as a unique society that provides a potential role model for others and is a likely candidate to be the globe's dominant force in political, economic, social, and cultural terms.

Were this not true, anti-Americanism would have been unnecessary or at least thoroughly unimportant. If the United States was just another country, one's attitude toward it mattered little and that nation required no special attention. But if America represented a different way of life and a system that might prove the basis for the world's future, that was a matter of the greatest importance that demanded the most intense scrutiny and passion.

There were three ways that anti-Americans thought the United States would become the main force to shape human civilization and how others lived; these go back as far as 1750, long before the word "globalization" was ever invented:

First, the United States would seem so attractive to foreign observers due to its innovations and success that others would copy it.

Second, American culture, technology, products, and ideas would spread actively throughout the world so as to become everywhere pervasive.

Third, U.S. military and economic power would dominate other countries directly, an idea that was strongly in evidence in anti-American thinking before the United States had much influence on the international scene.

Despite the differing emphases of various individuals, movements, and countries, these three factors were virtually always present. By the twenty-first century, they seemed omnipresent. The long-held prophecy of America's centrality to the world's future seemed to be coming true. On this point, the European and Middle East perspectives are surprisingly close. In 2004, the percentage of those believing that the United States sent forces into Iraq in order to dominate the world was 53 percent in France, 47 percent in Germany, 55 percent in Pakistan, 60 percent in Morocco, and 61 percent in Jordan.[3]

Only this belief in the idea that America presented a unique threefold threat to the world can explain why anti-Americanism became a consistently important idea in history when there was never any coherent doctrine of anti-Britishism, anti-Frenchism, anti-Russianism, or anti-

Germanism. These other countries had actively sought global hegemony, aggressively exported their cultures, built empires, started wars, and killed people around the planet. Yet no one felt the need to write thousands of books and articles to try to decipher their inner nature as a unique phenomenon. No political movements developed for which antagonism to these individual states was a central principle. No bodies of thought or ideologies were required to prove why one of these specific nations embodied a dangerous or perverted nature.[4]

In contrast, through the decades, as new schools of thought and issues succeeded one another, political leaders, cultural figures, and intellectuals had to adopt a view of America in line with their principles and consistent with what they wanted to do in their own countries. These groups then tried to persuade a wider audience to endorse their negative view of what America was offering and their own program for doing better than that.

Many other issues, of course, were also involved, though they often revolved around this central proposition. But anti-Americanism has been at its height when and where it was a useful political tool wielded by those whose interests were different or antagonistic to those of the United States. Thus, anti-American doctrine has historically been most powerful when sponsored by dictatorial regimes—Communist, fascist, Arab nationalist, and Islamist alike—which not only have a more or less rigorous state control of ideas and institutions but also are dominated by an ideology that saw itself as an alternative and rival to what the United States did and represented.

One problem for the school that says that anti-Americanism is merely a response to policy is that the attributes of American society and U.S. policy were often distorted—frequently, willfully so—out of all relationship to reality. Ignorance and honest misunderstanding were part of this picture but so was the deliberate manipulation of antagonistic groups pursuing their own interests.

Such an approach allowed these ruling elites in ideologically based dictatorships to deny that their country's real main enemy was their own governments. Instead, they were able to incite their people demagogically to support the regime in a supposed life-and-death struggle with U.S. imperialism. They argued that underdevelopment was not a result of their own mistakes or policies, nor was any major domestic change needed. Once the heavy hand of American imperialism was removed, rapid progress would be easy. In the meantime, anyone advocating liberal reforms, democracy, or human rights could be accused of acting as U.S. agents and subverting the nation's self-defense.

Anti-Americanism, then, is often a reflection on the nature of anti-Americans themselves—their worldview, deeds, and goals. They, not the United States, are often seekers of world conquest, apologists for dictatorship, distorters of truth, haters of the other, enemies of freedom, those holding onto privilege in their own societies, and defenders of a cultural elitism that serves their interests.

If one views the United States as irredeemably hostile and evil, anything it does will simply be interpreted within that context. Specific U.S. policies, whatever objection to them existed on their own merits, were merely symptoms of that country's aggressive intent, growing power, difference from one's own nation's worldview, and inferior nature.

In the late 1940s, Sayyid Qutb, a key architect of Islamism and Middle Eastern anti-Americanism, wrote of a U.S. intention to destroy Islam through spiritual and cultural colonialism. Any appearance to the contrary was merely intended to confuse Muslims about "the true nature of the struggle" and to extinguish "the flame of belief in their hearts. . . . The Believers must not be deceived, and must understand that this is a trick."[5] A half-century later, in justifying the September 11 attacks, the Saudi cleric Hammoud al-ʿUqla al-Shuʾaybi explained, "America is an [infidel] state that is totally against Islam and Muslims."[6]

The determination to find in America what is inferior and disliked is one revealing sign of anti-Americanism. It came into play whenever a given U.S. policy, for whatever reasons, became controversial. For example, did Europeans or Arabs oppose the United States over war with Iraq because they believed the action was an attempt to steal oil, enslave Muslims, and take over the world? Or did they think that America simply misunderstood the best manner to deal with the challenges presented by Saddam Hussein's regime and there were better ways to do so? These were both arguments against the war in Iraq, but the first is anti-American and the second is not.

But just as the policy-oriented school of explaining anti-Americanism has its problems, so does the values-determinant one. After all, the question remains why certain specific aspects of America are selected for disdain even by those who support a given concept—say, democracy—in general.

The dictatorships that sponsor anti-Americanism may hold values far from those of the United States, but the democracies of Western Europe are not so different from American society in many ways. Are, for example, French values really so profoundly different from those of the United States? Certainly, the basic concepts of democracy were often questioned in the nineteenth century, but this has not been true for a long time in Western societies at least.

The answer is found in the specific ways, often details, in which American characteristics represent unwelcome potential trends for other countries. Anti-Americanism arose, then, because even when characteristic American practices or institutions were shared by others, the United States was accused of going too far or in the wrong direction. It was the uniquely American adaptations of common Western ways that drew antagonism. In this sense, the United States is not hated because it is democratic but because American democracy is said to be too extreme or lacking the balance of a properly sophisticated elite. America is not reviled due to its "free-enterprise" economy but from a conviction that it has a dictatorial and soulless system with a culture considered to be junk-ridden and anti-intellectual. These claims may be wrong or right, exaggerated or distorted, but the aspects of America most often defined as negative are those the complainant wants to avoid in his own country.

Another part of the answer is that the main critique against America reflects an overall distaste for the general direction of societal evolution over the last two centuries. The key aspects include an unchecked democracy with the less educated masses having too much power, the loss of authority by the intellectual and cultural elite, workers made conservative by material privileges, the male/female balance out of whack, too rapid change and too little respect for tradition, a propensity to violence, an obsession with gadgets, a domination of machinery and technology, plus much more. As a result, in the contemporary world, modernization, globalization, industrialization, and Westernization are often just used as alternate names for Americanization.

At the same time, the real or supposed features of the critique can vary widely, sometimes even coming from opposite directions. As an American journalist put it:

> Fanatical Muslims despise America because it's all lapdancing and gay porn; the secular Europeans despise America because it's

all born-again Christians hung up on abortion. . . . America is also too isolationist, except when it's too imperialist. And even its imperialism is too vulgar and arriviste to appeal to real imperialists. . . . To the mullahs, America is the Great Satan, a wily seducer; to the Gaullists, America is the Great Cretin, a culture so self-evidently moronic that only stump-toothed inbred Appalachian lardbutts could possibly fall for it. . . . Too Christian, too Godless, too isolationist, too imperialist, too seductive, too cretinous.[7]

This is no exaggeration. Polls show, for example, that to secular Europeans, America is a religious country (78 percent of the French in one survey), while to Muslims, America is an atheistic land (only 10 percent of Jordanians thought it religious).[8] The bottom line for one determined to be anti-American is that whatever you don't like, that is what the United States represents.

Ironically, anti-Americanism actually subverted the kind of accurate and critical evaluation that would benefit both the United States and others. Confronted by so much distortion and hatred, Americans facing systematic hostility were more likely to disregard criticism as bias rather than as suggestions for improvement. Anti-Americans use that ideology to defend their own system's worst shortcomings rather than to improve their own societies. In addition, a doctrine of generally dismissing American ideas, institutions, or policies also made it harder for foreigners to pick and choose rationally what was worth copying, adapting, or rejecting from the United States.

Paradoxically, this situation also helps explain why those formerly engaged in the most direct, real conflict with the United States were often not very anti-American. From their own experience, they had learned that conflict with America was costly, that conciliation was advantageous, and that a stereotype of U.S. permanent hostility was not accurate. In Latin America, only Mexico's anti-Americanism could be said to be motivated by direct conflicts, and the same applies for most of Europe (except possibly Greece) and the Middle East as well (except possibly Iran). In Africa, which wanted more Americanization, the sins of slavery and U.S foreign policy had no impact.

Vietnam is not a hotbed of anti-Americanism, and neither is Panama, Nicaragua, or Chile. The U.S. defeat of Germany and Japan did not make them anti-American. Japan, after losing a devastating war with America, having two atomic bombs dropped on civilian targets and enduring an occupation (which includes the presence of American troops today, more than a half-century later), did not dwell on resentment. Instead, it absorbed huge elements of American politics and culture very effectively, reinforcing its own identity as it adapted to the modern world. But the most consistently anti-American country in Western Europe is France, the only major state there with which the United States has never fought a war.

In contrast, there was a great deal of continuity in anti-Americanism as an idea held by certain groups in specific places. The United States did pose a challenge to the world, an alternative model of society—long before its foreign policy was of any importance or its culture threatened to swamp the earth. And whenever people disliked any American policy or innovation, they had a 200-year-old anti-American framework within which to fit and magnify their criticism.

Indeed, there is a strong link between nineteenth-century anti-Americans and those of the two centuries that followed. America has always been detested as the prophet, herald, and exemplar of modernism, democracy, and mass culture. It was—as the founders of anti-Americanism and each succeeding generation put it—the greatest threat to the existing order in modern world history. The criticisms of romantics and aristocrats were magnified and made systematic by fascists and Communists, nationalists and traditionalists who did everything possible to discredit America as their strategic and allegedly civilizational rival.

Beginning in the early 1800s, the United States was ridiculed as a place where culture was nonexistent, money was king, democracy was a farce, and the unwashed masses ruled. Even then, before the United States had done anything on the world stage, there was tremendous fear that it would transform the world by its example. By the 1880s, this picture was sharpened considerably. The United States represented the forces of mass production, an assault on tradition, capitalism and advertising, the destruction of the individual, and the downfall of cultural standards. Especially after the U.S. victory over Spain in 1898, increasing attention was given to the idea that the United States was not only a role model but also a power developing the ability to force itself on others, conquer foreign lands, and even one day rule the whole world.

Being universally loved, Americans would constantly rediscover, was not such an easy goal to attain. A year after violent attacks on Vice

President Richard Nixon during a tour of Latin America, George Allen, director of the U.S. Information Agency, tried to explain these trends by drawing on his agency's extensive public opinion polling abroad:

> We continue to act like adolescents. We boast about richness, our bigness and our strength. We talk about our tall buildings, our motor cars and our incomes. Nations, like people, who boast can expect others to cheer when they fail. . . . There is considerable concern in many quarters lest they be swamped by American "cultural imperialism," by a way of life characterized by Coca-Cola, cowboys and comics. . . . If American tourists must chew gum they should be told at least to chew it as inconspicuously as possible.[9]

The central issue, however, was not how Americans chewed gum, but the fact that throughout the Cold War, the Soviet Union, Third World radical movements, and extreme left-wing Europeans saw the United States as the main enemy. In turn, Cold War battles led the United States into actions that greatly increased the scope of its international involvements that led to criticism, especially in Latin America. Antagonism to the United States was most often triggered by objections to its support for a given government, usually—sometimes accurately—described as a corrupt, unpopular dictatorship, or its opposition to a movement it identified as pro-Communist.

But the audience for anti-American slogans, especially in Europe, was limited since most people opposed Communism, viewed the United States as a protector against it, and often considered anti-Americanism as propaganda from those favoring not only America's enemies but their own as well. Some intellectuals were frustrated by the trampling of non-Communist democratic forces in the battle, though others were more tolerant of misdeeds taking place in the context of a life-and-death struggle with totalitarian forces.

When the Cold War ended, however, the USSR vanished but its anti-American case was globalized. America, the victor and sole remaining superpower, could credibly be considered capable of world conquest. The new situation intensified all the factors that led to a historic fear, hatred, and resentment of America. The publishing magnate Henry Luce had called the twentieth century the "American century." Yet it seemed likely that the twenty-first would better merit that title. Those who liked or hated this idea could at least agree that it would be an era of U.S. primacy as the globe's principal power, role model, and cultural influence.

In addition, new developments in technology and business methods—satellite television, the Internet, global franchising—also increased the immediacy of its cultural influence, making U.S. power more visible to everyone on a daily basis down to their very choice of television watching or dining.

While the United States was riding high, however, it was a moment of psychological vulnerability for Europeans and Muslims. The former were going through the difficult transition from national identities to European integration in order to fulfill an age-old dream of peace, harmony, and prosperity. It was clear that a broader European identity could be built faster and stronger if Europeans as a group set themselves apart from the United States by conceptual distinction and rivalry. In that way, inter-European quarrels would be avoided, unity augmented, and hostility directed outward. After all, this was always xenophobia's great appeal: everyone united against the outsider as the best way to ensure internal social harmony.

Public opinion polls reflected the fact that anti-Americanism became, to an almost unprecedented extent, a sentiment held by the masses, even majorities, in many countries. In the opening years of the twenty-first century, it had become nothing less than a fad or fashion, a new conventional wisdom—though how transitory was not clear. And this was true not only for the left but also in nationalist and conservative circles. "Above all," observed the German publisher Mathias Döpfner, anti-Americanism has become taken for granted, the accepted premise "of intelligent conversation."[10] A British journalist wrote, "These days you cannot say anything too bad about the Yanks and not be believed.[11]

The new look for anti-Americanism was a synthesis of ideas from each faction. From conservatives, it took a sense of superiority over the populist America of the antitraditional, secularized mass society and the democracy of grubby buffoons, which went back to the aristocratic anti-Americanism of the nineteenth century. From the left, anti-Americanism provided a new mechanism for trying to extend European influence to the world, proposing that Third World countries see Europe as a counterbalance to America. A conservative like French President Jacques Chirac could thus mount a nationalist foreign policy that would appeal to the European and Third World left, while French leftists would be reconciled with capitalism and bourgeois patriotism that, since they were made in Europe, were far better than the American version.

Similarly, the Muslim and especially Arab worlds were also in need of a new worldview. Increasingly aware that they were behind the West and not catching up, the dictatorial regimes were unable to win victories or solve problems. As a result, rulers who wanted to remain in power, intellectuals marketing their failed ideology, and Muslim clerics fearful of secularist trends all found it easy and advantageous to blame the United States. The cause of all their problems was not their own deficient systems and the bad choices they had made but rather American interference and enmity.

On one hand, there was a fair degree of consensus—especially outside the Middle East—that the best type of society, economy, and culture resembled America at least in general terms. On the other hand, those dissatisfied with the contemporary world and horrified by its apparent direction saw America as the ultimate threat jeopardizing their beloved way of life. Those favoring the status quo denounced the United States as a force for subversive change; those who wanted to transform their societies attacked the United States as a defender of the existing order. Both could join in seeing that country as the problem, simultaneously the source of reactionary paralysis and dangerous innovations.

The far left in particular needed a new ideology. Marxism had failed to create utopia where it ruled or to inspire revolution elsewhere. Even socialism was a dead issue in Europe and Latin America. No one could credibly continue to argue that humanity's problem was a class system and the solution was a proletarian revolution or state ownership of the economy. Making America rather than capitalism the villain that one was fighting seemed an admirable solution for this dead end.

For the extreme left, as well as Arab nationalists or Islamists, this new approach revitalized their failed ideologies and broadened their appeal. Around criticism of America, entire countries could unite, bringing left and right into a new nationalist consensus. French capitalists and workers, ultraconservatives with radical ideologues, traditionalists as well as anarchists, and patriots as well as self-proclaimed internationalists would all be in the same camp. "Progressive" human rights activists could march in defense of Third World dictators; Islamists and pan-Arab nationalists could join hands. Those who persecuted revolutionary Islamists at home could justify Usama bin Ladin's deeds.

In the process, too, many of them did not hesitate to revitalize anti-Semitism, another idea that had the power to unite people of widely disparate political views. That oldest xenophobic prejudice of all had been linked to anti-Americanism in the nineteenth century and again in fascist as well as later Soviet propaganda. As Bernard Wasserstein explains, both biases bring together disparate groups to vent "a hatred of the successful," are "fueled by envy and frustration," and attribute all problems to one main source, which is striving "to control and exploit humanity" in a "monstrous conspiracy."[12]

Indeed, the whole apparatus of anti-Semitism was borrowed to systematize anti-Americanism: the *Protocols of the Elders of Zion* was matched by materials "proving" that America sought world conquest, accusations that Jews performed ritual murder were modernized by tales of American genocide and homicide, medieval accusations that Jews had poisoned wells to cause plagues became a modern-day U.S. responsibility for the destruction of the environment, and the alleged Jewish murder of God was transmogrified into a supposed U.S.-led crusade to destroy Islam.

Some European and most Middle Eastern anti-Americans attributed the Bush administration's doings to a Jewish-Israeli cabal that was the true ruler of the United States.[13] In Germany, neo-Nazis and radical leftists wearing *kaffiyas* marched together in anti-American demonstrations and chanted the same slogans against globalization and waving the same Hizballah flags. Horst Mahler, leader of a right-wing party and former member of the far-left Baader-Meinhoff gang, said on September 12, 2001, that the attacks "on Washington and New York mark the end of the American century, the end of global capitalism, and also the end of the Jehovah cult and of Mammonism."[14]

In the context of all these developments, a growing group of people were prepared to see September 11 not merely as a terrorist act but also as a revolutionary deed against those responsible for the unjust global system. As Lee Harris wrote in evaluating this new ideology, "Here, for the first time, the world had witnessed the oppressed finally striking a blow against the oppressor . . . the dawn of a new revolutionary era."[15]

Many rationalizations could be made for this new reading of history. In Russia, the revolutionaries had betrayed the masses, but in the United States the left could accuse the masses of being traitors to their revolutionary duty. Accepting that there would be no proletarian uprising, and that no economic collapse would force them to rebel, left two possible conclusions. If cultural hypnotism and material bribery had persuaded the masses to accept the unjust American system, then the United States, possessing such power, was a terrible monster that might create a global anti-utopia that would put the same stable and prosperous but soulless and banal system into effect everywhere. But if, instead, the American people as a whole were now a willing partner in the system because they benefited from it, this meant they were an equally guilty accomplice of imperialism and thus the enemy of everyone else in the world.

Although few were aware of it, this new doctrine for the far left, Arab nationalists, and Islamists had a long gestation in anti-American history as well as through certain developments in German philosophy, French postmodernist utopianism, and Third World political economy.[16] Ironically, this doctrine's first part goes back to the "Frankfurt school," the gentlest, most open-minded of Marxists who rejected Stalinism. While they had little direct interest in America, their basic idea fit well with the classic anti-American argument that it was the epitome of a soulless machine society, buying off workers by useless gadgets and mental manipulation. Marx believed that progress would inevitably bring closer the day of revolution and a just socialist society. In contrast, the new view suggested that progress was an enemy that increased humanity's alienation and made it harder to attain the promised land of utopian communism.

Herbert Marcuse, one of this group's members who emigrated to America, developed the theory of "repressive tolerance" as an explanation for that country's success and the absence of proletarian revolution. He claimed that by discouraging people from wanting to overthrow it, the very openness and opportunity that bourgeois democracy offered was a form of oppression. Giving people rising living standards—the opposite of what Marx had predicted—was destroying them spiritually. The more freedom people had, the worse off they were. The true enemy, then, was not capitalism's failure but rather its success. Clearly, that conclusion pointed to America as the most dangerous society in the world.

The second layer came from French critical theory. Michel Foucault and other radical thinkers claimed that most intellectuals and cultural figures had participated in the cynical manipulations of ruling classes to keep down poor and repressed groups. Marxists had focused on the capitalists' monopoly of economic power; postmodernists pointed to their monopoly over information production. This set the stage for the argument that the main front of the U.S. threat, and where it must be fought, was over the invasion of its culture and ideas.

The third part of this doctrine was Third World political economy, which contributed the concept that underdevelopment was an artificial disaster created by the United States. America had become rich by making the rest of the world poor. It was not just responsible for exploiting the Third World but had actually stopped its progress. The United States was responsible for all the regimes that made people's lives miserable.

If these beliefs about the pernicious, powerful effect of America were true, then anti-Americanism was indeed the world's most important issue. It was vital to defend oneself against the American peril and to make a better future possible for humanity by defeating it. This worldview quickly replaced Marxism as the far left's ideology and simultaneously became a way to revitalize the nationalist or Islamist right. The enemy was American domination, not capitalist rule per se, and the battle against it must be waged by all people of other nations, not merely workers and peasants. This struggle requires an alliance of anti-American forces ranging from European intellectuals to Middle Eastern dictators.

At the same time, though, the new doctrine also provided a way to preserve traditional patriotic loyalty to one's own state as well, in a way that did not threaten continental unity. European countries could cooperate among themselves while at the same time could continue competing one on one with the United States in the battle for global cultural, political, and economic influence. Such a notion, however, had far less appeal in Britain or Germany than it did in France, for France was the only one of this trio that was not only the historic headquarters for European anti-Americanism but also saw itself both as the leader of Europe as a whole and as a better world leader than the United States.[17]

As Denis Lacorne wrote,

The competing universalist pretensions of their two revolutions, the particular arrogance of the French intelligentsia, and the contempt of the American political class for neo-Gaullist posturing will ensure that France and the United States remain rivals. This rivalry can only be asymmetrical: we French would like to civilize the world, but we are instead being globalized by the United States, even as our "civilization" is rejected by our European neighbors as excessively Francocentric.[18]

Jealousy is a potent force here, focusing the anger, resentment, and disbelief of people for whom nothing was going right against those who seemed to prosper so effortlessly. European intellectuals and artists had the added pain of knowing that their American counterparts have far larger audiences, resources, and income. The British historian Paul Johnson explained that the envy for "American wealth, power, success... [was] made all the more poisonous because of a fearful European conviction that America's strength is rising while Europe's is falling."[19]

This former attitude is most pronounced among intellectuals and cultural figures, always the main group promoting anti-Americanism. "Scratch an anti-American in Europe," said Denis MacShane, Britain's minister for Europe, "and very often all he wants is a guest professorship at Harvard, or to have an article published in the *New York Times*."[20] A left-wing British journalist confessed, "Everybody in our business here wonders whether he didn't make the mistake of a lifetime by not moving to the United States when he was 22."[21] Revel points out that "the news that America has accomplished something is the signal for us to say that that accomplishment is worthless."[22]

Even worse was the fear that the model of a society so anti-intellectual would catch on.[23] European political leaders may have honest disagreements and differing interests with America or even use anti-Americanism to whip up support occasionally. But it is the intellectual sector far more than the politicians who feel frightened, angry, and highly motivated. Anti-Americanism has been a class ideology for intellectuals just as surely as capitalism was that of the bourgeoisie. In terms of variety and living standards, American products and methods benefited British, French, and German consumers, but in cultural terms they threatened the monopoly over the market that had always been the main asset of the local intellectual and cultural elite.

Blaming things on America rationalizes their situation. In that case, the critics of mass society were not snobs protecting their interests but rather progressives and patriots. Instead of ridiculing British soap operas or greasy fish and chips, they could decry imported American equivalents—especially since workers who vote for the Labour Party consume American junk culture more than do wealthy people who vote Conservative. It thus becomes possible to assert that the masses are not fools without good taste but rather victims of inferior imported American products and values. Not only does this avoid a clash between elite and masses, but it also gives hope that the people might be won to better things if they are persuaded to reject the true, foreign culprit.

In this connection, too, anti-Americans can always fall back on the powerful myth of a "popular" elite culture, the same logical fallacy used for 200 years. The pretense is that being "French" for everyone—including all that country's workers and peasants—means consuming classical culture and eating haute cuisine. The tastes of the average American, who is presumably a Texas cowboy or Arkansas hillbilly, are compared to those of the top 1 percent of the European elite and predictably found less intellectually oriented and culturally sophisticated. If like would be compared to like, the average European's cultural level is probably close to that of his or her American counterpart, while the intellectual elites in both places probably also have similar preferences.

All in all, this battle over cultural control seems reminiscent of the nineteenth-century struggle between the aristocracy and its client intelligentsia against the rising business/manufacturing class. The former favored the handmade, higher quality work of artisans against the lower quality, cheaper, factory-produced goods that would raise the masses' living standards but purportedly lower society's overall tone. Today seems like a new round in this competition, which thus brings a revival of the old aristocratic-romantic cultural critique of America.

The real problem, however, was not the quality of American exports, which varied greatly, but the fact that they competed with all aspects of the local intelligentsia's work—books, movies, music—as a threat to success and commercial survival. Anti-Americanism was a way out for those fearing that they would lose any war of choice with American products, values, ideas, or institutions.

Worst of all was the fact that America is a place where intellectuals have a lower status and less exalted public role. Rather than being seen as respected minds given deference as representing humanity's highest impulses and greatest consciousness, they were viewed as a bunch of nerds who couldn't get dates. If Europe became more like America, the status of intellectuals there would take a nosedive.

No wonder European intellectuals shuddered and denounced such a place. Many of them had once turned to anticapitalism and now embraced anti-Americanism out of disappointment with what liberty had brought. Once the masses had more freedom and money, they were eager to satisfy material hungers and chase after cheap thrills. Relatively few wanted to be like the intellectuals or spend their time pursuing the "finer things of life."

As Arthur Koestler pointed out in 1951, this was merely the process of free choice at work:

> I loathe processed bread in cellophane, processed towns of cement and glass, and the Bible processed as a comic-strip; I loathe crooners and swooners, quizzes and fizzes... the Organization Man and *Reader's Digest*. But who coerced us into buying all this? The United States do not rule Europe as the British ruled India; they waged no Opium War to force their revolting "Coke" down our throats. Europe bought the whole package because Europe wanted it.[24]

Still, this situation was profoundly disillusioning to all those who had hoped for something better. If the masses truly wanted this stuff, there would be no utopia in the future but merely a growing surfeit of material goods and pleasures keyed to the lowest human lusts. Would one have to be resigned to the fact that this was human nature and thus inevitable, or could it be that some system was deliberately making people frivolous and foolish, buying things they did not need and watching sports or situation comedies rather than devoting their time to the latest philosophy book or art exhibit?

Yet this was precisely the portrait of the United States drawn by nineteenth-century European anti-American stereotypes, long before Americans invented or mastered the arts of mass production, advertising, marketing, franchising, and packaging. If the problem was merely coming from the American model that was being exported, there was still hope that it might be rejected and that a better alternative was possible than a lowest-common-denominator culture based on junk and base desires.

In their hearts, though, the European intelligentsia feared it impossible to win the battle, at least not by fighting fairly. "I don't think," explained the British writer Ian Jack, "there will be many people queuing up to heap their [American-made] clothes (or books) on bonfires" to reverse the flow of influence.[25]

It almost seemed as if America discovered some strange subliminal secret about mesmerizing the masses. American civilization is considered to be so potent that it has the alleged ability to take over people's brains and make them want to boogie. The pull of its music, films, and gadgets seemed irresistible, rendering everyone helpless to fight their attraction. Even the intellectuals could not trust themselves to resist. The Swiss philosopher Jeanne Hersch put it this way:

> The Americans make us uneasy because, without wishing us ill, they put things before us for taking ... so convenient that we accept them, finding perhaps that they satisfy our fundamental temptations. Masses of American products are imposed upon us by artificial means, especially where films are concerned. . . . Even when we can make a choice between products, we are influenced by a sort of force within ourselves, which we fear because it is indeterminate and indefinable.[26]

This is precisely what the ancestors of contemporary European anti-Americans feared as early as the 1830s. No wonder many in the Middle East think America has made a pact with the devil.

Yet the myth of a steadily advancing cultural imperialism is as misplaced as that of the conspiratorial designs of American political imperialism. Moreover, the battle to avoid being swamped by the worst of American culture—even within the United States itself—is far from unwinnable. Some, like Japan, adjust successfully through a combination of borrowing, adapting, and preserving their own tradition.

Of course, not only was the quality of American life and culture consistently underestimated—by pointing at the worst rather than the best—but so was the system's most enduring characteristic: its ability to improve itself and fix its problems. One of the main ways this happened was the fact—ignored by anti-Americans—that American culture and society were always ready to borrow from others.

Ironically, this willingness to import ideas included an eagerness by many Americans to seize on the trendiest forms of anti-Americanism produced by Europe and the Middle East. What could be more ironic than the fact that a postmodernist, America-faulting theory that the United States was taking over the world culturally and intellectually—invented mainly in France and the Middle East—gained hegemony among much of the American intelligentsia? What more graphic proof could there be of the multidirectional reality of cultural influences?[27]

Equally, America imported many other cultural products, goods, and ideas from other countries, or had them available on its own soil through large immigrant communities. To give a simple example, if people in European countries want to eat "American" food, they may go to a McDonald's, but if people in America want to eat French or Italian food, they have a choice of many thousands of such restaurants all owned by Americans.[28] Americans also listen to British popular music and watch British television shows, drink French wines and eat French cheeses, and buy Japanese electronic goods and cars, yet the United States is also a major producer of music, television shows, wine, and high technology, without living in fear of a foreign psychological takeover.

Another basis for anti-Americanism had been an additional double standard, the contrast between the ways in which U.S. and European foreign policies are portrayed. For centuries, Britain and France ruled the world, seizing colonies and massacring "natives" while, then and later, unapologetically imposing their distinctive ideas and institutions on Third World victims. In the twentieth century, the USSR played a similar role.

Despite these facts, there was never any phenomenon of anti-Britishism, anti-Frenchism, or anti-Russianism (as contrasted with anti-Communism). A distinction was always made between policy and state, state and society. Third World insurgents against British and French rule usually arose from among those who had most absorbed and accepted their ideas and cultures. The terrible French brutality in Indochina and Algeria is barely a memory in those countries, while Paris's continuing interventions in Africa to install new regimes and prop up dictators are not held to discredit it as a flawed state or society. Even Germany is forgiven for plunging the world into two wars and engaging in genocide. Meanwhile, though, the United States continues to be chastised for far more distant historic actions—its treatment of Native Americans, slavery, and ancient interventions in Latin America—which supposedly reveal its true imperialist and brutal essence.

While, of course, pro-American thinking in European countries often exceeded the contrary view, this, too, became a factor that stoked anti-Americanism. The more some people advocated copying, borrowing, or buying from America, the more others were horrified by this prospect. The real secret of the debate over America is that it was usually about what people should do within their own countries. Many people in the most anti-American places, like France or the Arab world, saw no contradiction between an acerbic view of America and admiring it as a society with a high living standard or good educational system. What they didn't like was the possibility that America's example or power might change their own lives or societies to an extent or in a direction that they did not want.

These arguments were so passionate because people were choosing what to accept or reject for themselves. Was copying particular features from America a road toward happiness or disaster, destroying one's identity or attaining a better life? If the stakes were not so close to home, what happened in America itself would have been an issue of only academic interest, like economic reform in Argentina or cultural trends in Zimbabwe. No one would get so heated, angry, and disputatious about something so remote from home.

Ironically but inevitably, the ones born in other lands who best knew America and were most favorable toward that country were those who had chosen to immigrate to the United States. For them, America was a land of opportunity, despite the setbacks and disillusionment that life there sometimes gave them. Gradually, they transmitted these positive impressions to those left behind, for example among relatives and home villages in Italy and Ireland. Over time, there may be a similar effect from those who have migrated most recently from Latin America, South and East Asia, and Africa.

But the main anti-Americanism-producing countries are less influenced by such factors. Mass emigration from Germany and Britain ended long ago. France never produced many immigrants to the United States, and perhaps the lack of such personal links and the lack of a sense of contributing to the shaping of America has been a significant factor for that country's general miscomprehension of it. The same problem applies to Arab and Muslim states from which few immigrants came until very recently and for whom the assimilation process has just begun.

What are some of the particular American traits that have produced so much misunderstanding and derision? First, there is an idealism bordering on enlightened altruism. In a cynical world, it nonetheless remains true that the United States is a country that wants to do good.

To Americans—and, yes, even American leaders—the idea of spreading democracy and proving that they are genuinely helping others is a major factor in foreign policy. Based on their own national experiences, Americans believe that improving peoples' lives is the key to stability and see gaining their goodwill as the route to peace and success. Once the small number of villains in another nation—Kosovo or Somalia, Iraq or Afghanistan—are killed or captured, they believe, the silent majority would prefer moderation. The American politicians' task is to persuade the public that they can do all these things. This was how the United States was to be made secure after September 11, 2001.

Second, Americans passionately embrace a powerful optimism. They expect that goodness will triumph, the world will improve, and everything will turn out right in the end. This is a progression that follows the pattern of their national experience. They did not learn that idea from seeing so many happy endings in Hollywood movies; rather, it was this trait that forced directors to meet the audience's demand for them.

Such optimism allows and encourages Americans to undertake great actions and tremendous risks. Often, they brush aside the endless advice that something cannot be done. Naturally, this led to mistakes and costly losses but hardly ever led to any real or lasting disaster. And U.S. history has repeatedly shown that this attitude succeeds in the end, producing stunning successes.

Third, the United States has a pragmatic, problem-solving mentality. Rather than muddling through or living with difficulties, Americans want to resolve them. In this search for solutions, ideology does not enchain Americans. And yet here, too, when failure does take place, there is a willingness to change assumptions and methods. Every time in U.S. history when there have been problems that anti-Americans defined as implicit in the country's nature—slavery and later racism, the need to develop culture and education in the early nineteenth century, and the uncontrolled capitalism of the late nineteenth century, for example—America has altered itself to solve them.

Finally, there must be mentioned a reluctance to engage in foreign entanglements. While it is easy to exaggerate an American preference for isolationism, there is no country in the world less interested in empire or world conquest. This was the tendency of the United States after the Cold War's end, when American foreign policy became focused on a series of humanitarian missions in places like Somalia, Bosnia, and Kosovo. But September 11, 2001, like the Japanese attack on Pearl Harbor on December 7, 1941, forced Americans into a very different era against their preferences.

Whatever America's faults, its unique characteristics point to one important conclusion that runs in the opposite direction from what anti-

Americans claim: this is not a country that wants to rule the world. And yet such a claim is the mantra of anti-Americanism.

Thus, to cite one example among millions, France's respected *Le Monde Diplomatique* published articles purveying conspiracy theories that identified globalization as an American attempt at world conquest, making the United States at least as bad as Nazi Germany or Stalinist Russia and worse than bin Ladin. The real axis of evil is said to be a U.S.-dominated economic system, an ideological "dictatorship" of American media and think tanks, and a post–September 11 military offensive that treats Europeans as "vassals" that are ordered "to kneel in supplication [as] the United States aspires to exercise absolute political power." Those taken prisoner in Afghanistan while fighting for bin Ladin and imprisoned in the "cages" of Guantánamo are examples of what the United States intends to do to Europeans who defy its imperial will.[29]

What is actually taking place, suggested Robert Kagan in his essay "Power and Weakness," is merely a division of labor between Europe and America.[30] Since America was now protecting Europe from the world's disruptive forces, Europe was then free to emphasize its high morality and opposition to using force because the United States dealt with threats that Europe did not have to confront.

Kagan explained, "Europe is turning away from power . . . into a self-contained world of laws and rules and transnational negotiation and cooperation. It is entering a post-historical paradise of peace and relative prosperity." The United States is left to deal with "the anarchic Hobbesian world where international laws and rules are unreliable and where true security, the defense and promotion of a liberal order still depend on the possession and use of military might." Thus, the Europeans could stereotype America as enjoying that role due to its "culture of death" and warlike temperament that was "the natural product of a violent society where every man has a gun and the death penalty reigns."[31]

European critics claimed that Americans see the world divided between good and evil, while Europeans perceive a more complex picture. Americans favor coercion by force; Europeans prefer persuasion through benefits. Thus, Europeans consider themselves more "tolerant, patient, peaceful and attuned to international law and economic attempts to encourage cooperation." Kagan suggests that the different roles are not a result of national character but of Europe's "retreat from responsibility" in the world, leaving the task of maintaining international order and dealing with dangerous threats to the United States. Yet far from being a recent development, these basic European stereotypes of America—as being violent, materialistic, morally simplistic, unsophisticated, too quick to act, and too wedded to change—are identical with its traditional anti-American themes going back to the early nineteenth century at a time when Europe was pleased to rule the globe and made no apologies for doing so.

At any rate, today Kagan points out that this European vision of America is a misleading image. For example, the portrayal of America as aggressive and unilateralist is contradicted by U.S. eagerness for Europe to take the lead in such crises as Bosnia and Kosovo. Only European failure to act decisively forced the United States to do so itself, since only American leadership could turn official European unity into actual cooperation. The attempt to prove that America was systematically driving for control and disregarding European feelings also ignored much evidence that belied its claims: the U.S. effort to build a wide coalition in the 1991 war against Iraq; its patient cooperation with other states in the decade-long UN sanctions program on Iraq; its long, strenuous work to resolve the Arab-Israeli conflict; its support for European unification; its sensitive handling of the USSR's dismantlement; and a dozen other matters. Even in the Iraq War, which seemed to fulfill all the nightmares about the United States dragging Europe into crisis, the U.S.-led coalition included support from Britain, Spain, Italy, and many central European countries, as well as from Germany's main opposition party.

Finally, of course, the most extreme anti-American exaggeration was that the United States might use its power against the Europeans themselves. The ultimate fear was not that the United States had bad policies but that it had bad intentions.

September 11 and the subsequent events were the first tests of the enhanced new anti-American doctrine. There was nothing intrinsically anti-American in opposition to or criticism of any specific U.S. policy, for example, the war on Iraq. The issue was not whether individuals or countries rejected what the United States wanted but whether in doing so they used anti-American stereotypes, distorted U.S. motives or actions, or tried to raise hatred against the United States itself. The anti-American interpretation was that this crisis provided additional proof that the

United States sought world conquest and behaved badly because of deep-seated, chronic shortcomings in American society.

This assumption was held to be equally true in Europe and the Middle East, as well as elsewhere in the world. Once set alight, anti-Americanism became a fad spread by the very technological innovations supposedly abetting American-dominated globalism. Suddenly, Japan's former prime minister Yasuhiro Nakasone demanded that the United States "renounce an arrogance that makes them behave as though they are the masters of the universe."[32] In China, a poll showed that 30 percent thought the United States was responsible for the SARS epidemic there.[33] And in 2004, Islamic leaders in three northern Nigerian states blocked critical polio inoculations for children, denouncing them as a U.S. plot to spread AIDS or infertility among Muslims.[34]

Incredibly, by adopting his false ideas, this reaction gave victory to a terrorist who had attacked America and murdered almost 3,000 people. Of course, most said, this was a regrettable crime. Many Europeans sympathized with the United States; others supported it even regarding the war in Iraq. Yet suddenly bin Ladin's basic concept of what was going on in the world was accepted by a significant European minority and by a majority in the Middle East.

The fact that George W. Bush was a conservative made him a far more credible target for being labeled by the left as a mad emperor bent on world domination. The fact that he had no intellectual pretensions, to say the least, fueled the intellectuals' contempt. The fact that he launched a war on Iraq without first obtaining world support was taken as proof of accusations already being fostered. Many Americans agreed with the most critical assessments of foreigners at a time when domestic partisan passions had been raised to a high level.

In short, Bush's personality and policies seemed to fulfill precisely the role that the anti-Americans were predicting and warning against. Signs of the new situation were already visible during Clinton's terms, the time during which the September 11 attacks were being planned, after all. But, combined with the post–Cold War situation of American power, the evolution of anti-Americanism itself, and September 11, the Bush era made for a critical mass that made anti-Americanism an explosive global phenomenon. The terms of abuse for Bush (a stupid cowboy, religious fanatic) and the United States (ignorant, brutal, arrogant, violent, erratic) were all from the classical texts. Whether or not this U.S. policy was wise or foolish, necessary or not—an issue completely outside the scope of this book—it neatly fit into existing hostile assumptions and some groups' interest in spreading them, guaranteeing that there would be a heightened anti-Americanism in response.

If these factors had not been in place, anti-Americanism would still have been a significant yet less noticeable and endemic factor. But the fact that U.S. positions fit with the preconceptions of an anti-Americanism that was ripe for rapid expansion, does not mean that its view and analysis are accurate. Anti-Americanism is not reinvented each time there is a president or policy others do not like. Thus, while criticisms of the United States or its leaders can be quite valid, anti-Americanism itself is based on a false, irrational case.

Over the course of history, there have been many variations of it ranging from the humorous and frivolous all the way to the murderous and dangerous. At a 1974 world food conference in Rome, Senator Daniel Moynihan recalled, "The scene grew orgiastic as speakers competed in their denunciation of the country that had called the conference, mostly to discuss giving away its own wheat."[35] Almost thirty years later, in the Gaza Strip, a U.S. government convoy was deliberately ambushed by Palestinian terrorists and three Americans killed as its passengers traveled to interview Palestinian candidates for Fulbright scholarships to study in the United States.

Certainly, anti-Americanism's overall impact should not be overstated. For much of its history, it was a curiosity found in the writings of travelers and novelists. There was almost always a pro-American side and anti-Americanism usually was just talk, with little effect on events. But after becoming systematized and augmented during the Cold War's battle of ideas, anti-Americanism's concepts finally took global center stage at the outset of the twenty-first century. In an age whose main symbol and shaping influence has become September 11, the lethality of such ideas is all too evident.

Certainly, any doctrine of such power and durability has a basis in reality. But anti-Americanism was a mixture of two different aspects of reality, drawing both from the nature and behavior of the United States itself and that of its critics. In the end, anti-Americanism was a response to the phenomenon of America itself, precisely because of that country's uniqueness and innovation, the success it has achieved, and the challenge it poses to all alternative ideologies or existing societies.

NOTES

Preface

1. The Carlyle quote is from his book *Latter-Day Pamphlets*, http://jollyroger .com/library/Latter-DayPamphletsbyThomasCarlyleebook.html. The Heine quote is from Wagner, "The Europeans' Image of America," in *America and Western Europe*, 24. The rest of the quotations about America can be found in "Nonstop English," http://nonstopenglish.com/reading/quotations/ index.asp?page=40&searchword=&search=America&author=&length.

Chapter 1

1. Commager and Giordanetti, *Was America a Mistake?*, 26.
2. Gerbi, *Dispute of the New World*, 381.
3. Crèvecoeur, "Letters from an American Farmer" http://old.jccc.net/~ vclark/doc8_1_1.htm.
4. Montesquieu, *Spirit of Laws*, 102.
5. Echeverria, *Mirage in the West*, 7.

6. Montesquieu, *Spirit of Laws*, 135.

7. For a biography of Buffon, see Jacques Roger, *Buffon: A Life in Natural History* (Ithaca, NY: Cornell University Press, 1997).

8. Gerbi, *Dispute of the New World*, 4.

9. Ibid.; Chinard, "18th Century Theories on America as Human Habitat," 30.

10. Jefferson, *Notes on the State of Virginia*, 47; Gerbi, *Dispute of the New World*, 3.

11. Chinard, "18th Century Theories on America as Human Habitat," 30; Gerbi, *Dispute of the New World*, 5.

12. Jefferson, *Notes on the State of Virginia*, 58–59; Chinard, "18th Century Theories on America as Human Habitat," 31.

13. Chinard, "18th Century Theories on America as Human Habitat," 32; Gerbi, *Dispute of the New World*, 7–8.

14. See Robert Leckie, *A Few Acres of Snow: The Saga of the French and Indian Wars* (New York: J. Wiley and Sons, 2000).

15. Chinard, "18th Century Theories on America as Human Habitat," 32–33.

16. Benson, *America of 1750*, Vol. 1, 56.

17. For example, in 1761, Abbé Arnaud in *Journal Etranger*; Chinard, "18th Century Theories on America as Human Habitat," 35. Like others, Kalm later changed his views of Americans and said that people multiply more quickly than in Europe. He praised the lower taxes and personal freedoms offered by the United States. Chinard, "18th Century Theories on America as Human Habitat," 34.

18. Commager and Giordanetti, *Was America a Mistake?*, 85.

19. Ibid, 93–102.

20. Gerbi, *Dispute of the New World*, 99; Chinard, "18th Century Theories on America as Human Habitat," 36.

21. Echeverria, *Mirage in the West*, 14; also Jefferson, *Notes on the State of Virginia*, 64; Commager and Giordanetti, *Was America a Mistake?*, 129–130.

22. Chinard, "18th Century Theories on America as Human Habitat," 36.

23. Commager and Giordanetti, *Was America a Mistake?*, 12–14.

24. Gerbi, *Dispute of the New World*, 330. See also Ceasar, *Reconstructing America*, 20.

25. Gerbi, *Dispute of the New World*, 331.

26. Hegel, *Introduction to Philosophy of History*, 81; Gerbi, *Dispute of the New World*, 425, 428–430.

27. Gerbi, *Dispute of the New World*, 436; Diner, *America in the Eyes of the Germans*, 9.

28. Hegel, *Introduction to Philosophy of History*, 86.

29. Ceaser, *Reconstructing America*, 170.

30. Gerbi, *Dispute of the New World*, 457–459.

31. Gerbi, *Dispute of the New World*, 160; Chinard, "18th Century Theories on America as Human Habitat," 38–39.

32. Commager, *America in Perspective*, 22.

33. Franklin, "Observations Concerning the Increase of Mankind, Peopling of Countries," http://bc.barnard.columbia.edu/~lgordis/earlyAC/documents/observations.html.

34. Ford, *Works of Thomas Jefferson*, Vol. 3, 458.

35. Jefferson, *Notes on the State of Virginia*, 268, 55.

36. Ford, *Works of Thomas Jefferson*, 268, n28.

37. Jefferson, *Notes on the State of Virginia*, 64–65.

38. Chinard, "18th Century Theories on America as Human Habitat," 36.

39. Gerbi, *Dispute of the New World*, 154–156; Chinard, "18th Century Theories on America as Human Habitat," 37–38.

40. Moore, *Complete Poems of Sir Thomas Moore*, http://sailor.gutenberg.org/etext05/7cptm10.txt.

41. Moore, "To Thomas Hume Esq, M.D," http://sailor.gutenberg.org/etext05/7cptm10.txt.

42. Hamilton, *Men and Manners in America*, quoted in Gerbi, *Dispute of the New World*, 491.

43. Darwin, *Journal of Researches*, 173.

44. "Der Amerikamude," cited in Nordholt, "Anti-Americanism in European Culture," 16.

45. Gerbi, *Dispute of the New World*, 375–376.

46. Ibid.

47. Nordholt, "Anti-Americanism in European Culture," 15.

48. Ceasar, *Reconstructing America*, 170.

49. Diner, *America in the Eyes of the Germans*, 36.

50. Ibid.

51. Keats, "To (What Can I Do to Drive Away)," http://www.4literature.net/John_Keats/To__What_can_I_do_to_drive_away_/.

52. Hollyday, *Anti-Americanism in the German Novel, 1841–1861*, 34.

53. Saustrup, "Hoffman von Fallersleben, August Heinrich," http://www.tsha.utexas.edu/handbook/online/articles/view/HH/fho88.html.

54. This variety of anti-Americanism is discussed at greater length in chapter 2.

55. Echeverria, *Mirage in the West*, 217.

56. Strauss, *Menace in the West*, 205.

57. Roger, *L'Ennemi Américain*, 17.

58. Auden, "Introduction," in James, *American Scene*, xiv.

Chapter 2

1. Fairlie, *Spoiled Child of the Western World*, 50.
2. Nordholdt, "Anti-Americanism in European Culture," 12 n19.
3. Schlesinger, "America Experiment or Destiny?", 512–513.
4. Tatum, *United States and Europe 1815–1823*, 219.
5. Roger, *Rêves et cauchemars Américains*, 24.
6. Quoted in Berger, *British Traveler in America, 1836–1860*, 107.
7. Nordholdt, "Anti-Americanism in European Culture," 13.
8. Ibid., 10.
9. Fay, *American Experiment*, 4.
10. Gerbi, *Dispute of the New World*, 326–327.
11. Fay, *American Experiment*, 239.
12. Gerbi, *Dispute of the New World*, 330.
13. Ceaser, *Reconstructing America*, 78.
14. Nordholdt, "Anti-Americanism in European Culture," 10.
15. Echeverria, *Mirage in the West*, 128.
16. Ibid.
17. Diner, *America in the Eyes of the Germans*, 38.
18. Louis Marie Turreau de Linières, *Aperçu sur la situation politique des Etats-Unis d'amérique* (Paris, 1815), 137–138, quoted in Echeverria, *Mirage in the West*, 247.
19. Ceasar, *Reconstructing America*, 78.
20. Beaujour, *Sketch of the United States of North America at the Commencement of the Nineteenth Century, from 1800 to 1810* (London, 1814), described in Stearn, *Broken Image*, 14–15.
21. Echeverria, *Mirage in the West*, 248.
22. Roger, *Rêves et cauchemars Américains*, 25.
23. Nordholdt, "Anti-Americanism in European Culture," 9.
24. Wagner, "Europeans' Image of America," 24.
25. Hollyday, *Anti-Americanism in the German Novel, 1841–1861*, 153–160.
26. Ibid., 27.
27. Ibid., 29–31.
28. Ibid., 53–61.
29. Ibid., 61.
30. Quoted in Echeverria, *Mirage in the West*, 252.
31. De Tocqueville, *Democracy in America*, Vol. 1, http://xroads.virginia.edu/~HYPER/DETOC/ch1_17.htm.
32. Ibid., http://xroads.virginia.edu/~HYPER/DETOC/1_ch15.htm.

33. Ibid.

34. Ibid.

35. Ibid.

36. Ibid.

37. Ibid.

38. Ibid., Vol. 2, http://xroads.virginia.edu/~HYPER/DETOC/ch2_13.htm.

39. Ibid.

40. G. D. Warburton, *Hochelega* (London, 1846), cited in Berger, *British Traveler in America, 1836–1860*, 106.

41. Sinclair, *History of New Zealand*, 60–62.

42. Ibid.

43. Ibid.

44. Marryat, *Diary in America*, Series 1, Vol. 1, "Introduction," http://www.blackmask.com/books74c/diaryone.htm.

45. Ibid., Series 2, Vol. 2, Chapter 2, http://www.athelstane.co.uk/marryat/diaramer/diaru/diaru10.htm.

46. Ibid., Series 2, Vol. 2, Chapter 10, http://www.athelstane.co.uk/marryat/diaramer/diaru/diaru18.htm.

47. Op cit.

48. Ibid., Series 2, Vol. 1, Chapter 5, http://www.athelstane.co.uk/marryat/diaramer/diarz/diarz06.htm.

49. Op cit.

50. Ibid., Series 1, Vol. 3, Chapter 48, http://www.athelstane.co.uk/marryat/diaramer/diary/diary48.htm.

51. Ibid., Series 1, Vol. 1, Chapter 22, http://www.blackmask.com/books74c/diaryone.htm#1_0_23.

52. Gerbi, *Dispute of the New World*, 484–485.

53. Echeverria, *Mirage in the West*, 252; and Gerbi, *Dispute of the New World*, 342.

54. Gerbi, *Dispute of the New World*, 326–327.

55. Francis Grose, *Classical Dictionary of the Vulgar Tongue* (London, 1785), quoted in Heilman, *America in English Fiction*, 348.

56. Marryat, *Diary in America*, Series 1, Vol. 2, Chapter 23, http://www.athelstane.co.uk/marryat/diaramer/diary/diary23.htm.

57. Discussion of this issue, which does not indicate anti-Americanism as such but repugnance with that indefensible institution, is not included in this book.

58. Dickens, *American Notes*, 91–92; Nevins, *America through British Eyes*, 207–208.

59. Diner, *America in the Eyes of the Germans*, 38.

60. Trollope, *Domestic Manners of the Americans*, 12.

61. Gerbi, *Dispute of the New World*, 478, n133.

62. Conrad, *Imagining America*, 32. Although Trollope gave lip service to there being many positive things about America—nine hundred and ninety-nine out of a thousand, she said at one point—she did not seem to find many.

63. Schama, "Unloved American," http://www.newyorker.com/fact/content/ ?030310fa_fact.

64. Sadlier, "Introduction," Trollope, *Domestic Manners of the Americans*, xii–xiii.

65. Trollope, *Domestic Manners of the Americans*, 39

66. T. Wemyss Reid, *Life of Lord Houghton*, Vol. 1 (London, 1890), 158f, as quoted in Pelling, *America and the British Left*, 4.

67. Conrad, *Imagining America*, 4.

68. Trollope, *Domestic Manners of the Americans*, 363.

69. Nordholdt, "Anti-Americanism in European Culture," 13.

70. Saint-Méry, *Moreau de St. Méry's American Journey 1793–1798*, 281–287.

71. Hollyday, *Anti-Americanism in the German Novel*, 33.

72. Karl Muller, *Des Lebens Wandlungen*, cited in Hollyday, *Anti-Americanism in the German Novel 1841–1861*, 39.

73. Baker, *America Perceived*, 40–44.

74. Conrad, *Imagining America*, 67.

75. Wilde, "Woman of No Importance," http://www.4literature.net/Oscar _Wilde/Woman_of_No_Importance/3.html.

76. James F. Muirhead, *Land of Contrasts* (London).

77. Anthony Trollope, *North America*, http://www.worldwideschool.org/library/ books/geo/geography/northamericavolumei/chap9.html.

78. Marryat, *A Diary in America*, Series 1, Vol. 3, Chp. XLVIII, http://www .athelstane.co.uk/marryat/diaramer/diary/diary48.htm.

79. Dickens, *American Notes*, 137.

80. Ibid., 127–128. At the time there was a popular myth that, when frightened, the ostrich put its head into the ground and thought no one could see it.

81. Dickens, *Dickens' Digest*, 350–351.

Chapter 3

1. Siegfried, *America Comes of Age*, 190.

2. Pelling, *America and the British Left*, 161.

3. Paul de Rousiers, *La Vie Américaine* (Paris: Diderot, 1892), 2, cited in Roger, *L'Ennemi Américain*, 188–189.

4. Fairlie, *Spoiled Child of the Western World*, 50–52.

5. Kroes, "Great Satan versus the Evil Empire," 38.

6. Lawrence, *Plumed Serpent*, 73–74.
7. McPherson, *Antietam: Crossroads of Freedom*, 57.
8. On Marx, see chapter 5.
9. Jordan and Pratt, *Europe and the Civil War*, 225.
10. Ibid., 251.
11. July 17 and August 15, 1862; quoted in McPherson, *Antietam: Crossroads of Freedom*, 58.
12. Ibid., 143.
13. Ibid., 144.
14. Jordan and Pratt, *Europe and the Civil War*, 139.
15. American Park Network (APN) web site, http://www.americanparknetwork .com/parkinfo/sl/history/liberty.html.
16. Mead, "Why Do They Hate Us? Two Books Take Aim at French Anti-Americanism," http://www.foreignaffairs.org/20030301fareviewessay10345/ walter-russell-mead/why-do-they-hate-us-two-books-take-aim-at-french-anti -americanism.html.
17. Ory, "From Baudelaire to Duhamel," 46.
18. Ibid.
19. Ibid.
20. Sorman, "United States: Model or Bête Noire?" 214.
21. Roger, *Rêves et cauchemars Américains*, 28, 96.
22. Mead, "Why Do they Hate Us? Two Books Take Aim at French Anti-Americanism," http://www.foreignaffairs.org/20030301fareviewessay10345/ walter-russell-mead/why-do-they-hate-us-two-books-take-aim-at-french-anti -americanism.html.
23. Zeldin, "Pathology of Anti-Americanism," 36.
24. Clark, *Less Than Kin*, 126.
25. As quoted in Baker, *America Perceived*, 160.
26. Ibid., 160–161.
27. Ibid., 161–162.
28. Ceasar, *Reconstructing America*, 164–165.
29. Cross, *Emergence of Liberal Catholicism in America*, 194.
30. Ibid., 192–194.
31. Pelling, *America and the British Left*, 3.
32. Sorman, "United States: Model or Bete Noire?" 214.
33. Arnold, *Civilization in the United States*, 172–173.
34. Stearn, *Broken Image*, 148–149.
35. Spengler, *Decline of the West*, Vol. 2, 475.
36. Jones, *Life and Work of Sigmund Freud*, 269.
37. Ibid., 270.
38. Arnold, *Civilization of the United States*, 171.

39. In the novel, Lucien Leuwen. Roger, *L'Ennemi Américain*, 84–85.
40. Hamsun, *Cultural Life of Modern America*, 18.
41. Ibid., 8.
42. Ibid., 106.
43. Commager, *America in Perspective*, 312.
44. Wilde, "Impressions of America," http://www.december2001.com/oscar wilde/impressionsofamerica.html.
45. Ibid.
46. Ibid.
47. Ibid.
48. James, *American Scene*, 67.
49. Ibid., 77.
50. Ibid., 2–3.
51. Ibid., 25.
52. Schama, "Unloved American," http://www.newyorker.com/fact/content/ ?030310fa_fact.
53. F. Gaillardet, *L'Aristocratie en Amérique*, 3, 348, cited in Roger, *L'Ennemi Américain*, 153–154.
54. Valéry, *Regards sur le monde actuel* (Paris, 1960), 914, cited in Roger, *L'Ennemi Américain*, 202.
55. Roger, *L'Ennemi Américain*, 202.
56. See Edmund Morris, *Theodore Rex* (New York, 2000), which contains scores of positive statements by European leaders on Roosevelt, perhaps because they saw him as someone with views—though not personal behavior—similar to their own.
57. E. de Mandat-Grancey, *En visite chez l'Oncle Sam* (1891), 68, cited in Roger, *L'Ennemi Américain*, 145.
58. Emile Barbier, *Voyage au pays des dollars* (Paris, 1893), 336–337, cited in Roger, *L'Ennemi Américain*, 188–189.
59. A. Ruz, *La Question Cubaine* (Paris, 1898), 46, cited in Roger, *L'Ennemi Américain*, 192–193; author's interview with Philippe Roger, January 20, 2003.
60. Brogan, "From England," 3–4.
61. Fairlie, *Spoiled Child of the Western World*, 54.
62. Ian Jack, "This Land Is Their Land," http://books.guardian.co.uk/review/ story/0,12084,908950,00.html.
63. Zeldin, "Pathology of Anti-Americanism," 37.
64. Wells, *Future of America*, 210, 257–258.
65. J.-L. Chastanet, *L'Oncle Shylock ou l'impérialisme américain à la conquête du monde* (1927), 9–10.
66. Judt, *Past Imperfect*, 190–192.

67. Gasset, *Revolt of the Masses* (New York, 1932), 151–152.

68. On this issue regarding Germany, see chapter 5.

69. Strauss, *Menace in the West*, 193–194.

70. Louis Aragon, *La Revolution surrealiste*, cited in Roger, *L'Ennemi Américain*, 439.

71. Strauss, *Menace in the West*, 192.

72. Ibid., 190.

73. Romier, *Who Will Be Master: Europe or America?* (London, 1931), quoted in ibid., 202.

74. Ibid., 100.

75. Ibid., 202.

76. Ibid., 206–207.

77. Kuisel, *Seducing the French*, 113.

78. E. Barbier, *Voyage au pays des dollars* (Paris, 1893), 126–128, cited in Roger, *L'Ennemi Américain*, 250–251.

79. Ory, "From Baudelaire to Duhamel," 46.

80. Strauss, *Menace in the West*, 208.

81. Cited in ibid., 3.

82. Morand, *New York*, 301.

83. Ibid., 305–306.

84. Duhamel, *Scènes de la Vie Future*, 52.

85. Ibid., 54, 80.

86. Ibid., 58–59.

87. Ibid., 69, 72, 245.

88. Ibid., 37.

89. Ibid., 48.

90. Miller, *Airconditioned Nightmare*, 156–157.

91. Ibid., 20.

92. Ibid., 24.

Chapter 4

1. Barghoorn, *Soviet Image of the United States*, 3–5.

2. Dostoyevsky, *Devils (The Possessed)*, 147–148, 247–248, 253–254, 270.

3. Barghoorn, *Soviet Image of the United States*, 3–5.

4. Marx, "Address of the International Working Men's Association to Abraham Lincoln, President of the United States of America," http://www.marxists.org/history/international/iwma/documents/1864/lincoln-letter.htm.

5. Ibid.

6. Marx and Aveling, *Working-Class Movement in America*, 12–14.

7. Ibid., 86–87, 154–165.

8. Gorky, *City of the Yellow Devil*, 8–10.

9. Ibid., 17.

10. Ibid., 135.

11. Ibid., 88–89.

12. Lenin, *Collected Works*, Vol. 23 (1929 ed.), 292, as quoted in Shub, *Lenin*, 391.

13. Barghoorn, *Soviet Image of the United States*, 15.

14. Lenin, *On the United States of America*, 334–335.

15. Barghoorn, *Soviet Image of the United States*, 17.

16. Ilin, *New Russia's Primer*, 16–17.

17. Ibid., 13–14.

18. Ashby, *Scientist in Russia*, 246–247.

19. Barghoorn, *Soviet Image of the United States*, 25–27.

20. Ilf and Petrov, *Little Golden America*, 84.

21. Ibid., 12, 20–21, 29–30.

22. Ibid., 108.

23. Ibid., 173.

24. Ibid., 376–377.

25. Ibid., 376–377.

26. Ibid., 29–30. Indeed, in earlier times, big-city milk and meat came from animals grazing in its streets, with a much lower quality and real health hazards.

27. Ibid., 102.

28. Ibid., 370.

29. Ibid., 380.

30. Quoted in Barghoorn, *Soviet Image of the United States*, 46.

31. Ibid., 121–122.

32. Letter to Sydney Hook, June 8, 1956, quoted in Wilford, *CIA, The British Left, and the Cold War*, 216.

33. Parks, *Culture, Conflict and Coexistence*, 119.

34. Ibid., 120.

35. Barghoorn, *Soviet Image of the United States*, 227–228.

36. Ibid., 120.

37. Ibid., 114–121.

38. Viktor Konetskii, *Elpidifor Peskarev*, DN, 2 (1977), cited in Maurice Friedberg, "Reading for the Masses," *USIA Report*, June 25, 1981, 72–73.

39. Voprosy literatury, 7, 1980, 4, cited in Friedberg, "Reading for the Masses," 71.

40. T. N. Denisova, "Sovremennyi amerikanskii roman," *Sotsial 'nokriticheskie traditsii* (Kiev: "Naukova dumka," 1976), 143, cited in Friedberg, "Recent Soviet Criticism of American Literature (#2)," 11.

NOTES

41. Burlatskii, "SshA i SSSR" (The United States and the USSR), http://www
    .washprofile.org/arch0403/07.30%20-%20burlatskiy.html.
42. "Soviet Propaganda Alert," October 15, 1981, 1–11.
43. Ibid.
44. Shiraev and Zubok, *Anti-Americanism in Russia: From Stalin to Putin*, 23.
45. Moscow World Service, November 13, 1986, and *Pravda*, October 31, 1986,
    6, quoted in *Soviet Propaganda Alert*, no. 34 (January 16, 1987): 13.
46. *Soviet Propaganda Alert* (October 15, 1981): 1–11. See chapter 2.
47. Bucar, *Truth about American Diplomats*, 128.
48. *Soviet Propaganda Alert* (October 15, 1981): 1–11.
49. Ibid., 12.
50. Biddiss, *Gobineau Selected Political Writings*, 161.
51. Ibid., 162.
52. See chapter 1.
53. Ceaser, *Reconstructing America*, 123.
54. Ibid., 103–106.
55. Ibid., 173–175.
56. Ibid., 187.
57. Ibid., 197–201.
58. Heidegger, *Introduction to Metaphysics*, 35.
59. Ibid., 46.
60. Ceaser, *Reconstructing America*, 189, 192, 193.
61. Diner, *America in the Eyes of the Germans*, 72–73.
62. Ibid., 56.
63. Ibid., 70, 97–98.
64. Ibid., 81, 95.
65. Ibid., 81, 92–93.
66. Ibid., 87.
67. Ibid., 70–71.
68. Compton, *Swastika and the Eagle*, 17, 35.
69. The dinner party was described in Rauschning, *Voice of Destruction*, 68–71.
70. Ibid.
71. Ibid.
72. Bormann, *Hitler's Secret Conversations 1941–1944*, 155.
73. Ibid.
74. Ibid., 491.
75. Ibid., 491–492.
76. Burdett, "Different Visions of Space: Italian Fascist Writers and the United
    States," http://www.cf.ac.uk/euros/newreadings/volume5/burdett.html.
77. Campana, "Un Colloquio con Mussolini."
78. Probably the most important difference was that the Communists could

never fully acknowledge America's economic success—or, at least, claimed that it benefited only a small minority—while the more usual claim was that this technological and material "progress" had created an even more objectionable society.

Chapter 5

1. Of course, it is possible to say that use of the term "America" for the United States is in itself an example of an arrogant expropriation of the type that could produce anti-Americanism. But since it is commonly accepted, this term will be used in this book, while the names South America or Latin America will be applied for that part of the New World.
2. Fitzgerald, *Political Thought of Bolivar*, 118.
3. Smith, *Talons of the Eagle*, 96.
4. Ibid.
5. Reid, *Spanish American Images of the United States 1790–1960*, 109.
6. Text in Toscano and Hiester, *Anti-Yankee Feelings in Latin America*, 17.
7. Text, ibid., 21.
8. Galeano, *Las Venas Abiertas de América Latina*, 10.
9. For more information on Mexican-U.S. relations, see John S. D. Eisenhower, *So Far from God: The U.S. War with Mexico, 1846–1848* (Norman, Oklahoma, 2000). For more information on Diaz, see Paul H. Garner, *Porfirio Diaz* (Cambridge, UK, 2001).
10. Grayson, "Anti-Americanism in Mexico," 35.
11. Smith, *Talons of the Eagle*, 111–112.
12. Reid, *Spanish American Images of the United States 1790–1960*, 157–158.
13. Toscano and Hiester, *Anti-Yankee Feelings in Latin America*, 53, 55.
14. Ibid., 55.
15. Reid, *Spanish American Images of the United States 1790–1960*, 194–195.
16. Darío, "To Roosevelt," http://www.worldpolicy.org/globalrights/nicaragua/1904-Dar%C3%ADo-english.html.
17. Reid, *Spanish American Images of the United States 1790–1960*, 195.
18. Ibid., 155–156.
19. Rangel, *Latin-Americans*, 36–38.
20. Text in Toscano and Hiester, *Anti-Yankee Feelings in Latin America*, 163.
21. Neruda, "United Fruit Company," http://subbacultcha.angelcities.com/unitedfruit.html.
22. Text in Toscano and Hiester, *Anti-Yankee Feelings in Latin America*, 165.
23. Rangel, *Latin-Americans*, 80–90.
24. Text in Toscano and Hiester, 43–45, 165.

25. Fuentes, "Prologue," *Ariel*, 16.
26. Rodó, *Ariel*, 31, 58.
27. Ibid., 51, 56, 58, 80.
28. Ibid., 81.
29. Ibid., 95–98.
30. Ibid., 59.
31. Ibid., 79.
32. Rubén Darío had used the Caliban image for America in the 1890s. Reid, *Spanish American Images of the United States 1790–1960*, 194–195.
33. Rodó, *Ariel*, 31, 58.
34. Reid, *Spanish American Images of the United States 1790–1960*, 154.
35. Rippy, "Introduction," Manuel Ugarte, *Destiny of a Continent*, xii.
36. Ugarte, *Destiny of a Continent*, 9.
37. Reid, *Spanish American Images of the United States 1790–1960*, 233.
38. Ugarte, *Destiny of a Continent*, 11–12.
39. Ibid., 16.
40. Ibid., 139–140.
41. Ibid., 141.
42. Text, Toscano and Hiester, *Anti-Yankee Feelings in Latin America*, 95–96.
43. Smith, *Talons of the Eagle*, 109–110.
44. From 1945 to 1951.
45. Arévalo, *Shark and the Sardines*, 9–10, 13.
46. Ibid., 17–43.
47. Although this title could be awarded to the People's Republic of China, North Korea, and several Middle Eastern dictatorships, it was a far more important issue for Cuba from the time of the revolution onward.
48. Goodsell, *Fidel Castro's Personal Revolution in Cuba: 1959–1973*, http://www.fordham.edu/halsall/mod/1962castro.html.
49. Ibid.
50. Guevara, *Guerrilla Warfare* (New York, 1961), 119.
51. Falcoff, *Culture of Its Own*, 56–57.
52. Rangel, *Latin-Americans*, 58–59.
53. Galeano, *Las Venas Abiertas de América Latina*, 8, 224–255.
54. Paz, *Tiempo Nublado*, 159.
55. Yergin and Stanislaw, *Commanding Heights*, 232–244.
56. Rangel, *Latin-Americans*, 44.
57. Galeano, *Las Venas Abiertas de América Latina* 3, 215.
58. Rangel, *Latin-Americans*, 87.
59. Ibid., 44.
60. Ibid., 44–46.
61. Ibid., 114.

62. Ibid., 58–59.

63. *Washington Post*, July 7, 1980, A-1 and A-12, quoted in Grayson, "Anti-Americanism in Mexico," 41.

64. *Washington Post*, December 28, 1981, A-21, described by Grayson, "Anti-Americanism in Mexico," 31–32.

65. Gastón García Cantú, "El Dilema del presente," *Excelsior*, July 13, 1987, 1, quoted in Pastor and Castañeda, *Limits to Friendship*, 123.

66. Pastor and Castañeda, *Limits to Friendship*, 29–30, 57, 76.

67. Ibid., 60.

68. *New York Times* poll, "Mexico Survey," October 28–November 4, 1986. Partial results of the poll were published in the *New York Times*, November 16–17, 1986, cited in Pastor and Castañeda, *Limits to Friendship*, 16–17, 59.

69. Pastor and Castañeda, *Limits to Friendship*, 140.

70. Ibid., 145–148.

71. Ibid., 192.

72. "Perceptions of US Are Nuanced among Those Who Know Us Best," U.S. Information Agency, Office of Research and Media Affairs, August 5, 1996.

73. Office of Research, U.S. Information Agency, "World Publics Have Mainly Positive Image of U.S. But Recognize Various Bilateral Tensions," Office of Research, U.S. Information Agency (January 29, 1993); Office of Research and Media Reaction, U.S. Information Agency "America as Global Actor: The U.S. Image Around the World," Office of Research and Media Reaction, U.S. Information Agency (January 1995), 25–30.

74. Hollander, *Anti-Americanism*, 359.

Chapter 6

1. Toynbee, *America and the World Revolution*, 208–209.

2. Obviously there are exceptions, like the Philippines, for example, but they were very limited ones.

3. Buchwald, "Why We Dislike Americans."

4. Pinter, "Degree Speech to the University of Florence," http://alt.venus.co .uk/weed/current/pinter3.htm.

5. Barzini, *Americans Are Alone in the World*, 84–85, 205.

6. Wagner, "America and Western Europe," 25.

7. Kenneth Tynan, "Letter to a Young Man," *Encounter* 9, no. 4 (October 1957), 19–23, cited in Wilford, *CIA, the British Left and the Cold War*, 273.

8. Laski, *American Democracy: A Commentary and an Interpretation* (London, 1949). The authors wish to thank Hugh Wilford for his help. For an ac-

count of the relationship between Britain and the American South, see Wilford, "The South and the British Left, 1930–1960."

9. Quoted in Brome, *J. B. Priestley*, 209.
10. Hollander, *Anti-Americanism*, 376.
11. Greene, *Quiet American*, 31, 140.
12. Wheatcroft, "Dickens to Le Carré," http://www.freerepublic.com/focus/ f-news/1055651/posts.
13. For a complete account of this struggle within the Labour Party, see Wilford, "South and the British Left, 1930–1960," 163–186.
14. Haseler, *Anti-Americanism*, 8.
15. Morgan, *Anti-Americans*, 216.
16. Revel, *L'Obsession anti-Américaine*, 19.
17. Zeldin, "Foreword," *Rise and Fall of Anti-Americanism*, xi.
18. Kuisel, *Seducing the French*, 24–25.
19. Revel, *L'Obsession anti-Américaine*, 19.
20. Ibid., 98.
21. Kuisel, *Seducing the French*, 40–41.
22. Ibid.
23. Winock, "Cold War," 73.
24. Kuisel, *Seducing the French*, 43.
25. Albert Beguin, "Réflexions sur l'Amerique, l'Europe, la neutralité," *Esprit* (June 1951), 886, quoted in Kuisel, *Seducing the French*, 115.
26. "Les Flammes de Budapest," *Esprit* (December 1956), quoted in Judt, *Past Imperfect*, 196.
27. Kuisel, *Seducing the French*, 116.
28. Ibid., 45.
29. Lacorne and Rupnik, "France Bewitched by America," 19.
30. Ibid.
31. Ibid.
32. Pierre-Antoine Cousteau, *L'Amérique Juive* 37, (n.d.), cited in Roger, *Rêves et cauchemars américains*, 41.
33. August Leclerc, "Flegme Yankee," *Le Réveil du Nord*, May 6, 1944, 1, quoted in Roger, *Rêves et cauchemars américains*, 41.
34. Thompson, "Prologue to Conflict," 16.
35. Roger, *Rêves et cauchemars américains*, 289–290.
36. Ibid., 294–295.
37. Kuisel, *Seducing the French*, 146.
38. Ibid., 148.
39. Bohlen, *Witness to History 1929–1969*, 510–511.
40. Judt, *Past Imperfect*, 202.

41. Rupnik and Humbertjean, "Images of the United States in Public Opinion," 79.

42. Deutsch, Macridis, Edinger, and Merritt, *France, Germany and the West Alliance*, 71.

43. De Beauvior, *America Day by Day*, 43.

44. Ibid.

45. Ibid., 308.

46. Ibid., 386.

47. Siegfried, *America at Mid-Century*, 6–7.

48. Ibid., 6–7.

49. Ibid., 352–356.

50. Sartre, *Situations III*, 81–82.

51. Ibid., 82–84.

52. Lacorne and Rupnik, "Intro: France Bewitched by America," 21.

53. Winock, "Cold War," 70.

54. Granjon, "Sartre, Beauvoir, Aron," 122.

55. Ibid., 117.

56. Roger, *Rêves et cauchemars Américains*, 57.

57. Judt, *Past Imperfect*, 201.

58. Revel, *L'Obsession anti-Américaine*, 193.

59. Schama, "Unloved American," http://www.newyorker.com/fact/content/?030310fa_fact.

60. Kahn, *Big Drink*, 20–27.

61. Kuisel, *Seducing the French*, 55–63.

62. Ibid.

63. Ibid., 104.

64. Ibid., 64.

65. Ibid.

66. Ibid., 65.

67. Strauss, *Menace in the West*, 272–273.

68. Lacorne and Rupnik, "Intro: France Bewitched by America," 23.

69. Ibid.

70. Rapin, "An Interview with the Linguist Claude Hagège," http://www.france.diplomatie.fr/label_france/ENGLISH/FRANCO/HAGEG/hageg.html.

71. R. Debray, *Modeste Contribution aux discourse et ceremonies officielles du dixième anniversaire* (Paris: Maspéro, 1978), 51–52, cited in Roger, *L'Ennemi Américain*, 523.

72. Revel, *L'Obsession anti-Américaine*, 202.

73. For more information about Védrine and his views, see Hubert Védrine with Dominique Moïsi, *France in an Age of Globalization* (Washington, D.C., 2001).

74. Lacorne and Rupnik, "Intro: France Bewitched by America," 18–19.

75. Kuisler, *Seducing the French*, 219–220.

76. Author's interviews in Paris, January 16–20, 2003.

77. Author's interview with Philippe Roger, January 20, 2003.

78. Aron, *Opium of the Intellectuals*, 228–229.

79. Revel, *L'Obsession Anti-Américaine*, 30.

80. Strauss, *Menace in the West*, 255.

81. Rapin, "Interview with the Linguist Claude Hagège," http://www.france
.diplomatie.fr/label_france/ENGLISH/FRANCO/HAGEG/hageg.html.

82. Hollander, *Anti-Americanism*, 385.

83. Baudrillard, *America*, 23.

84. Wheatcroft, "Dickens to Le Carré," http://www.freerepublic.com/focus/
f-news/1055651/posts.

85. Andrew Irving and David Scott, "British Public's Perceptions of Relationship between the U.K. and U.S. and Selected Political Issues," Office of Research, United States Information Agency, May 1988, i–xi.

86. Ibid., 30.

87. Hollander, *Anti-Americanism*, 389.

88. Moorehead, *Bertrand Russell*, 523. See Hollander, *Anti-Americanism*, 374–
375, for a similar statement.

Chapter 7

1. Al-'Awad, *Tishrin*, http://memri.org/bin/articles.cgi?Page=archives&Area=ia
&ID=IA13403.

2. Rushdie, "Anti-Americanism Has Taken the World by Storm," http://www
.guardian.co.uk/print/0,3858,4350590-108920,00.html.

3. Ajami, "Anti-Americans," http://www.travelbrochuregraphics.com/extra/the
_anti_americans.htm.

4. Ajami, "Stranger in the Arab-Muslim World," 60.

5. Gerges, "Tragedy of Arab-American Relations," http://www.csmonitor.com/
2001/0918/p9s1-coop.html.

6. Ajami, "Stranger in the Arab-Muslim World," 59.

7. Calvert, "The World Is an Undutiful Boy! Sayyid Qutb's American Experience," 94.

8. Ibid., 97.

9. Ibid., 99.

10. Ibid., 11.

11. Abdel-Malek, *America in an Arab Mirror*, 14–15.

12. Ibid., 18.

13. Ibid., 91–92.

14. Ibid., 135, 137.

15. "Sayyid Qutb's America," *All Things Considered*, National Public Radio, May 6, 2003, http://discover.npr.org/features/feature.jhtml?wfId=1253796.

16. Rubin and Rubin, *Anti-American Terrorism and the Middle East*, 128.

17. Cited in Abdel-Malek, *America in an Arab Mirror*, 94–95.

18. Ajami, "Stranger in the Arab-Muslim World," 56.

19. Republic of Iraq Television, September 12, 2001, translated by FBIS.

20. Rubin, *Arab States and the Palestine Conflict*, 216–233.

21. Podeh, "Lie That Won't Die: Collusion, 1967," http://www.meforum.org/article/587.

22. U.S. Archives, Record Group 59, report on the meeting by U.S. Embassy in Jordan, September 4, 1969.

23. Sobel, *Palestinian Impasse*, 227.

24. Interview with Arafat, *Le Quotidien de Paris*, September 15, 1981.

25. For a discussion of Arafat's views and relations with the United States, see Barry Rubin and Judith Colp Rubin, *Yasir Arafat: A Political Biography*.

26. Rubin and Rubin, *Anti-American Terrorism and the Middle East*, 113.

27. See Saddam Hussein, "Strategy for the Arab World," in Rubin and Rubin, *Anti-American Terrorism and the Middle East*, 119–123.

28. Ayatollah Ruhollah Khomeini, "United States Will Not Intervene Militarily," cited in ibid., 106–107.

29. There are parallels here to French anti-Americanism. See chapter 8.

30. Amin, "American Ideology," http://weekly.ahram.org.eg/2003/638/focus.htm.

31. Ibid.

32. Ibid.

33. Editorial, *al-Akhbar*, August 19, 2002. Excerpt and translation in "Another Crisis in Egypt-U.S. Relations As Reflected in the Egyptian Media," MEMRI Special Dispatch No. 413, August 21, 2002, http://memri.org/bin/articles.cgi?Page=archives&Area=sd&ID=SP41302.

34. Al-Jazira, "Opposite View," October 27, 2002, http://www.aljazeera.net/programs/op_direction/articles/2002/10/10-27-1.htm.

35. Awwad, al-Ayyam, http://memri.org/bin/articles.cgi?Page=archives&Area=sr&ID=SR01403.

36. *Al-Sharq al-Awsat*, December 12, 2001. Excerpt and translation in "Radical Islamist Profiles (3): Ayman Muhammad Rabi' Al-Zawahiri: The Making of an Arch Terrorist," MEMRI Inquiry and Analysis Series No. 127, March 11, 2003, http://www.memri.org/bin/articles.cgi?Page=archives&Area=ia&ID=IA12703#_ednref31; on the Egyptian Islamist view of America and Zawahiri's writings, see Barry Rubin, *Islamic Fundamentalists in Egyptian Politics* (New York, 2003).

NOTES

37. Altallah Abd Al-Abu Al-Subh, "Clinton's Visit to Israel and the Palestinian Authority," *al-Risala*, December 3, 1998 as cited in Rubin and Rubin, *Anti-American Terrorism and the Middle East*, 130.

38. Amin, "American Ideology," http://weekly.ahram.org.eg/2003/638/focus.htm.

39. *Jumhur-ye EIslami*, August 17, 2002. Excerpt and translation in "Iranian Conservative Daily: 'America Is the New Nazism,'" MEMRI Special Dispatch No. 417 (August 30, 2002), http://memri.org/bin/articles.cgi?Page=archives&Area=sd&ID=SP41702. The article appeared a few days after Iran's Supreme Leader Ali Khamenei compared Bush to Hitler in a speech.

40. Habid, *Okaz*, http://www.memri.org/bin/articles.cgi?Page=subjects&Area=middleeast&ID=SP51303.

41. *Jumhur-ye EIslami*, August 17, 2002, excerpt and translation in MEMRI Special Dispatch No. 417, August 30, 2002, http://memri.org/bin/articles.cgi?Page=archives&Area=sd&ID=SP41702.

42. *Al-Ahram*, January 13, 2003, excerpt and translation in "Egypt Rethinks Its Nuclear Program Part I: Scientific and Technological Capability vs. International Commitments," MEMRI Inquiry and Analysis Series No. 118, January 17, 2003, http://memri.org/bin/articles.cgi?Page=archives&Area=ia&ID=IA11803.

43. See "Egypt Air Crash: The Hidden Hand behind the Disaster," *al-Ahram*, April 2, 2000, http://www.albalagh.net/current_affairs/egypt_crash.shtml.

44. Teimourian, interview, *The World Today*, Australian Broadcasting Company, http://www.abc.net.au/worldtoday/s686685.htm.

45. Ali al-Husseini al-Khamene'i, "Second Speech to Organization of Islamic Countries Meeting," cited in Rubin and Rubin, *Anti-American Terrorism and the Middle East*, 128.

46. "Humaid Blasts West for Double Standard," *Arab News*, October 29, 2002, http://aljazeerah.info/News%20archives/2002%20News%20archives/Oct%202002%20News/Oct%2029,%202002%20News.htm.

47. Abdel-Bari Atwan, interview, *al-Jazira television*, October 12, 2003: cited in Abdallah, "Causes of Anti-Americanism in the Arab World: A Socio-Political Perspective," 69–70. See also al-Makdisi, "Anti-Americanism in the Arab World: An Interpretation of a Brief History," http://www.historycooperative.org/journals/jah/89.2/makdisi.html.

48. Amayreh, "Why I Hate America," http://www.memri.org/bin/articles.cgi?Page=archives&Area=sd&ID=SP30301.

49. For a detailed discussion of these events, see Rubin and Rubin, *Arafat*.

50. Ursan, *Al-Usbu' al-Adabi*, http://www.memri.org/bin/articles.cgi?Page=archives&Area=sd&ID=SP27501.

51. Ibid.

52. Amayreh, "Why I Hate America," http://memri.org/bin/articles.cgi?Page= archives&Area=sd&ID=SP30301.

53. BBC-TV, "Iraq Hails Attack on US," September 12, 2001, http://news.bbc.co .uk/1/hi/world/middle_east/1540216.stm.

54. al-Hawali, "Open Letter to President Bush," http://www.netcomuk.co.uk/ ~magamiet/Articles%2C_lectures/Open%20letter%20to%20Bush.htm.

55. "Prince" *60 Minutes*, CBS-TV, October 28, 2001; "Saudi Arabia: The Double-Act Wears Thin," *The Economist*, September 27, 2001.

56. Hafedh al-Shaykh, *Akhbar al-Khalij*, September 12, 2001, found in Murray Kahl, "Terror Strikes U.S.: 'An Act of War,' How Will Americans Respond," September 12, 2001, http://www.chretiens-et-juifs.org/article.php ?voir%5b%5d=839&voir%5b%5d=3736#_Toc525035372.

57. *Reuters*, September 11, 2001.

58. Juzo, *Al-Hayat*, http://www.memri.org/bin/articles.cgi?Page=archives&Area =sd&ID=SP27201.

59. Bin Ladin was shortly thereafter expelled from Sudan and found sanctuary in Afghanistan. His manifesto originally appeared in *al-Quds al-Arabi*. Translation in Rubin and Rubin, *Anti-American Terrorism and the Middle East*, 137–139.

60. *Reuters*, September 11, 2001.

61. Ibid.

62. As described in "U.S. Ambassador to Cairo Takes on Conspiracy Theories in the Egyptian Press," MEMRI No. 423, October 1, 2002, http://www .memri.org/bin/articles.cgi?Page=countries&Area=egypt&ID=SP42302.

63. *Al-Usbu'*, September 23, 2002, excerpt and translation in "U.S. Ambassador to Cairo Takes on Conspiracy Theories in the Egyptian Press," MEMRI Special Dispatch No. 423, October 1, 2002, http://www.memri.org/bin/ articles.cgi?Page=countries&Area=egypt&ID=SP42302.

64. For example, his speech of November 7, 1979. Text in U.S. Department of Commerce, Foreign Broadcast Information Service (FBIS), November 8, 1979.

65. Hawi, *Al-Safir*, September 15, 2001, translated by FBIS.

66. "Eye-Witness to the Crime," *Al-Ahram Al-Arabi*, May 20, 2002. Excerpt and translation in "Egyptian Government Paper Accuses America of Gulf War Atrocities," MEMRI Special Dispatch Series No. 99, June 8, 2000, http://www.memri.org/bin/articles.cgi?Page=archives&Area=sd&ID=SP9900.

67. Nafi, "Disturbing Phenomenon in the U.S. Media," http://memri.org/bin/ articles.cgi?Page=archives&Area=sd&ID=SP29201#_edn1.

68. Duweidar, "World in the Hands of a Devil," http://memri.org/bin/articles .cgi?Page=archives&Area=sd&ID=SP48203.

69. Mahmoud, "May the Cannibals be Cursed!" http://memri.org/bin/articles .cgi?Page=archives&Area=sd&ID=SP55903.

70. "Najaf Massacre and the National Unity Required in Iraq," *Al-Ahram*, editorial, August 31, 2003. Excerpt and translation in "Egyptian Government Daily Al-Ahram: The U.S. Is Behind the Najaf Bombing," MEMRI Special Dispatch No. 562, September 1, 2003, http://memri.org/bin/articles.cgi?Page =archives&Area=sd&ID=SP56203.

71. "Poll: Muslims Call U.S. 'Ruthless, Arrogant,' " CNN, February 26, 2002, http://edition.cnn.com/2002/US/02/26/gallup.muslims/; Andrea Stone, "Many in Islamic World Doubt Arabs Behind 9/11," *USA Today*, February 27, 2002, http://www.usatoday.com/news/sept11/2002/02/27/usa-poll.htm.

72. Pew Global Attitudes Project, "Views of a Changing World 2003/War with Iraq Further Divides Global Publics," June 3, 2003, 29, http://people-press .org/reports/display.php3?ReportID=185.

73. Dunham, "It's Not Americans That Arabs Hate," http://www.businessweek .com/bwdaily/dnflash/apr2002/nf20020415_0109.htm; Tessler, "Do Islamic Orientations Influence Attitudes toward Democracy in the Arab World: Evidence from the World Values Survey in Egypt, Jordan, Morocco, and Algeria," http:/conconflicts.ssrc.org/mideast/tessler/pf/; James J. Zogby, "What Arabs Think: Values, Beliefs and Concerns: Report of Zogby International Commissioned by the Arab Thought Foundation," September 2002.

74. Nicolas Francis, Moises Naim, Abdel Monem, and Said Aly, "Anti-Americanism: What's New, What's Next?" World Economic Forum annual meeting, February 1, 2002, http:/www.weforum.org/site/knowledgenavigator .nsf/Content/Anti-Americanism:%20What's%20New,%20What's%20Next? _2002?open&country_id=&region_id=701002.

75. Reuters, October 3, 2002.

76. "Khomeini Comes to America," American Enterprise Institute, September 26, 2003, http://www.aei.org/events/filter.,eventID.630/transcript.asp.

77. Nassar, "Interview with Saddam Hussein," http://memri.org/bin/articles.cgi ?Page=archives&Area=sd&ID=SP43702.

78. Al-Jazira. Excerpted and translated in "Qatar's Al-Jazirah TV Resumes Critical Tone toward US in Iraq," Foreign Broadcast Information Service (FBIS), December 12, 2003.

79. Murad, *Al-Akhbar*, http://memri.org/bin/articles.cgi?Page=archives&Area= sd&ID=SP46903.

80. *Al-Hayat Al-Jadida*, March 6, 2003. Excerpt and translation in "PA Youth Movement Verdict in 'Field Trial': President Bush Guilty of War Crimes," MEMRI Special Dispatch No. 477, March 7, 2003, http://memri.org/bin/ articles.cgi?Page=archives&Area=sd&ID=SP47703.

81. *Tishrin*, March 27, 2003.

82. Ibid., April 10, 2003.

83. Al-Fanik, "Imminent U.S. Aggression," http://memri.org/bin/articles.cgi ?Page=archives&Area=sd&ID=SP48203.

84. Al-Faisal, "America the Forgiven," http://www.arabnews.com/?page=1§ion= 0&article=32938&d=3&m=10&y=2003.

Chapter 8

1. Pew Global Attitudes Project, "America's Image Further Erodes, Europeans Want Weaker Ties," http://people-press.org/reports/display.php3?ReportID= 175PEW.

2. BBC, "Israeli Anger Over EU 'Threat' Poll," http://news.bbc.co.uk/1/hi/ world/middle_east/3237277.stm.

3. Pew Global Attitudes Project, "Year after Iraq War," http://www.pewtrusts .com/pdf/pew_global_attitudes_year_war_031604.pdf, 7–8.

4. Ibid., 22.

5. Ali, "Tariq Ali on the 'United Nations of America,'" http://www.greenleft .org.au/back/2003/527/527p22.htm.

6. Loach, "Marching Off to Peace," http://www.observer.co.uk/comment/story/ 0,6903,796615,00.html.

7. Ash, "Peril of Too Much Power," http://www.mtholyoke.edu/acad/intrel/ bush/ash.htm/.

8. Lenin, *On the United States of America*, 334–335.

9. *Après l'Empire* (2003), cited in Aster, "La Maladie Française," 3–4.

10. USIA Office of Research, "World Publics Have Mainly Positive Image of U.S. but Recognize Various Bilateral Tensions," January 29, 1993.

11. USIA Office of Research, "Western European Public Opinion Roundup on U.S. and NATO, Spring 1993," April 19, 1993.

12. USIA Office of Research and Media Reaction, "America as Global Actor: The U.S. Image around the World," January 1995, 4–8, 25–30.

13. USIA Office of Research, "The U.S. Image 2000: Global Attitudes Towards the U.S. in the New Millennium," November 2000, 22.

14. Lloyd, "How Anti-Americanism Betrays the Left," http://observer.guardian .co.uk/worldview/story/0,11581,668425,00.html.

15. Rushdie, "Rethinking the War on American Culture," http://www.uwm.edu/ ~wash/rushdie.htm.

16. Alibhai-Brown, "America Has Descended into Madness," http://argument .independent.co.uk/regular_columnists/yasmin_alibhai_brown/story.jsp?story =415816.

17. Burchill, "Suffering under Uncle Sam," http://www.guardian.co.uk/ Columnists/Column/0,5673,368817,00.html.
18. Rushdie, "Rethinking the War on American Culture," http://www.uwm.edu/ ~wash/rushdie.htm/.
19. Magnet, "London Peace Marchers Say: Long Live the Intifada," http://www .city-journal.org/html/eon_2_17_03jm.html.
20. Van Elteren, "America Life by Proxy: Dutch Youth and Their Sense of Place," 131.
21. Ibid.
22. Ibid., 132
23. Ibid., 163.
24. Ibid., 143.
25. Sardar and Davies, *Why Do People Hate America?*, 131.
26. McKay, "Afterward: Downsizing America," 161–162.
27. Guillaume, *Le Complot des maîtres du pouvoir* (The Plot of Our Rulers) (Paris, 1999), cited by Schütz, "Euro-skepticism and Anti-Americanism Erupt in Europe," http://www.culturekiosque.com/nouveau/books/ europeanunion.html.
28. See chapter 6.
29. Bové and Dufour, *World Is Not for Sale*, 55.
30. Mamère and Warin, *Non Merci, Oncle Sam!*, 9.
31. Ibid., 9–10.
32. The 1871 Franco-Prussian War plus World War I and II.
33. Mamère and Warin, *Non Merci, Oncle Sam!*, 15.
34. Ibid., 14.
35. Ibid., 11.
36. Riotta, "Transatlantic Chill?" B5.
37. Friedman, "Ah, Those Principled Europeans," http://www.cubaliberal.org/ archivo-03-01/03_02_02-a.htm.
38. See chapter 3.
39. Islam, "When Two Tribes Go to War," http://observer.guardian.co.uk/bush/ story/0,8224,982331,00.html/.
40. Lacorne, "Barbaric Americans," 54.
41. Ibid.
42. Riotta, "Transatlantic Chill?" B5.
43. U.S. Information Agency Office of Research, July 6, 1990.
44. USIA Opinion Research Memorandum, January 27, 1994.
45. USIA Briefing Paper, February 13, 1998.
46. ROMIR, "Western Attitudes Toward Russia as Perceived by Russians," November 13–14, 1999, cited in Shiraev and Zubok, *Anti-Americanism in Russia: From Stalin to Putin*, 71.

47. Office of Research, Department of State, "Russians Still Struggling with Loss of Superpower Status and U.S. Global Dominance," July 15, 2002.

48. Chugayev, "War in Iraq Destroys Myths About America," http://www.cdi .org/russia/250-3.cfm.

49. Center for Defense Information, "Poll Shows Saddam More Popular Than Bush Among Russians," http://www.cdi.org/russia/251-2.cfm.

50. Nikolayev, "Basic Lessons of the Iraqi War," http://www.cdi.org/russia/ 254-10.cfm.

51. Grishina, "Anti-Americanism Winning over Russia's Elite," http://www .therussiajournal.com/index.htm?obj=3969.

52. See chapter 3. A work that deals with this revival is James P. Scanlan, ed., *Russian Thought after Communism: The Recovery of a Philosophical Heritage* (New York: M.E. Sharpe, 1994).

53. Shiraev and Zubok, *Anti-Americanism in Russia*, 66–69, 72.

54. Nikos Dimou in *Ethnos*, November 14, 1999, and Nikos Vardiambasis in *Eleftherotypia*, November 13, 1999, cited in Dimitras, "Greeks' Persistent Anti-Americanism," http://www.aimpress.org/dyn/trae/archive/data/199912/91205 -017-trae-ath.htm.

55. Michas, "America the Despised," http://www.nationalinterest.org/issues/67/ Michas.html, 94–102.

56. Cornwell, "By George!," http://news.independent.co.uk/world/americas/story .jsp?story=463147.

57. Revel, *L'Obsession anti-Américaine*, 63–64.

58. Kettle, "U.S. Bashing: It's All the Rage in Europe," http://www .washingtonpost.com/ac2/wpdyn?pagename=article&node=&contentId= A26468-2001Jan6&notFound=true.

59. PEW Global Attitudes Project, "America Admired, Yet Its New Vulnerability Seen As Good Thing, Say Opinion Leaders," http://people-press.org/ reports/display.php3?ReportID=145.

60. Revel, *L'Obsession anti-Américaine*, 130.

61. Ibid., 131–132.

62. Colombiani, "We Are All Americans," http://www.worldpress.org/1101we_are _all_americans.htm.

63. Quoted in Ajami, "Falseness of Anti-Americanism," http://www .foreignpolicy.com/users/login.php?story_id=166&URL=http://www .foreignpolicy.com/story/cms.php?story_id=166.

64. See Giovanna Borradori, *Philosophy in a Time of Terror: Dialogues with Jurgen Habermas and Jacques Derrida* (Chicago, 2003).

65. *Reuters*, July 23, 2003.

66. Hale, "Global Warmth for U.S. after 9/11 Turns to Frost," http://www.usatoday.com/news/nation/2002-08-14-1a-cover_x.htm.

67. Theil, "Great 9/11 Conspiracy," http://bulletin.ninemsn.com.au/bulletin/eddesk.nsf/All/7C0C9C0FE6AD4F42CA256DA200146E47!open.

68. Rosenfeld, "Anti-Americanism and Anti-Semitism: A New Frontier of Bigotry," http://www.ajc.org/InTheMedia/Publications.asp?did=902, 4.

69. Clinton, "Chelsea Clinton Speaks Out for the First Time in a Personal Account of the September 11 Tragedy and Its Aftermath," http://www.digitalfreeway.com/talkmedia/december2001/Chelsea_excl.html.

70. Beard, "11 September," http://www.lrb.co.uk/v23/n19/mult01_.html.

71. Kaletsky, "Arrogance and Fear: An American Paradox," http://www.casi.org.uk/discuss/2002/msg00208.html.

72. Kaldor, "Beyond Militarism, Arms Races and Arms Control," http://www.ssrc.org/sept11/essays/kaldor.htm.

73. Meacher, "This War on Terrorism Is Bogus," http://www.guardian.co.uk/comment/story/0,3604,1036571,00.html.

74. Raven, "Bully with a Bloody Nose Is Still a Bully," http://www.guardian.co.uk/Columnists/Column/0,5673,553672,00.html.

75. Ibid.

76. Maxwell, "Anti-Americanism in Brazil," http://www.cfr.org/pdf/correspondence/xMaxwell.php.

77. Alberts, "PM Links Attacks to 'Arrogant West,' " http://www.freerepublic.com/focus/f-news/749357/posts.

78. Revel, *L'Obsession Anti-Américaine*, 162–163.

79. Ganley, "Journalist Lambasts French War Coverage," *Associated Press*, December 30, 2003.

80. Finn, "U.S.-Style Campaign with Anti-U.S. Theme," http://www.newsmine.org/archive/dissent/foreign/germany/german-anti-us-campaign.txt.

81. Rosenfeld, "Anti-Americanism and Anti-Semitism: A New Frontier of Bigotry," http://www.ajc.org/InTheMedia/Publications.asp?did=902, 4.

82. Ali, "Re-Colonizing Iraq," http://www.newleftreview.net/NLR25501.shtml.

83. Ibid.

84. Ali, "Interview," http://www.progressive.org/0901/intv0102.html.

85. Monbiot, "Logic of Empire," http://www.guardian.co.uk/bush/story/0,7369,769755,00.html.

86. Ibid.

87. *Le Monde*/TFI poll, April 1, 2003.

88. Hale, "Global Warmth for U.S. after 9/11 Turns to Frost," http://www.usatoday.com/news/nation/2002-08-14-1a-cover_x.htm.

89. Pinter, "God Bless America," http://globalresearch.ca/articles/PIN301A.html.

90. Eugenio Scalfari, *La Repubblica*, August 24, 2003.

91. Barbara Spinelli, *La Stampa*, August 24, 2003.

92. Le Carré, "United States of America Has Gone Mad," http://www
.commondreams.org/views03/0115-01.htm.

93. Applebaum, "America, the Gulag," http://www.washingtonpost.com/ac2/wp
-dyn?pagename=article&node=&contentId=A42230-2003Jun10&notFound
=true.

94. Summerfield, "Canadians Love Americans, Dislike Their Government";
"Canadians Approve of the US, Disapprove of President George W. Bush,"
Environics Research Group/Focus, July 11, 2003, http://erg.environics.net/
news/default.asp?aID=524.

95. Drabble, "I Loathe America, and What It Has Done to the Rest of the
World," http://www.telegraph.co.uk/opinion/main.jhtml?xml=/opinion/
2003/05/08/do0801.xml.

96. Quick quote, February 10, 2003; all other quotes, Australian parliamentary
debates transcript, March 19, 2003.

97. Fallaci, *The Rage and the Pride*, 67, 149–151.

98. Esler, "The Danger of This Infantile Anti-Americanism," http://argument
.independent.co.uk/commentators/story.jsp?story=406294.

99. "Anti-Americanism in Old Europe: A Dialogue with Bernard-Henri Lévy,"
http://www.digitalnpq.org/global_services/global%20viewpoint/02-04-03levy
.html. Revel's book was on the best-seller list. There was also Bernard-
Henri Lévy's *Who Killed Daniel Pearl?* and two books by André Glucks-
mann, *Dostoyevsky in Manhattan* and *West vs. West.*

Chapter 9

1. Hollander, *Anti-Americanism*, 336.

2. Moynihan, *Dangerous Place*, 76.

3. PEW Global Attitudes Project, "A Year after the Iraq War," 20, http://www
.pewtrusts.com/pdf/pew_global_attitudes_year_war_031604.pdf.

4. This is equally true of what might be called pro-Americanism. Similarly, it
would be possible to write a book like this one on the influence and inspiration of the United States—but not of these other countries—in creating
pro-American forces that tried to copy its methods and institutions elsewhere, not only in the Third World but also throughout Europe.

5. Qutb, *Ma'alim fi al-Tariq*, http://www.masmn.org/Books/Syed_Qutb/
Milestones/001.htm.

6. Quoted in Paz, "Islamists and Anti-Americanism," http://meria.idc.ac.il/
journal/2003/issue4/jv7n4a5.html.

7. Steyn, "It's 'Peace' Psychosis in a Nut's Hell," http://opinion.telegraph.co .uk/opinion/main.jhtml?xml=/opinion/2003/11/18/do1802.xml.

8. Ajami, "Falseness of Anti-Americanism," http://www.foreignpolicy.com/ users/login.php?story_id=166&URL=http://www.foreignpolicy.com/story/ cms.php?story_id=166.

9. McPherson, "Latin American Anti-Americanism and U.S. Responses: Venezuela 1958," www.driskellcenter.umd.edu/programs/2002-2003/conf/washla/ papers/McPherson.pdf.

10. Döpfner, "Bush ist dumm und böse," http://www.welt.de/data/2004/04/21/ 267596.html.

11. Aaronovitch, "Lost from the Baghdad Museum: Truth," http://www .guardian.co.uk/Iraq/Story/0%2C2763%2C974193%2C00.html.

12. Wasserstein, "Anti-Semitism and Anti-Americanism," http://chronicle.com/ free/v48/i05/05b00502.htm.

13. Safire, "German Problem," http://de.indymedia.org/2002/09/30138.shtml.

14. Halevi, "Twin Hatreds: Anti-Americanism and Anti-Semitism," GLORIA Center Conference on Anti-Americanism, September 17, 2003.

15. Harris, "Intellectual Origins of America-Bashing," http://www.policyreview .org/deco2/harris.html.

16. By way of comparison, Marx traced the origins of his ideology to the trio of German philosophy, French utopianism, and British political economy.

17. For a good discussion of this issue that shows the limits of anti-Americanism in Germany, see Richard Bernstein, "German Question," *New York Times Magazine*, May 2, 2004.

18. Lacorne, "Barbaric Americans," 55.

19. Johnson, "Anti-Americanism Is Racist Envy," http://www.forbes.com/ columnists/global/2003/0721/017.html.

20. Frankel, "Sneers From Across the Atlantic: Anti-Americanism Moves to W. Europe's Political Mainstream," A1.

21. Frum, "America in the Dock," *Daily Telegraph*, October 21, 2002, http:// news.telegraph.co.uk/opinion/main.jhtml?xml=/opinion/2002/10/21/do2101 .xml&sSheet=/opinion/2002/10/21/ixopinion.html.

22. Revel, *Neither Marx nor Jesus*, 139.

23. Haseler, *Varieties of Anti-Americanism*, 42–45.

24. Koestler, *Lotus and Robot*, 277.

25. Jack, "This Land Is Their Land," http://books.guardian.co.uk/review/story/ 0,12084,908950,00.html.

26. Kuisel, *Seducing the French*, 114.

27. There is a valid reason for portraying criticism from foreigners as anti-Americanism while that same sentiment coming from Americans—and quoted abroad—is not so classified. There is a natural dichotomy in any in-

group/out-group relationship in which self-criticism, even when apparently vitriolic, is based on a certain context and set of assumptions that makes it objectively less sweeping and hostile.

28. An increasingly multicultural Europe also has such features, yet that is precisely the point: why do a relatively small number of American restaurants pose a threat when many more "foreign" eateries do not?

29. Ramonet, "Other Axis of Evil," http://mondediplo.com/2002/03/01axis.

30. Kagan, "Power and Weakness," http://www.policyreview.org/JUN02/kagan .html.

31. Ibid.

32. Frachon, "America Unloved," http://www.worldpress.org/europe/ 0202lemonde_eye.htm.

33. Worldnet Daily.com, "Mystery Superflu: China Blames U.S. for SARS," May 9, 2003, http://www.worldnetdaily.com/news/article.asp?ARTICLE_ID= 32493.

34. Associated Press, "Thousands Push Polio Vaccine in Africa," February 22, 2004.

35. Moynihan, *Dangerous Place*, 32.

BIBLIOGRAPHY

Books

Abdel-Malek, Kamal, ed. *America in an Arab Mirror: Images of America in Arabic Travel Literature.* New York, 2000.

Adams, Henry. *The Education of Henry Adams.* New York, 1942.

Adams, Michael. *Fire and Ice: The United States, Canada and the Myth of Converging Values.* Toronto, 2003.

Ali, Tariq. *The Clash of Fundamentalisms: Crusades, Jihads and Modernity.* London, 2002.

Arévalo, Juan Jose. *The Shark and the Sardines.* New York, 1961.

Arnold, Matthew. *Civilization in the United States.* Boston, 1888.

———. *Discourses in America.* London, 1885.

Aron, Raymond. *The Opium of the Intellectuals.* New York, 1962.

Ashby, Eric. *Scientist in Russia.* Middlesex, U.K., 1947.

Aveling, Edward, and Eleanor Marx. *The Working-Class Movement in America.* London, 1891.

Baker, William J. *America Perceived: A View from Abroad in the 19th Century.* West Haven, Conn., 1977.

Barghoorn, Frederick C. *Soviet Image of the United States.* New York, 1950.

Barzini, Luigi. *Americans Are Alone in the World.* New York, 1953.

Baudrillard, Jean. *America.* London, 1988.

Beichman, Arnold. *Nine Lies about America.* New York, 1972.

Beloff, Max. *The Foreign Policy of Soviet Russia 1929–1941.* Vols. 1 and 2. Oxford, U.K., 1949.

Benson, Adolph, ed. *The America of 1750; Peter Kalm's Travels in North America: The English Version of 1770.* Vols. 1 and 2. New York, 1966.

Berger, Max. *The British Traveler in America, 1836–1860.* New York, 1943.

Biddiss, Michael D. *Father of Racist Ideology.* London, 1970.

———, ed. *Gobineau, Selected Political Writings.* London, 1970.

Blanchard, Mary. *Oscar Wilde's America.* New Haven, Conn., 1998.

Blumenthal, Henry. *American and French Culture, 1800–1900.* Baton Rouge, La., 1975.

Bohlen, Charles. *Witness to History 1929–1969.* New York, 1973.

Bonn, M. J. *The American Adventure: A Study of Bourgeois Civilization.* New York, 1934.

Bormann, Martin. *Hitler's Secret Conversations 1941–1944.* New York, 1953.

Bové, José, and François Dufour. *The World is Not for Sale: Farmers against Junk Food.* London, 2001.

Brome, Vincent. *J. B. Priestley.* London, 1988.

Browder, Robert Paul. *The Origins of Soviet-American Ideology.* Princeton, N.J., 1953.

Bucar, Annabelle. *The Truth About American Diplomats.* Moscow, 1949.

Carlyle, Thomas. *Latter-Day Pamphlets.* http://www.gutenberg.net/etext97/latda10.txt.

Ceaser, James W. *Reconstructing America.* New Haven, Conn., 1997.

Chastanet, J. L. *L'Oncle Shylock ou l'impérialisme Américain à la conquête du monde.* Paris, 1927.

Chateaubriand, Françoise-René. *Memoires.* New York, 1961.

Chesterton, G. K. *What I Saw in America.* New York, 1923.

Clark, William. *Less Than Kin.* Boston, 1957.

Colombiani, Jean-Marie. *Tous Américains? Le monde après le 11 Septembre 2001.* Paris, 2002.

Commager, Henry Steele, ed. *America in Perspective: The United States through Foreign Eyes.* New York, 1947.

Commager, Henry Steele, and Elmo Giordanetti, eds. *Was America a Mistake? An Eighteenth Century Controversy.* New York, 1967.

Compton, James. *The Swastika and the Eagle.* London, 1968.

Conrad, Peter. *Imagining America.* New York, 1980.

Crèvecoeur, Jean de. *Letters from an American Farmer.* http://old.jccc.net/ ~vclark/doc8_1_1.htm.

Cross, Robert D. *The Emergence of Liberal Catholicism in America.* Cambridge, Mass., 1958.

Crozier, Michel. *The Trouble with America.* Berkeley, Calif., 1984.

Darwin, Charles, *Journal of Researches into the Natural History and Geology of the Countries Visited during the Voyage of H.M.S. Beagle Round the World, under the Command of Capt. Fitz Roy, R.N.* London, 1845.

De Beauvoir, Simone. *America Day by Day.* Berkeley, Calif., 1999.

De Tocqueville, Alexis. *Democracy in America.* Vols. 1 and 2. http://xroads .virginia.edu/~HYPER/DETOC/toc_indx.html.

Deutsch, Karl. W., Roy C. Macridis, Lewis J. Edinger, and Richard L. Merritt, *France, Germany, and the Western Alliance: A Study of Elite Attitudes on European Integration and World Politics.* New York, 1967.

Dickens, Charles. *American Notes.* New York, 1985.

———. *The Dickens Digest.* New York, 1943.

Diner, Dan. *America in the Eyes of the Germans: An Essay on Anti-Americanism.* Princeton, N.J., 1996.

Dorfman, Ariel, and Armand Mattelart. *How to Read Donald Duck: Imperialist Ideology in the Disney Comic.* New York, 1991.

Dostoyevsky. *The Devils (The Possessed).* London, 1971.

Duhamel, Georges. *Scènes de la Vie Future.* Paris, 1930.

Eastman, Max. *Great Companions: Critical Memoirs of Some Famous Friends.* New York, 1959.

Echeverria, Durand. *Mirage in the West: A History of the French Image of American Society to 1815.* New York, 1966.

Erb, Richard D., and Stanley R. Ross, eds. *United States Relations with Mexico: Context and Content.* Washington, D.C., 1981.

Evans, J. Martin. *America: The View from Europe.* San Francisco, Calif., 1976.

Fairlie, Henry. *The Spoiled Child of the Western World.* New York, 1976.

Falcoff, Mark. *A Culture of Its Own.* New Brunswick, N.J., 1998.

Fallaci, Oriana. *The Rage and the Pride.* New York, 2001.

Fay, Bernard. *The American Experiment.* New York, 1929.

Fischer, Louis. *The Soviets in World Affairs: A History of Relations between the Soviet Union and the Rest of the World.* Vols. 1 and 2. Princeton, N.J., 1951.

Fitzgerald, Gerald E., ed. *The Political Thought of Bolivar.* The Hague, Netherlands, 1971.

Ford, Paul Leicester, ed. *Works of Thomas Jefferson.* Vol. 3. New York, 1904.

Friedenberg, Edgar Z., ed. *The Anti-American Generation.* New York, 1971.

Fuentes, Carlos. *The Buried Mirror: Reflections on Spain and the New World.* New York, 1992.

Galeano, Eduardo. *Las Venas Abiertas de América Latina.* Mexico City, Mexico, 1986.

Gasset, José Ortega y. *The Revolt of the Masses.* New York, 1932.

George, Alexander, ed. *Western State Terrorism.* New York, 1991.

Gerbi, Antonello. *The Dispute of the New World: The History of a Polemic, 1750–1900.* Pittsburgh, Penn., 1973.

Goodsell, James Nelson. *Fidel Castro's Personal Revolution in Cuba: 1959–1937.* New York, 1975. http://www.fordham.edu/halsall/mod/1962castro.html.

Gorky, Maxim. *The City of the Yellow Devil.* Moscow, 1972.

Graham, Greene. *The Quiet American.* London, 1982.

Granatstein, J. L. *Yankee Go Home?,* Toronto, Canada, 1996.

Guevara, Che. *Guerrilla Warfare.* New York, 1961.

Hacker, Andrew. *The End of the American Era.* New York, 1970.

Hamsun, Knut. *The Cultural Life of Modern America.* Cambridge, Mass., 1969.

Handlin, Oscar. *The Distortion of America.* New Brunswick, N.J., 1996.

Hardt, Michael, and Antonio Negri. *Empire.* Cambridge, Mass, 2000.

Haseler, Stephen. *Anti-Americanism: Steps on a Dangerous Path.* London, 1986.

———. *The Varieties of Anti-Americanism.* Washington, D.C., 1985.

Hegel, George Wilhelm Friedrich. *The Philosophy of History.* New York, 1900.

Heidegger, Martin. *An Introduction to Metaphysics.* New Haven, Conn., 1959.

Heilman, Robert B. *America in English Fiction.* Baton Rouge, La., 1937.

Hollander, Paul. *Anti-Americanism: Irrational & Rational.* Brunswick, N.J., 1995.

Hollyday, G. T. *Anti-Americanism in the German Novel, 1841–1861.* Berne, Switzerland, 1977.

Hurstfield, Julian G. *America and the French Nation, 1939–1945.* Chapel Hill, N.C., 1986.

Ilf, Ilya, and Eugene Petrov. *Little Golden America.* New York, 1937.

Ilin, M. *New Russia's Primer: The Story of the Five Year Plan.* Cambridge, Mass., 1931.

Jack, Ian. *Granta 77: What We Think of America.* London, 2002.

James, Henry. *The American Scene.* New York, 1946.

Jefferson, Thomas. *Notes on the State of Virginia.* Chapel Hill, N.C., 1955.

Jones, Ernest. *The Life and Work of Sigmund Freud.* New York, 1961.

Jones, Howard Mumford. *America and French Culture.* Chapel Hill, N.C., 1927.

Jordan, Donaldson, and Edwin Pratt. *Europe and the American Civil War.* New York, 1931.

Joseph, Franz M, ed. *As Others See Us: The United States through Foreign Eyes.* Princeton, N.J., 1959.

Judt, Tony. *Past Imperfect: French Intellectuals, 1944–1956*. Berkeley, Calif., 1992.

Julien, Claude. *America's Empire*. New York, 1973.

Kafka, Franz. *Amerika*. New York, 1946.

Kahn, E. J., Jr. *The Big Drink*. New York, 1950.

Kaiser, Karl, and Hans-Peter Schwartz, eds. *America and Western Europe: Problems and Prospects*. Lexington, Mass., 1978.

Kamalipour, Yahya R., ed. *Images of the U.S. around the World: A Multicultural Perspective*. Albany, N.Y., 1999.

Kipling, Rudyard. *American Notes*. New York, 1891. http://www.selfknowledge .com/amrnt10.htm.

Koestler, Arthur. *The Lotus and Robot*. New York, 1961.

Kroes, Rob, and Maarten Van Rossem, eds. *Anti-Americanism in Europe*. Amsterdam, 1986.

Kuisel, Richard F. *Seducing the French: The Dilemma of Americanization*. Berkeley, Calif., 1993.

Lacorne, Denis, Jacques Rupnik, and Marie-France Toinet, eds. *The Rise and Fall of Anti-Americanism: A Century of French Perception*. New York, 1990.

Lacouture, Jean. *De Gaulle*. London, 1970.

Lawrence, D. H. *The Plumed Serpent*. New York, 1951.

Leiken, Robert S. *Why Nicaragua Disappeared*. New York, 2003.

Lenin, Vladimir. *On the United States of America*. Moscow, 1967.

Lyon, John, and Phillip R. Sloan, eds., *From Natural History to the History of Nature: Readings from Buffon and His Critics*. Notre Dame, Indiana, 1981.

Mamère, Noël, and Olivier Warin. *Non Merci, Oncle Sam!* Paris, 1999.

Marryat, Frederick. *A Diary in America*. Series 1, Vols. 2 and 3, and Series 2, Vols. 1–3. http://www.athelstane.co.uk/marryat/diaramer/diaramer.htm.

Marti, Jose. *Marti on the U.S.A.* Carbondale, Ill., 1966.

Martineau, Harriet. *Retrospect of Western Travel*. Vol. 1. New York, 1838.

Marx, Leo. *The Machine in the Garden: Technology and the Pastoral Idea in America*. New York, 1964.

McKay, George, ed. *Yankee Go Home (& Take Me with U)*. Sheffield, U.K., 1977.

McPherson, James M. *Antietam: Crossroads of Freedom*. New York, 2002.

Mereness, Newton D. *Travels in the American Colonies 1690–1788*. New York, 1916.

Miller, Henry. *Airconditioned Nightmare*. Vol. 1. New York, 1945.

Montesquieu, Charles de. *The Spirit of Laws*. New York, 1990.

Moore, Thomas. *The Complete Poems of Sir Thomas Moore*. http://sailor .gutenberg.org/etext05/7cptm10.txt.

Moorehead, Caroline. *Bertrand Russell: A Life*. New York, 1963.

Morand, Paul. *New York*. New York, 1930.

Moreau de Saint-Méry, Mederic Louis Elie. *Moreau de St. Méry's American Journey 1793–1798.* Garden City, N.Y., 1947.

Morgan, Thomas B. *The Anti-Americans.* London, 1967.

Moynihan, Daniel Patrick. *A Dangerous Place.* New York, 1978.

Nevins, Allan, ed. *America through British Eyes.* New York, 1948.

O'Gorman, Edward. *The Invention of America.* Bloomington, Ind., 1961.

Parks, J. D. *Culture, Conflict and Coexistence: American-Soviet Cultural Relations, 1917–1958.* Jefferson, N.C., 1983.

Pastor, Robert A., and Jorge C. Castañeda. *Limits to Friendship: The United States and Mexico.* New York, 1988.

Paxton, Robert, and Nicholas Wohl, eds. *De Gaulle and the United States: A Centennial Reappraisal.* Oxford, U.K., 1994.

Paz, Octavio. *The Labyrinth of Solitude.* New York, 1985.

———. *Tiempo Nublado.* Barcelona, Spain, 1983.

Pelling, Henry. *America and the British Left.* London, 1956.

Pells, Richard. *Not like US: How Europeans Have Loved, Hated, and Transformed American Culture since World War II.* New York, 1997.

Pfaff, William. *Barbarian Sentiments.* New York, 1989.

Qutb, Sayyid. *Ma'alim fi al-Tariq.* English translation, http://www.masmn.org/Books/Syed_Qutb/Milestones/001.htm.

Rangel, Carlos. *The Latin-Americans: Their Love-Hate Relationship with the United States.* New York, 1977.

———. *Third World Ideology and Western Reality: Manufacturing Political Myth.* New Brunswick, N.J., 1986.

Rauschning, Hermann. *The Voice of Destruction.* New York, 1940.

Reid, John T. *Spanish American Images of the United States 1790–1960.* Gainesville, Fla., 1977.

Revel, Jean-François, *L'Obsession Anti-Américaine.* Paris, 2002.

———. *Without Marx or Jesus: The New American Revolution Has Begun.* Garden City, N.Y., 1971.

Roazen, Paul. *Freud: Political and Social Thought.* New Brunswick, N.J., 1999.

Rodó, José Enrique. *Ariel.* Austin, Texas, 1988.

Roger, Jacques. *Buffon: A Life in Natural History.* Ithaca, N.Y., 1997.

Roger, Philippe. *Rêves et cauchemars Américains: Les Etats-Unis au Miroir De l'opinion Publique Française, 1945–1953.* Paris, 1998.

———. *L'Ennemi Américain.* Paris, 2002.

Romier, Lucien. *Who Will Be Master: Europe or America?* New York, 1928.

Rubin, Barry. *The Arab States and the Palestine Conflict.* New York, 1982.

———. *How Others Report Us.* Beverly Hills, Calif., 1979.

Rubin, Barry, and Judith Colp Rubin. *Anti-Americanism in the Middle East: A Documentary Reader.* New York, 2002.

———. *Arafat: A Political Biography.* New York, 2003.

Rubinstein, Alvin Z., and Donald E. Smith, eds. *Anti-Americanism in the Third World: Implications for U.S. Foreign Policy.* New York, 1985.

Santayana, George. *Character and Opinion of the United States.* New York, 1921.

Sardar, Ziauddin, and Merryl Wyn Davies. *Why Do People Hate America?* Cambridge, U.K., 2002.

Sartre, Jean-Paul. *Situations III.* Paris, 1949.

Schmidt, Hugo. *Nikolaus Lenau.* New York, 1971.

Schmitt, Karl M. *Mexico and the United States, 1821–1973: Conflict and Coexistence.* New York, 1974.

Schopenhauer, Arthur. *The World as Will and Idea.* New York, 1961.

Schulte Nordholt, Jan Willem. *The Dutch Republic and American Independence.* Chapel Hill, N.C., 1982.

Servan-Schreiber, J. J. *The American Challenge.* New York, 1968.

Shaw, George Bernard. *The Political Madhouse in America and Nearer Home.* London, 1933.

Shiraev, Eric, and Vladislav Zubok. *Anti-Americanism in Russia: From Stalin to Putin.* New York, 2000.

Shlapentokh, Vladimir. *Soviet Public Opinion and Ideology.* New York, 1986.

Shub, David. *Lenin.* New York, 1948.

Siegfried, André. *America At Mid-Century.* New York, 1955.

———. *America Comes of Age.* New York, 1927.

Simmons, James C. *Star-Spangled Eden.* New York, 2000.

Sinclair, Keith. *A History of New Zealand.* Auckland, New Zealand, 2000.

Smith, Peter H. *Talons of the Eagle: Dynamics of U.S.–Latin American Relations.* New York, 1996.

Sobel, Lester, ed. *Palestinian Impasse: Arab Guerrillas and International Terror.* New York, 1977.

Spengler, Oswald. *The Decline of the West.* Vols. 1 and 2. New York, 1926.

Stearn, Gerald Emanuel, ed. *Broken Image: Foreign Critiques of America.* London, 1975.

Strauss, David. *Menace in the West: The Rise of French Anti-Americanism in Modern Time.* Westport, Conn., 1978.

Tatum, Edward. *The United States and Europe 1815–1823.* Berkeley, Calif., 1936.

Thornton, Thomas Perry, ed. *Anti-Americanism: Origins and Context.* Newbury Park, Calif., 1988.

Tomlinson, John. *Cultural Imperialism.* Baltimore, Md., 1991.

Toscano, F., and James Hiester, eds. *Anti-Yankee Feelings in Latin America: An Anthology of American Writings from Colonial to Modern Times in Their Historical Perspective.* Washington, D.C., 1982.

Toynbee, Arnold J. *America and the World Revolution.* New York, 1962.

Trollope, Anthony. *North America.* Vol. 1. http://www.worldwideschool.org/library/books/geo/geography/northamericavolumei/toc.html.

Trollope, Frances. *Domestic Manners of the Americans.* New York, 1927.

Trommler, Frank, and Joseph McVeigh, eds. *America and the Germans.* Vol. 1. Philadelphia, 1985.

Ugarte, Manuel. *Destiny of a Continent.* New York, 1925.

Ward, Joseph P., ed. *Britain and the American South: From Colonialism to Rock and Roll.* Jackson, Miss., 2003.

Waugh, Evelyn. *The Loved One: An Anglo-American Tragedy.* Boston, 1948.

Wells, H. G. *The Future in America.* New York, 1974.

Whitaker, Arthur P., and David C. Jordan. *Nationalism in Contemporary Latin America,* 1966.

Wilford, Hugh. *The CIA, The British Left, and the Cold War.* London, 2003.

Wister, Fanny Kemble, ed. *Fanny, the American Kemble: Her Journals and Unpublished Letters.* Tallahassee, Fla., 1972.

Yergin, Daniel, and Joseph Stanislaw. *Commanding Heights.* New York, 2002.

Zinn, Howard. *On History.* New York, 2001.

Articles and Chapters

Aaronovitch, David. "Lost from the Baghdad Museum: Truth." *Guardian.* June 10, 2003. http://www.guardian.co.uk/Iraq/Story/0%2C2763%2C974193%2C00.html.

Abdallah, Abdel Mahdi. "Causes of Anti-Americanism in the Arab World: A Socio-Political Perspective." *MERIA Journal,* 7, no. 4 (December 2003): 62–73.

Ajami, Fouad. "The Anti-Americans." *Wall Street Journal,* July 3, 2003. http://www.travelbrochuregraphics.com/extra/the_anti_americans.htm.

———. "The Falseness of Anti-Americanism." *Foreign Policy* (September/October 2003). http://www.foreignpolicy.com/users/login.php?story_id=166&URL=http://www.foreignpolicy.com/story/cms.php?story_id=166.

———. "The Sentry's Solitude." *Foreign Affairs* (November/December 2001). http://www.foreignaffairs.org/20011101facomment5770/fouad-ajami/the-sentry-s-solitude.html.

———. "Stranger in the Arab-Muslim World." *Wilson Quarterly* (spring 2001), 56–60.

Al-'Awad, Abd al-Fattah. Article in *Teshreen,* March 22, 2003. Excerpt and translation in "Syrian Government and Media on the War in Iraq." *MEMRI Inquiry and Analysis Series No. 134,* April 21, 2003. http://memri.org/bin/articles.cgi?Page=archives&Area=ia&ID=IA13403#_edn13.

Al-Faisal, Reem. "America the Forgiven." *Arab News*, October 3, 2003. http://www.arabnews.com/?page=1§ion=0&article=32938&d=3&m=10&y= 2003.

Al-Fanik, Fahd. "The Imminent U.S. Aggression." *al-Ra'i*, March 19, 2003. Excerpt and translation in "Ultimatum to Iraq—The Reaction of the Arab Press." *MEMRI Special Dispatch No. 482*, March 20, 2003. http://memri.org/ bin/articles.cgi?Page=archives&Area=sd&ID=SP48203.

Al-Hawali, Safar bin Abd al-Rahman. "An Open Letter to President Bush." October 15, 2001. http://www.netcomuk.co.uk/~magamiet/Articles%2C_lectures/ Open%20letter%20to%20Bush.htm.

Alberts, Sheldon. "PM Links Attacks to 'Arrogant West.'" *National Post*, September 12, 2002. http://www.freerepublic.com/focus/f-news/749357/posts.

Ali, Tariq. Interview. *Progressive Magazine* (January 2002). http://www .progressive.org/0901/intv0102.html.

———. "Re-Colonizing Iraq." *New Left Review 21* (May–June 2003). http://www .newleftreview.net/NLR25501.shtml.

———. "Tariq Ali on the 'United Nations of America'." *Green Left Weekly*, February 26, 2003. http://www.greenleft.org.au/back/2003/527/527p22.htm.

Alibhai-Brown, Yasmin. "America Has Descended into Madness." *The Independent*, June 16, 2003. http://argument.independent.co.uk/regular_columnists/ yasmin_alibhai_brown/story.jsp?story=415816.

Amayreh, Khalid. "Why I Hate America." *Palestine Times* (November 2001). Excerpt and translation in "Terror in America: Palestinian Islamist Journalist: 'Why I Hate America'." *MEMRI Special Dispatch No. 303*, November 27, 2001. http://www.memri.org/bin/articles.cgi?Page=archives&Area=sd&ID= SP30301.

Amiel, Barbara. "Anti-Americans Are Really against Liberal Democracy." http:// www.guardian.co.uk/Iraq/Story/0%2C2763%2C974193%2C00.html.

Amin, Samir. "The American Ideology." *Al-Ahram Weekly*, May 15–21, 2003. http://weekly.ahram.org.eg/2003/638/focus.htm.

Applebaum, Anne. "America, the Gulag." *Washington Post*, June 11, 2003. http:// www.washingtonpost.com/ac2/wp-dyn?pagename=article&node=&contentId =A42230-2003Jun10&notFound=true.

Arafat, Yassir. Interview. *Le Quotidien de Paris*, September 15, 1981.

Arnon, Robert. "From France." In *As Others See Us: The United States through Foreign Eyes*, edited by Franz M. Joseph. Princeton, N.J., 1959.

Ash, Timothy Garton. "The Peril of Too Much Power." *New York Times*, April 9, 2002. http://www.mtholyoke.edu/acad/intrel/bush/ash.htm.

Astier, Henri. "La Maladie Française." *Times Literary Supplement*, January 10, 2003, 3–4.

Auden, W. H. "Introduction." In Henry James, *The American Scene*. New York, 1946.

Awwad, Abdallah. Article in *al-Ayyam*, April 11, 2003. Excerpt and translation in "Arab and Muslim Media Reactions to the Fall of Baghdad." *MEMRI Special Report No. 14*, April 11, 2003. http://memri.org/bin/articles.cgi?Page=archives&Area=sr&ID=SR01403/.

Beard, Mary. "11-September—Some LRB Writers Reflect on the Reasons and Consequences." *London Review of Books*, October 4, 2001, 20.

Brogan, Denis. "From England." In *As Others See Us: The United States through Foreign Eyes*, edited by Franz M. Joseph. Princeton, N.J., 1959.

Brooks, David. "Among the Bourgeoisophobes." *Weekly Standard* 007, no. 30, (April 15, 2002). http://www.weeklystandard.com/Content/Public/Articles/000/000/001/102gwtnf.asp.

Buchwald, Art. "Why We Dislike Americans," *Paris Herald Tribune*, August 19 and 20, 1957.

Burchill, Julie. "Suffering under Uncle Sam." *The Guardian*, September 16, 2000. http://www.guardian.co.uk/Columnists/Column/0,5673,368817,00.html.

Burdett, Charles. "Different Visions of Space: Italian Fascist Writers and the United States." *Cardiff University New Readings*, 5 (March 28, 2001). http://www.cf.ac.uk/euros/newreadings/volume5/burdett.html.

Burlatskii, Fedor. "SshA i SSSR (The U.S. and the USSR)." *Washington Profile*, July 30, 2003. http://www.washprofile.org/arch0403/07.30%20-%20burlatskiy.html.

Calvert, John. "The Islamist Syndrome of Cultural Confrontation." *ORBIS* (September 2002): 333–349.

———. " 'The World Is an Undutiful Boy': Sayyid Qutb's American Experience." *Islam and Christian-Muslim Relations* 11, no. 1 (2000): 87–103.

Campana, Michele. "Un Colloquio con Mussolini: Parole Profetiche Sulle due potenti forze che minacciano l'Italia." *Meridiano d'Italia*, 6, no. 5 (February 4, 1951).

Chinard, Gilbert. "18th Century Theories on America as Human Habitat." *Proceedings of the American Philosophical Society* 91, no. 1 (February 1947): 27–57.

Chugayev, Sergei. "War in Iraq Destroys Myths about America." *Komsomolskaya Pravda*, no. 53 (March 2003). http://www.cdi.org/russia/250-3.cfm.

Clinton, Chelsea. "Chelsea Clinton Speaks Out for the First Time in a Personal Account of the September 11 Tragedy and Its Aftermath." *Talk Magazine* (December 2001–January 2002). http://www.digitalfreeway.com/talkmedia/december2001/Chelsea_excl.html.

Colombiani, Jean-Marie. "We Are All Americans." *Le Monde*, September 12, 2001. Translation in *World Press Review* 48, no. 11 (November 2001). http://www.worldpress.org/1101we_are_all_americans.htm.

Cornwell, Rupert. "By George!" *The Independent*, November 13, 2003. http://
news.independent.co.uk/world/americas/story.jsp?story=463147.

Darío, Rubén. "To Roosevelt." 1904. http://www.worldpolicy.org/globalrights/
nicaragua/1904-Dar%C3%ADo-english.html.

Dimitras, Panayote Elia. "The Greeks' Persistent Anti-Americanism." *AIM Athens* (December 1999). http://www.aimpress.org/dyn/trae/archive/data/199912/
91205-017-trae-ath.htm.

Döpfner, Mathias. "Bush ist dumm und böse." *Die Welt*, April 21, 2004. http://
www.welt.de/data/2004/04/21/267596.html.

Doran, Charles F., and James Patrick Sewell. "Anti-Americanism in Canada?" In
Anti-Americanism: Origins and Context, edited by Thomas Perry Thornton.
Newbury Park, Calif, 1988.

Drabble, Margaret. "I Loathe America, and What It Has Done to the Rest of
the World." *Daily Telegraph*, May 8, 2003. http://www.telegraph.co.uk/
opinion/main.jhtml?xml=/opinion/2003/05/08/do0801.xml.

Dunham, Richard S. "It's Not Americans That Arabs Hate." *Business Week Online*, April 15, 2002. http://www.businessweek.com/bwdaily/dnflash/apr2002/
nf20020415_0109.htm.

Duweidar, Jalal. "The World in the Hands of a Devil." *Al-Akhbar*, March 19,
2003. Translation in *MEMRI Special Dispatch No. 482*, March 20, 2003. http://
memri.org/bin/articles.cgi?Page=archives&Area=sd&ID=SP48203.

Environics Research Group/Focus Canada. "Canadians Approve of the US, Disapprove of President George W. Bush." July 11, 2003. http://erg.environics
.net/news/default.asp?aID=524.

Esler, Gavin. "The Danger of This Infantile Anti-Americanism." *Independent*,
May 15, 2003. http://argument.independent.co.uk/commentators/story.jsp
?story=406294.

Fallaci, Oriana. "Anger and Pride." *Corriere della Sera*, September 29, 2001.
http://www.corriere.it/speciali/fallaci/fallaci1.shtml.

Finn, Peter. "U.S.-Style Campaign with Anti-U.S. Theme." *Washington Post*,
September 19, 2002.

Frachon, Alain. "America Unloved." *Le Monde*, November 24, 2001. Translation
in *World Press Review* 48, no. 12 (December 2001). http://www.worldpress
.org/europe/0202lemonde_eye.htm.

Frankel, Glenn. "Sneers From Across the Atlantic." *Washington Post*, February
11, 2003, A1.

Franklin, Benjamin. "Observations Concerning the Increase of Mankind, Peopling of Countries (1751)." http://bc.barnard.columbia.edu/lgordis/earlyAC/
documents/observations.html.

Friedberg, Maurice. "Reading for the Masses: Soviet Popular Fiction: 1976–1980."
USIA Report, June 25, 1981.

————. "Recent Soviet Criticism of American Literature (#2)." Office of Research, U.S. International Communication Agency, August 15, 1979.

Friedman, Thomas. "Ah, Those Principled Europeans." *New York Times,* February 2, 2003. http://www.cubaliberal.org/archivo-03-01/03_02_02-a.htm.

Frum, David. "America in the Dock." *Daily Telegraph,* October 22, 2002. http://www.telegraph.co.uk/opinion/main.jhtml?xml=/opinion/2002/10/22/do2203.xml&sSheet=/opinion/2002/10/22/ixop.html&secureRefresh=true&_requestid=380421.

————. "America in the Dock." *Daily Telegraph,* October 21, 2002. http://news.telegraph.co.uk/opinion/main.jhtml?xml=/opinion/2002/10/21/do2101.xml&sSheet=/opinion/2002/10/21/ixopinion.html.

Fuentes, Carlos. "Prologue." In José Enrique Rodó, *Ariel.* Austin, Texas, 1988.

Ganley, Elaine. "Journalist Lambasts French War Coverage." *Associated Press,* December 30, 2003.

Gerges, Fawaz. "The Tragedy of Arab-American Relations." *Christian Science Monitor,* September 18, 2001. http://www.csmonitor.com/2001/0918/p9s1-coop.html.

Gopnik, Adam. "The Anti-Anti-Americans." *New Yorker,* September 1, 2003. http://www.newyorker.com/printable/?fact/030901fa_fact1.

Granjon, Marie-Christine. "Sartre, Beauvoir, Arnon: An Ambiguous Affair." In *The Rise and Fall of Anti-Americanism: A Century of French Perception,* edited by Denis Lacorne, Jacques Rupnik, and Marie-France Toinet. New York, 1990.

Grayson, George W. "Anti-Americanism in Mexico." In *Anti-Americanism in the Third World: Implications for U.S. Foreign Policy,* edited by Alvin Z. Rubinstein and Donald E. Smith. New York, 1985.

Grishina, Natalya. "Anti-Americanism Winning over Russia's Elite." *Russia Journal,* December 19, 2000. http://therussiajournal.com/index.htm?obj=3969.

Habid, Ayam. Article in *Okaz,* May 27, 2003. Translation in *MEMRI No. 513,* June 1, 2003. http://memri.org/bin/articles.cgi?Page=subjects&Area=middleeast&ID=SP51303.

Hale, Ellen. "Global Warmth for U.S. after 9/11 Turns to Frost." *USA Today,* August 14, 2002. http://www.usatoday.com/news/nation/2002-08-14-1a-cover_x.htm.

Halevi, Yossi Klein. "Twin Hatreds: Anti-Americanism and Anti-Semitism." GLORIA Center Conference on Anti-Americanism, September 17, 2003.

Harris, Lee. "The Intellectual Origins of America-Bashing." *Policy Review,* no. 116 (December 2002 and January 2003). http://www.policyreview.org/dec02/harris.html.

Hawi, George. Article in *Al-Safir,* September 15, 2001. Translated by Foreign Broadcast Information Service (FBIS).

Horowitz, Irving Louis. "Latin America, Anti-Americanism, and Intellectual Hubris." In *Anti-Americanism in the Third World: Implications for U.S. Foreign Policy*, edited by Alvin Z. Rubinstein and Donald E. Smith. New York, 1985.

Irving, Andrew, and David Scott. "British Public's Perceptions of Relationship Between the U.K. and U.S. and Selected Political Issues." Office of Research, United States Information Agency, May 1988.

Islam, Faisal. "When Two Tribes Go to War." *The Guardian*, June 22, 2003. http://observer.guardian.co.uk/bush/story/0,8224,982331,00.html/.

ITAR-TASS. "Poll Shows Saddam More Popular than Bush among Russians." *Center for Defense Information, Russia Weekly*, no. 251, April 4, 2003. http://www.cdi.org/russia/251-2.cfm.

Jack, Ian. "This Land Is Their Land." *The Guardian*, March 8, 2003. http://books.guardian.co.uk/review/story/0,12084,908950,00.html.

Johnson, Paul. "Anti-Americanism Is Racist Envy." *Forbes*, July 21, 2003. http://www.forbes.com/columnists/global/2003/0721/017.html.

Juzo, Mustafa. Article in *Al-Hayat*, September 17, 2001. Excerpt and translation in "Terror in America: Lebanese Professor: It Is Permissible to Rejoice over 'the Penetrating of the Bastion of American Colonialism'; 'Everyone Gloated at the Misfortune of the American Administration, while Its Leaders Scrambled to Find a Place to Hide.'" *MEMRI Special Dispatch Series No. 272*, September 20, 2001. http://www.memri.org/bin/articles.cgi?Page=archives&Area=sd&ID=SP27201.

El-Kaffas, Nasr. "Chirac! Visas!" *Al-Ahram Weekly*, March 6–12, 2003. http://weekly.ahram.org.eg/2003/628/re6.htm.

Kagan, Robert. "Politicians with Guts." *Washington Post*, January 31, 2003, A27.

———. "Power and Weakness." *Policy Review*, No. 113 (June–July 2002). http://www.policyreview.org/JUN02/kagan.html.

Kagarlitsky, Boris. "Roots of Anti-Americanism." *Moscow Times*, April 9, 2002. http://www.tni.org/archives/kagarlitsky/roots.htm.

Kaldor, Mary. "Beyond Militarism, Arms Races and Arms Control." Essay prepared for the Nobel Peace Prize Centennial Symposium, December 6–8, 2001. http://www.ssrc.org/sept11/essays/kaldor.htm.

Kaletsky, Anatole. "Arrogance and Fear: an American Paradox." [London] *Times*, February 7, 2002. http://www.casi.org.uk/discuss/2002/msg00208.html.

Keats, John. "To (What Can I Do to Drive Away)" http://www.4literature.net/John_Keats/To_What_can_I_do_to_drive_away_/.

Kettle, Martin. "U.S. Bashing: It's All the Rage in Europe." *Washington Post*, January 7, 2001. http://www.washingtonpost.com/ac2/wp-dyn?pagename=article&node=&contentId=A26468-2001Jan6&notFound=true.

Kroes, Robert. "The Great Satan versus the Evil Empire Anti-Americanism in the Netherlands." In *Anti-Americanism in Europe*, edited by Robert Kroes and Maarten van Rossem. Amsterdam, Netherlands, 1986.

Lacorne, Denis. "The Barbaric Americans." *Wilson Quarterly* (spring 2001): 51–55.

Lacorne, Denis, and Jacques Rupnik. "Intro: France Bewitched by America." In *The Rise and Fall of Anti-Americanism: A Century of French Perception,* edited by Denis Lacorne, Jacques Rupnik, and Marie-France Toinet. New York, 1990.

Le Carré, John. "The United States of America Has Gone Mad." [London] *Times,* January 15, 2003. http://www.commondreams.org/views03/0115-01.htm.

Lévy, Bernard-Henri. "Anti-Americanism in the Old Europe: A Dialogue with Bernard-Henri Lévy." *New Perspectives Quarterly* 20, no. 2 (spring 2003). http://www.digitalnpq.org/global_services/global%20viewpoint/02-04-03 levy.html.

Lloyd, John. "How Anti-Americanism Betrays the Left." *Guardian,* March 17, 2002. http://observer.guardian.co.uk/worldview/story/0,11581,668425,00.html.

Loach, Ken, "Marching Off to Peace." *The Observer,* September 22, 2002. http://www.observer.co.uk/comment/story/0,6903,796615,00.html.

Magnet, Julia. "London Peace Marchers Say: Long Live the Intifada." *City Journal,* February 17, 2003. http://www.city-journal.org/html/eon_2_17_03jm.html.

Mahmoud, Fatma Abdallah. "May the Cannibals Be Cursed!" *Al-Akhbar,* August 6, 2003. Excerpt and translation in "Columnist in Leading Egyptian Government Daily: U.S. Forces in Iraq Strip the Flesh from Their Victims' Corpses," *MEMRI Special Dispatch No. 559,* August 28, 2003. http://memri.org/bin/articles.cgi?Page=archives&Area=sd&ID=SP55903.

Makdisi, Ussama. "Anti-Americanism in the Arab World: An Interpretation of a Brief History," *The Journal of American History* 89, no. 2 (2002). http://www.historycooperative.org/cgi-in/justtop.cgi?act=justtop&url=http://www.historycooperative.org/journals/jah/89.2/makdisi.html.

Margalit, Avishai, and Ian Buruma. "Occidentalism." *The New York Review of Books,* January 17, 2002. http://research.yale.edu/wwkelly/restricted/Japan_journalism/NYRB_020107.htm.

Marx, Karl. "Address of the International Working Men's Association to Abraham Lincoln, President of the United States of America." January 28, 1865. http://www.marxists.org/history/international/iwma/documents/1864/lincoln-letter.htm.

Maxwell, Kenneth. "An Anti-Americanism in Brazil." *Correspondence: An International Review of Culture & Society,* no. 9 (spring 2002). http://www.cfr.org/pdf/correspondence/xMaxwell.php.

McKay, George. "Afterword: Downsizing America." In *Yankee Go Home (& Take Me with U),* edited by George McKay. Sheffield, 1977.

McPherson, Alan. "Latin American Anti-Americanism and U.S. Responses: Venezuela 1958." Washington Area Symposium on the History of Latin America, The David C. Driskell Center for the Study of the African Diaspora, October 14, 2002. http://ww.driskellcenter.umd.edu/programs/2002-2003/conf/washla/papers/McPherson.pdf.

Meacher, Michael. "This War on Terrorism Is Bogus." *Guardian*, September 6, 2003. http://www.guardian.co.uk/comment/story/0,3604,1036571,00.html.

Mead, Walter Russell, "Why Do They Hate Us? Two Books Take Aim at French Anti-Americanism." *Foreign Affairs* (March–April 2003). http://www.foreignaffairs.org/20030301fareviewessay10345/walter-russell-mead/why-do-they-hate-us-two-books-take-aim-at-french-anti-americanism.html;.

Michas, Takis. "America the Despised." *The National Interest*, no. 67 (June 29, 2002). http://www.nationalinterest.org/issues/67/Michas.html.

Monbiot, George. "The Logic of Empire." *The Guardian*, August 6, 2002. http://www.guardian.co.uk/bush/story/0,7369,769755,00.html.

Abd Al-Mun'im Murad, Mahmoud. "The Iraq Crisis (2)." *Akhbar Al-Yaum*, January 9, 2003. Translation in *MEMRI No. 469*, February 14, 2003. http://memri.org/bin/articles.cgi?Page=archives&Area=sd&ID=SP46903.

Nafi, Ibrahim. "Disturbing Phenomenon in the U.S. Media." *Al-Ahram*, October 19, 2001. Translation in *MEMRI No. 292*, October 26, 2001. http://memri.org/bin/articles.cgi?Page=archives&Area=sd&ID=SP29201#_edn1.

Naim, Moises. "The Perils of Lite Anti-Americanism." *Foreign Policy* (May–June 2003). http://www.foreignpolicy.com/story/story.php?storyID=13696.

Nassar, Sayyid. "Interview with Saddam Hussein." *Al-Usbou'*, November 4, 2002. Translation in *MEMRI Special Dispatch No. 437*, November 5, 2002. http://memri.org/bin/articles.cgi?Page=archives&Area=sd&ID=SP43702.

Neruda, Pablo. "United Fruit Company." http://subbacultcha.angelcities.com/unitedfruit.html.

Nikolayev, Andrei. "Basic Lessons of the Iraqi War." *Pravda*, no. 47 (April 2003). *CDI Russia Weekly #254*, April 25, 2003. http://www.cdi.org/russia/254-10.cfm.

Nordholdt, J. W. Schulte. "Anti-Americanism in European Culture: Its Early Manifestations." In *Anti-Americanism in Europe*, edited by Rob Kroes and Maarten van Rossem. Amsterdam, Netherlands, 1986.

Ory, Pascal. "From Baudelaire to Duhamel." In *The Rise and Fall of Anti-Americanism: A Century of French Perception*, edited by Denis Lacorne, Jacques Rupnik, and Marie-France Toinet. New York, 1990.

Paz, Reuven. "Islamists and Anti-Americanism." *Middle East Review of International Affairs*, 7, no. 4 (December 2003). http://meria.idc.ac.il/journal/2003/issue4/jv7n4a5.html.

Pei, Minxin. "The Paradoxes of American Nationalism." *Foreign Policy* (May–June 2003). http://www.foreignpolicy.com/story/story.php?storyID=13631.

Petre, Jonathan. "Terrorists Can Have Serious Moral Goals, Says Williams." *Daily Telegraph,* October 15, 2003. http://www.telegraph.co.uk/news/main .jhtml?xml=/news/2003/10/15/wbish15.xml&sSheet=/portal/2003/10/15/ ixportaltop.html.

PEW Global Attitudes Project. "America Admired, Yet Its New Vulnerability Seen As Good Thing, Say Opinion Leaders." December 19, 2001. http:// people-press.org/reports/display.php3?ReportID=145.

———. "America's Image Further Erodes, Europeans Want Weaker Ties." March 18, 2003. http://people-press.org/reports/display.php3?PageID=680.

———. "A Year After Iraq War." March 16, 2004. http://www.pewtrusts.com/ pdf/pew_global_attitudes_year_war_031604.pdf.

Pinter, Harold. "Degree Speech to the University of Florence." September 10, 2001. http://alt.venus.co.uk/weed/current/pinter3.htm.

———. "God Bless America," *The Guardian,* January 22, 2003. http:// globalresearch.ca/articles/PIN301A.html.

Podeh, Elie. "The Lie That Won't Die: Collusion, 1967," *Middle East Quarterly* 11, no. 1 (winter 2004). http://www.meforum.org/article/587.

Ramonet, Ignacio. "The Other Axis of Evil." *Le Monde Diplomatique* (March 2002). http://mondediplo.com/2002/03/01axis.

Rapin, Anne. "An Interview with the Linguist Claude Hagège." *Label France,* no. 26 (December 1996). http://www.france.diplomatie.fr/label_france/ENGLISH/ FRANCO/HAGEG/hageg.htmla.

Raven, Charlotte. "A Bully with a Bloody Nose Is Still a Bully." *The Guardian,* September 18, 2001. http://www.guardian.co.uk/Columnists/Column/ 0,5673,553672,00.html.

Riotta, Gianni. "Transatlantic Chill? Blame Europe's Power Failure." *Washington Post,* January 26, 2003.

Rippy, J. Fred. "Introduction." In Manuel Ugarte, *Destiny of a Continent.* New York, 1925.

Roett, Riordan. "Anti-Americanism in the Southern Cone of Latin America." In *Anti-Americanism: Origins and Context,* edited by Thomas Perry Thornton. Newbury Park, Calif., 1988.

Rosenfeld, Alvin H. "Anti-Americanism and Anti-Semitism: A New Frontier of Bigotry." *American Jewish Congress.* http://www.ajc.org/InTheMedia/ Publications.asp?did=902.

Roy, Arundhati. "The Algebra of Infinite Justice." *The Guardian,* September 29, 2001. http://www.guardian.co.uk/Archive/Article/0,4273,4266289,00.html.

Rubinstein, Alvin Z., and Donald E. Smith. "Anti-Americanism: Anatomy of a Phenomenon." In *Anti-Americanism in the Third World: Implications for U.S. Foreign Policy,* edited by Alvin Z. Rubinstein and Donald E. Smith. New York, 1985.

Rupnik, Jacques, and Muriel Humbertjean. "Images of the United States in Public Opinion." In *The Rise and Fall of Anti-Americanism: A Century of French Perception,* edited by Denis Lacorne, Jacques Rupnik, and Marie-France Toinet. New York, 1990.

Rushdie, Salman. "Anti-Americanism Has Taken the World by Storm." *Guardian,* February 6, 2002. http://www.guardian.co.uk/print/0,3858,4350590 -108920,00.html.

———. "Rethinking the War on American Culture." *New York Times,* March 5, 1999. http://www.uwm.edu/~wash/rushdie.html.

———. "The US Has an Ideological Enemy Harder to Defeat than Militant Islam." *The Guardian,* February 6, 2002.

Sadlier, Michael. "Introduction." In Frances Trollope, *Domestic Manners of the Americans.* New York, 1927.

Safire, William. "The German Problem." *New York Times,* September 19, 2002. http://de.indymedia.org/2002/09/30138.shtml.

Saustrup, Anders S. "Hoffman Von Fallersleben, August Heinrich." *The Handbook of Texas Online.* http://www.tsha.utexas.edu/handbook/online/articles/ print/HH/fho88.html.

Schama, Simon. "The Unloved American." *New Yorker,* March 10, 2003. http:// www.newyorker.com/fact/content/?030310fa_fact.

Schlesinger, Arthur, Jr. "America Experiment or Destiny?" *American Historical Review* 82, no. 3 (June 1977).

Schutz, Marco. "Euro-Skepticism and Anti-Americanism Erupt in Europe." *Culture Kiosque,* June 16, 2001. http://www.culturekiosque.com/nouveau/books/ europeanunion.html.

al-Shaykh, Hafedh. Article in *Akhbar al-Khalij,* September 12, 2001. In Murray Kahl, "Terror Strikes U.S.: 'An Act of War,' How Will Americans Respond," September 12, 2001. http://www.chretiens-et-juifs.org/Geopolitique/US_attack _survey.htm.

Sorman, Guy. "United States: Model or Bête Noire?" In *The Rise and Fall of Anti-Americanism: A Century of French Perception,* edited by Denis Lacorne, Jacques Rupnik, and Marie-France Toinet. New York, 1990.

Steyn, Mark. "It's 'Peace' Psychosis in a Nut's Hell." *Daily Telegraph,* November 18, 2003, http://opinion.telegraph.co.uk/opinion/main.jhtml?xml=/opinion/ 2003/11/18/do1802.xml.

Stone, Andrea. "Many in Islamic World Doubt Arabs Behind 9/11." *USA Today,* February 27, 2002. http://www.usatoday.com/news/sept11/2002/02/27/usat-poll .htm.

Summerfield, Robin. "Canadians Love Americans, Dislike Their Government." *The [Montreal] Gazette,* March 10, 2003.

Teimourian, Hazhir. Interview in "Arab Opinion on U.S.-Led Attack." *The*

World Today, Australian Broadcasting Company, September 26, 2002. http://
www.abc.net.au/worldtoday/s686685.htm.

Tessler, Mark. "Do Islamic Orientations Influence Attitudes toward Democracy
in the Arab World: Evidence from the World Values Survey in Egypt, Jordan,
Morocco, and Algeria." *International Journal of Comparative Sociology* (spring
2003). http://conconflicts.ssrc.org/mideast/tessler/pf/.

Theil, Stefan. "The Great 9/11 Conspiracy." *Newsweek,* September 17, 2003.
http://bulletin.ninemsn.com.au/bulletin/eddesk.nsf/All/7C0C9C0FE6AD4F42C
A256DA200146E47!open.

Thompson, Christopher. "Prologue to Conflict: De Gaulle and the United
States, from First Impressions through 1940." In *De Gaulle and the United
States: A Centennial Reappraisal,* edited by Robert Paxton and Nicholas
Wohl. Oxford, U.K, 1994.

Toinet, Marie-France. "Does Anti-Americanism Exist?" In *The Rise and Fall of
Anti-Americanism: A Century of French Perception,* edited by Denis Lacorne,
Jacques Rupnik, and Marie-France Toinet. New York, 1990.

U.S. Department of State. Report on the Meeting by U.S. Embassy in Jordan.
U.S. Archives, Record Group 59, September 4, 1969.

Ursan, Ali Uqleh. Editorial. "Terror in America: Syrian Arab Writers Association
Chairman: I Felt Like Someone Delivered from the Grave; My Lungs Filled
with Air and I Breathed in Relief, as I'd Never Breathed Before." *Al-Usbu' al-
Adabi,* September 15, 2001. Translation in *MEMRI Special Dispatch 275,* September 25, 2001. http://www.memri.org/bin/articles.cgi?Page=archives&Area=
sd&ID=SP27501.

Vaknin, Sam. "To Give with Grace: Why Central and East Europe Hates the
West." *Central Europe Review* 2, no. 11 (March 20, 2000). http://www.ce
-review.org/00/11/vaknin11.html.

Van Elteren, Mel. "America Life by Proxy: Dutch Youth and Their Sense of
Place." In *Yankee Go Home & Take Me with U,* edited by George McKay.
Sheffield, U.K., 1977.

Vulliamy, Ed. "Farewell America." *The Observer,* August 24, 2003. http://observer
.guardian.co.uk/review/story/0,6903,1028186,00.html.

Wagner, Wolfang. "The Europeans' Image of America." In *America and Western
Europe: Problems and Prospects,* edited by Karl Kaiser and Hans-Peter
Schwartz. Lexington, Mass., 1978.

Wasserstein, Bernard. "Anti-Semitism and Anti-Americanism." *Chronicle of
Higher Education,* September 28, 2001. http://chronicle.com/free/v48/i05/
05b00502.htm.

Wheatcroft, Geoffrey. "Dickens to Le Carré." *New York Times,* January 11, 2004.
http://www.freerepublic.com/focus/f-news/1055651/posts.

Wilde, Oscar. "Impressions of America." London, July 10, 1883. http://www
.december2001.com/oscarwilde/impressionsofamerica.html.

Wilford, Hugh. "The South and the British Left, 1930–1960." In *Britain and the American South: From Colonialism to Rock and Roll,* edited by Joseph P. Ward, 163–186. Oxford, University of Mississippi Press, 2003.

Winock, Michel. "The Cold War." In *The Rise and Fall of Anti-Americanism: A Century of French Perception,* edited by Denis Lacorne, Jacques Rupnik, and Marie-France Toinet. New York, 1990.

Zeldin, Theodore. "Foreword: The Pathology of Anti-Americanism." In *The Rise And Fall Of Anti-Americanism: A Century of French Perception,* edited by Denis Lacorne, Jacques Rupnik, and Marie-France Toinet. New York, 1990.

INDEX

intellectuals: British anti-Americanism, 132; Bush hated by, 202; European anti-Americanism, 26, 53–55, 72–73, 233; fear of mass culture dominance, 235; French anti-Americanism, 8, 66, 133–140, 143, 145, 149–150; Latin American anti-Americanism, 101, 107, 110, 114, 117–118; Soviet criticisms supported by European, 86–87; status of, in Europe versus America, 140, 234; value of anti-Americanism to, 233–235

Internet, 149

Iran: American intervention in 1953, 165; hostage incident (1980), 152; politics of anti-Americanism in, 157–158, 174; public opinion on America in, 181, 182; religious/cultural opposition to America in, 158, 167; state policy of anti-Americanism, 157–158; as threat to world peace, 188; war with Iraq, 166

Iraq, 166, 173, 174, 180. *See also* Iraq War (2003); Persian Gulf War (1991)

Iraq War (2003): American imperialism and, 209–214, 221; coalition in, 241; and increased anti-Americanism, 188; Middle Eastern response to, 180–185; moral considerations behind, 48; Russia on, 199; world response to, 209–218

The Iron Heel (London), 51

Irwin, Julia, 216

Islam: America as enemy of, 158, 167, 169, 175, 176, 223; America as patron of, 165; anti-Americanism as umbrella concept for, 161; Bin Ladin and Islamic revolution, 204–205; Qutb and revolutionary, 161. *See also* Muslims

isolationism, 63, 239

Israel: American relations with, 165, 173–174, 178; Arab-Israeli war (1967), 165; as enemy of Middle East, 157, 159, 173

Italy: Ethiopian defeat of, 60; fascism in, 98; McDonald's protests in, 195; post-WWII support for America in, 129; public opinion on America in, 188, 192

Jack, Ian, 235

Jackson, Andrew, 34

Jacquemont, Victor, 26, 35

James, Henry, viii, 58–59, 65

Japan: defeat of Russians by, 60; relation to American culture of, 236

al-Jazira (television network), 169, 183

jazz, Nazi criticism of, 95

Jefferson, Thomas, viii, 11, 13, 13–14, 27

Jewish World Domination? (Bonhard), 94

Jews: associated with Americans, 53, 94–95, 137; blamed for modernity, 53; fascism and, 94–95. *See also* anti-Semitism; Israel

Jobert, Michel, 147–148

Johnson, Paul, 233

Johnson, Samuel, viii

Joliot-Curie, Irène, 135

Jones, Ernest, 55

Jordan, 181, 221

Jospin, Lionel, 203

Juan in America (Linklater), 97

Julien, Claude, 150

The Jungle (Sinclair), 51

Kagan, Robert, 240–241

Kaldor, Mary, 206, 212

Kaletsky, Anatole, 206

Kalm, Peter, 10

Kant, Immanuel, 12, 26

Keats, John, 17

Kennedy, John, 89

al-Khamene'i, Ali al-Husseini, 164, 171

Khomeini, Ayatollah Ruholla, 158, 167, 172, 179

Khomeini, Hussein, 182

Khrushchev, Nikita, 88

"Kill the Yankee" (song), 200

Koestler, Arthur, 145, 235

Komsomolskaya Pravda (newspaper), 199

Konetskii, Viktor, 88

Korean War, 134, 143

Kosovo, 200–201, 207, 241

Kurnberger, Ferdinand, 16, 29–30

Kuwait, 166, 172, 181

Laboulaye, Edouard René Lefebvre de, 49

Labour Party (Britain), 131–132

Lacorne, Denis, 232

Lafayette, Marquis de, 13, 26, 62

Lafontaine, Oskar, 210

Lang, Jack, 150